Quick-Stitch

Crochet™

EDITED BY JUDY CROW

the Needlecraft Shop®

Quick-Stitch Crochet

EDITOR Judy Crow
ART DIRECTOR Brad Snow
PUBLISHING SERVICES MANAGER Brenda Gallmeyer

MANAGING EDITOR Brenda Stratton
ASSISTANT ART DIRECTOR Nick Pierce
COPY SUPERVISOR Michelle Beck
COPY EDITOR Nicki Lehman
TECHNICAL EDITOR Mary Ann Frits
TECHNICAL ARTIST Nicole Gage

GRAPHIC ARTS SUPERVISOR Ronda Bechinski
BOOK DESIGN Nick Pierce
GRAPHIC ARTISTS Vicki Staggs, Jessi Butler
PRODUCTION ASSISTANTS Marj Morgan

PHOTOGRAPHY SUPERVISOR Tammy Christian
PHOTOGRAPHY Matthew Owen
PHOTO STYLIST Tammy Steiner

CHIEF EXECUTIVE OFFICER David McKee
BOOK MARKETING DIRECTOR Dwight Seward

PRINTED IN CHINA
FIRST PRINTING: 2008
LIBRARY OF CONGRESS NUMBER: 2007928288
HARDCOVER ISBN: 978-1-57367-294-8
SOFTCOVER ISBN: 978-1-57367-295-5

DRGbooks.com

123456789

Welcome!

Crochet is a popular craft. Many people like it because they feel it relaxes them as they sit and peacefully work on a project. Others like it because of its versatility—after all you find crochet items in every room of the house, crocheted accessories, clothing and much more. Still others like it because of the many beautiful yarns and threads available to use.

Whatever the reason you like crochet, we all like the easy and quick patterns. With societies busy schedules, today crafters are looking for fast, simple projects with great end results. The designs in this book are ideal for the crafter on the go! We have a wide variety of projects from home décor, gifts and wearables. Each item was selected with the busy crocheter in mind, so grab your hooks and start stitching!

Judy Crow

Afghan Beauty

Fashionable Accessories

1

Around the House

To really make a house your home, you need to add a personal touch. Stitch these easy designs to add warmth, comfort and beauty to your home. Personalize each design by changing colors to match your decor.

Hot Pot Mates

Large Lid Grabber

DESIGN BY NINA MARSH

SKILL LEVEL
EASY

FINISHED SIZE
4½ x 8½ inches, unfolded

MATERIALS
- Medium (worsted) weight cotton yarn: 1 oz/50 yds/28g chocolate MEDIUM
- Size G/6/4mm crochet hook or size needed to obtain gauge
- Tapestry needle

GAUGE
4 sc = 1 inch; 4 sc rows = 1 inch

PATTERN NOTE
Weave in ends as work progresses.

Instructions

FIRST SIDE
Row 1 (RS): Ch 15, sc in 2nd ch from hook, sc in each rem ch across, turn. *(14 sc)*

Rows 2–17: Ch 1, sc in each sc across, turn.

Row 18: Ch 1, working in **front lps** *(see Stitch Guide)* only, sc in each sc across, turn.

Rows 19–28: Ch 1, sc in each sc across, turn. At end of row 28, fasten off.

2ND SIDE
Row 1 (RS): With RS facing and working in unused lps on opposite side of foundation ch, make slip knot on hook and join with sc in first ch, sc in each rem ch across, turn. *(14 sc)*

Rows 2–17: Ch 1, sc in each sc across, turn.

Row 18: Ch 1, working in front lps only, sc in each sc across, turn.

Rows 19–28: Ch 1, sc in each sc across, turn.

Edging
Working around outer edge, ch 1, sc in each st and in end of each row and work 2 sc in each corner, join in first sc, fasten off.

ASSEMBLY
Fold each end over to WS at row 18, matching sts, working in **back lps** *(see Stitch Guide)* only, sew 12 rows on each side tog forming a pocket at each end.

Small Lid Grabber

DESIGN BY NINA MARSH

SKILL LEVEL
EASY

FINISHED SIZE
3½ x 8½ inches, unfolded

MATERIALS
- Medium (worsted) weight cotton yarn: 1¼ oz/63 yds/35g lime MEDIUM
- Size G/6/4mm crochet hook or size needed to obtain gauge
- Tapestry needle

GAUGE
4 sc = 1 inch; 4 sc rows = 1 inch

PATTERN NOTES
Weave in ends as work progresses.

Instructions

FIRST SIDE
Row 1 (RS): Ch 11, sc in 2nd ch from hook, sc in each rem ch across, turn. *(10 sc)*

Rows 2–17: Ch 1, sc in each sc across, turn.

Row 18: Ch 1, working in **front lps** *(see Stitch Guide)* only, sc in each sc across, turn.

Rows 19–28: Ch 1, sc in each sc across, turn. At end of row 28, fasten off.

2ND SIDE
Row 1 (RS): With RS facing and working in unused lps on opposite side of beg ch, make slip knot on hook and join with sc in first ch, sc in each rem ch across, turn. *(10 sc)*

Rows 2–17: Ch 1, sc in each sc across, turn.

CONTINUED ON PAGE 40

Towel Edgings

DESIGNS BY JO ANN LOFTIS

Blue Towel Edging

SKILL LEVEL   ◼◼◻◻ EASY

FINISHED SIZE
1 inch wide

MATERIALS
• Elmore-Pisgah Peaches & Crème medium (worsted) weight cotton yarn (2½ oz/122 yds/71g per ball): 1 ball #26 light blue
• Size I/9/5.5mm crochet hook or size needed to obtain gauge
• Tapestry needle
• Sewing needle
• Cotton dish towel
• Matching sewing thread

GAUGE
4 sts = 1 inch

PATTERN NOTE
Weave in ends as work progresses.

Instructions

Row 1 (WS): Make ch to desired length in multiple of 6 plus 2 at end, sc in 2nd ch from hook, sc in each rem ch across, turn.

Row 2 (RS): Ch 1, sc in first sc, *sk next 2 sc, 5 dc in next sc, sk next 2 sc, sc in next sc, rep from * across, fasten off.

FINISHING
Sew Edging to 1 short end of towel.

Chocolate Towel Edging

SKILL LEVEL   ◼◼◻◻ EASY

FINISHED SIZE
1½ inch wide

MATERIALS
• Elmore-Pisgah Peaches & Crème medium (worsted) weight cotton yarn (2½ oz/122 yds/71g per ball): 1 ball #121 chocolate
• Size I/9/5.5mm crochet hook or size needed to obtain gauge
• Tapestry needle
• Sewing needle
• Cotton dish towel
• Matching sewing thread

GAUGE
4 sts = 1 inch

PATTERN NOTE
Weave in ends as work progresses.

Instructions

Row 1 (WS): Make ch to desired length in multiple of 8 plus 2 at end, sc in 2nd ch from hook, sc in each rem ch across, turn.

Row 2 (RS): Ch 1, sc in first sc, *sk next 3 sc, (tr, ch 1) 6 times in next sc, tr in same sc, sk next 3 sc, sc in next sc, rep from * across, fasten off.

FINISHING
Sew piece to 1 short end of towel.

Yellow & White Towel Edging

SKILL LEVEL   ◼◼◻◻ EASY

FINISHED SIZE
1⅝ inch wide

MATERIALS
• Elmore-Pisgah Peaches & Crème medium (worsted) weight cotton yarn (2½ oz/122 yds/71g per ball): 1 ball each #10 yellow and #1 white
• Size I/9/5.5mm crochet hook or size needed to obtain gauge
• Tapestry needle
• Sewing needle
• Cotton dish towel
• Matching sewing thread

GAUGE
4 sts = 1 inch

PATTERN NOTE
Weave in ends as work progresses.

Instructions

Row 1 (RS): With yellow, make ch to desired length in multiple of 7 plus 1 at end, sc in 2nd ch from hook, sc in each rem ch across, turn.

Row 2: Ch 1, sc in first sc, 2 dc in next sc, 2 tr in next sc, 2 dtr in next sc, 2 tr in next sc, 2 dc in next sc, sc in next sc, *sc in next sc, 2 dc in next sc, 2 tr in next sc, 2 dtr in next sc, 2 tr in next sc,

2 dc in next sc, sc in next sc, rep from * across, fasten off.

Row 3: With white, make slip knot on hook and join with sc in first sc, sc in each rem sc across, fasten off.

FINISHING
Sew piece to 1 short end of towel.

White & Daisy Ombré Towel Edging

SKILL LEVEL
EASY

FINISHED SIZE
1½ inch wide

MATERIALS
- Elmore-Pisgah Peaches  & Crème medium (worsted) weight cotton yarn (2½ oz/122 yds/71g per ball): 1 ball #1 white
- Elmore-Pisgah Peaches & Crème medium (worsted) weight cotton yarn (2 oz/ 98 yds/57g per ball): 1 ball #165 daisy ombré
- Size I/9/5.5mm crochet hook or size needed to obtain gauge
- Tapestry needle
- Sewing needle
- Cotton dish towel
- Matching sewing thread

GAUGE
4 sts = 1 inch

PATTERN NOTES
Weave in ends as work progresses.

Join rounds with a slip stitch unless otherwise stated.

Instructions

Rnd 1 (RS): With white, make ch to desired length in multiple of 6 plus 1 at end, 3 sc in 2nd ch from hook, sc in each ch to last ch, 3 sc in last ch, working in unused lps on opposite side of foundation ch, sc in each ch across, join in beg ch-1, fasten off.

Row 2: Now working in rows, with daisy ombré, make slip knot on hook and join with sc in 2nd sc, *sk next 2 sc, 7 dc in next sc, sk next 2 sc, sc in next sc, rep from * to first sc of last 3-sc group, fasten off, leaving rem sc unworked.

FINISHING
Sew piece to 1 short end of towel. ∎

11

Kitchen Duo

Dishcloth

DESIGN BY LORI ZELLER

SKILL LEVEL
EASY

FINISHED SIZE
10 inches square

MATERIALS

- Medium (worsted) weight cotton yarn: 2 oz/100 yds/56g each light yellow and yellow
- Size I/9/5.5mm crochet hook or size needed to obtain gauge
- Tapestry needle

GAUGE
Rnds 1 & 2 = 2¼ inches

PATTERN NOTES
Weave in ends as work progresses.

Join rounds with a slip stitch unless otherwise stated.

Chain-3 at beginning of double crochet row or round counts as first double crochet unless otherwise stated.

Instructions

Rnd 1 (RS): With light yellow, ch 4, join in first ch to form a ring, ch 1, [sc in ring, ch 2] 8 times, join in first sc. *(8 sc)*

Rnd 2: Sl st in first ch-2 sp, ch 1, sc in same sp, ch 3, dc in last sc made, *sc in next ch-2 sp, ch 3, dc in last sc made, rep from * around, join in first sc, fasten off. *(8 sc, 8 dc, 8 ch-3 sps)*

Rnd 3: With yellow, make slip knot on hook and join with sc in any ch-3 sp, ch 3, sc in same sp, ch 2, sc in next ch-3 sp, ch 2, *(sc, ch 3, sc) in next ch-3 sp, ch 2, sc in next ch-3 sp, ch 2, rep from * around, join in first sc. *(12 sc, 8 ch-2 sps, 4 ch-3 sps)*

Rnd 4: Sl st in first ch-3 sp, **ch 3** *(see Pattern Notes)*, (dc, ch 2, 2 dc) in next ch sp *(beg dc corner)*, ch 1, sk next ch-2 sp, dc in next sc, working behind dc just made, dc in sk ch-2 sp, ch 1, dc in next ch-2 sp, working behind dc just made, dc in last sc, ch 1, *(2 dc, ch 2, 2 dc) in next ch-3 sp *(dc corner)*, ch 1, sk next ch-2 sp, dc in next sc, working behind dc just made, dc in sk ch-2 sp, ch 1, dc in next ch-2 sp, working behind dc just made, dc in last sc, ch 1, rep from * around. *(32 dc)*

Rnd 5: Sl st in next dc and in next ch-3 sp, ch 3, (dc, ch 2, 2 dc) in same sp, ch 1, dc in next ch-1 sp, working behind dc just made, dc in 2nd dc of previous 2-dc group, ch 1, 2 dc in next ch-1 sp, ch 1, sk next ch-1 sp, dc in next dc, working behind dc just made, dc in sk ch-1 sp, ch 1, *corner in next ch-3 corner sp, ch 1, dc in next ch-1 sp, working behind dc just made, dc in 2nd dc of previous 2-dc group, ch 1, 2 dc in next ch-1 sp, ch 1, sk next ch-1 sp, dc in next dc, working behind dc just made, dc in sk ch-1 sp, ch 1,

rep from * around, join in 3rd ch of beg ch-3. *(40 dc)*

Rnd 6: Sl st in next dc and in next ch-2 sp, ch 1, (sc, ch 3, sc) in same sp *(sc corner made)*, [ch 3, sc in next ch sp] 4 times, ch 3, *sc corner in next ch-2 corner sp, [ch 3, sc in next ch-sp] 4 times, ch 3, rep from * around, join in first sc, fasten off. *(24 sc)*

Rnd 7: With light yellow, make slip knot on hook and join with sc in last ch-3 sp made, ch 3, dc in last sc made, *sc in next ch-3 sp, ch 3, dc in last sc made, sc in same ch-3 sp as before, [ch 3, dc in last sc made, sc in next ch-3 sp] 5 times, ch 3, dc in last sc made, rep from * twice, sc in next ch-3 sp, ch 3, dc in last sc made, sc in same ch-3 sp as before, [ch 3, dc in last sc made, sc in next ch-3 sp] 4 times, ch 3, dc in last sc made, join in first sc, fasten off. *(28 sc, 28 dc)*

Rnd 8: With yellow, make slip knot on hook and join in 2nd ch-3 sp made on last rnd, ch 3, (2 dc, ch 2, 3 dc) in same sp *(beg 3-dc corner made)*, ch 1 [2 dc in next ch-3 sp, ch 1] 6 times, *(3 dc, ch 2, 3 dc) in next ch-3 *(beg 3-dc corner made)*, ch 1, [2 dc in next ch-3 sp, ch 1] 6 times, rep from * around, join in 3rd ch of beg ch-3. *(72 dc)*

Rnd 9: Sl st in each of next 2 dc and in next ch-2 sp, ch 1, sc corner in same sp, [ch 3, sc in next ch-1 sp] 7 times, ch 3, *sc corner in next ch-2 corner sp, [ch 3, sc in next ch-1 sp] 7 times, ch 3, rep from * around, join in first sc. *(36 sc)*

Rnd 10: Sl st in next ch-3 sp, beg dc corner in same sp, ch 1, [2 dc in next ch-3 sp, ch 1] 8 times, *dc corner in next ch-2 sp, ch 1, [2 dc in next ch-3 sp, ch 1] 8 times, rep from * around, join in 3rd ch of beg ch-3. *(80 dc)*

Rnd 11: Sl st in next dc and in next ch-2 sp, ch 1, sc corner in same sp, ch 2, [sc in next ch-1 sp, ch 2] 9 times, *sc corner in next ch-2 corner sp, ch 2, [sc in next ch-1 sp, ch 2] 9 times, rep from * around, join in first sc. *(44 sc)*

Rnd 12: Sl st in next ch-3 sp, ch 1, sc corner in same sp, ch 1 [working over next ch-2 sp, work (sc, ch 3, sc) in sp between dc of next 2-dc group on 2nd row below, ch 1] 10 times, *sc corner in next ch-3 corner sp, ch 1, [working over next ch-2 sp, work (sc, ch 3, sc) in sp between dc of next 2-dc group on 2nd row below, ch 1] 10 times, rep from * around, join in first sc, fasten off. *(88 sc)*

Scrubbie
DESIGN BY DENISE ROTHBERG

SKILL LEVEL

EASY

FINISHED SIZE
7½ inches across

MATERIALS
• Medium (worsted) weight cotton yarn: 1 oz/50 yds/28g yellow ½ oz/25 yds/14g brown
• Size G/6/4mm crochet hook or size needed to obtain gauge
• Tapestry needle
• Yellow scrub disk

GAUGE
Rnd 1 = 5 inches across

PATTERN NOTES
Weave in ends as work progresses.

Join rounds with a slip stitch unless otherwise stated.

Chain-2 at beginning of half double crochet round counts as first half double crochet unless otherwise stated.

Instructions

Rnd 1: With brown, make slip knot on hook and working around outer center edge of scrub disk, join with sc in any lp on scrub disk, work 39 sc evenly spaced around edge, join in first sc, turn. *(40 sc)*

Rnd 2: Ch 2 *(see Pattern Notes)*, 2 hdc in next sc, *hdc in next sc, 2 hdc in next sc, rep from * around, join in 2nd ch of beg ch-2, fasten off. *(60 hdc)*

Rnd 3: Join yellow in 2nd ch of beg ch-2 of previous rnd, ch 2, (dc, 3 tr, dc, hdc) in same ch, sk next st, sc in next st, sk next st, *(hdc, dc, 3 tr, dc, hdc) in next st, sk next st, sc in next st, sk next st, rep from * around, join in 2nd ch of beg ch-2. *(15 sc, 30 hdc, 30 dc, 45 tr)*

Rnd 4: Ch 1, sc in each of first 3 sts, (sc, ch 3, sc) in next st, sc in each of next 3 sts, sl st in next sc, *sc in each of next 3 sts, (sc, ch 3, sc) in next st, sc in each of next 3 sts, sl st in next sc, rep from * around, join in first sc, fasten off. *(15 sl sts, 119 sc)* ■

Rag Place Setting

DESIGNS BY CYNTHIA HARRIS

SKILL LEVEL
EASY

FINISHED SIZES
Table runner: 18 x 10½ inches
Coaster: 4½ inches in diameter

MATERIALS
- 1 yd of 45-inch wide cotton material
- Size N/15/10mm crochet hook or size needed to obtain gauge
- Tapestry needle
- Safety pin

GAUGE
Gauge is not important for this project.

PATTERN NOTES
Weave in ends as work progresses.

Join rounds with a slip stitch unless otherwise stated.

Chain-3 at beginning of double crochet row or round counts as first double crochet unless otherwise stated.

PREPARING RAG STRIPS
Cut or tear material into ½-inch-wide strips. Join strips by either of the following 2 methods.

Method 1: Splice strips together by either hand- or machine-stitching the ends together.

Method 2: Make a small slit at the end of 2 strips. The slit should be cut lengthwise approximately ½ inch from the end of the strip and should only be big enough to allow the next strip to pass through it. Hold 2 strips with the slits together then take end without slit and lace it through the 2 slits. Pull the strip completely through the holes and pull tight to make the splice as small as possible.

Continue to join strips, roll into a ball. Strips will be worked as if crocheting with yarn.

Instructions

PLACE MAT
Note: Piece is worked in continuous rnds unless otherwise stated. Mark beg of rnds with safety pin.

Rnd 1 (RS): Ch 13, 2 sc in 2nd ch from hook, sc in each of next 10 chs, 4 sc in last ch, working on opposite side of foundation ch, sc in each of next 10 chs, 2 sc in last ch. *(28 sc)*

Rnd 2: 2 sc in each of next 2 sc, sc in each of next 10 sc, 2 sc in each of next 4 sc, sc in each of next 10 sc, 2 sc in each of next 2 sc. *(36 sc)*

Rnd 3: *[Sc in next sc, 2 sc in next sc] twice, sc in each of next 10 sc, [2 sc in next sc, sc in next sc] twice, rep from * once. *(44 sc)*

Rnd 4: *[Sc in next sc, 2 sc in next sc] twice, sc in each of next 14 sc, [2 sc in next sc, sc in next sc] twice, rep from * once. *(52 sc)*

Rnd 5: *[Sc in next sc, 2 sc in next sc] twice, sc in each of next 18 sc, [2 sc in next sc, sc in next sc] twice, rep from * once. *(60 sc)*

Rnd 6: *[Sc in next sc, 2 sc in next sc] twice, sc in each of next 22 sc, [2 sc in next sc, sc in next sc] twice, rep from * once. *(68 sc)*

Rnd 7: *[Sc in next sc, 2 sc in next sc] twice, sc in each of next 26 sc, [2 sc in next sc, sc in next sc] twice, rep from * once. *(76 sc)*

Rnd 8: *[Sc in next sc, 2 sc in next sc] twice, sc in each of next 30 sc, [2 sc in next sc, sc in next sc] twice, rep from * once. *(84 sc)*

Rnd 9: Sc in each sc around, join in first sc.

Rnd 10: Ch 1, **reverse sc** *(see illustration)* in each sc, join in first reverse sc, fasten off.

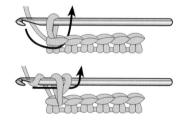

Reverse Single Crochet

COASTER
Rnd 1 (RS): Ch 3, join in first ch to form ring, **ch 3** *(see Pattern Notes)*, 11 dc in ring, join in 3rd ch of beg ch-3. *(12 dc)*

Rnd 2: Ch 3, dc in same ch, 2 dc in each rem dc, join in 3rd ch of beg ch-3, fasten off. *(24 dc)* ∎

Charger Place Mat

DESIGN BY CINDY ADAMS

SKILL LEVEL
EASY

FINISHED SIZE
18 inches in diameter

MATERIALS
- Bernat Cottontots medium (worsted) weight cotton yarn (3½ oz/ 171 yds/100g per ball): 1 ball #90615 sunshine
- Size H/8/5mm crochet hook or size needed to obtain gauge
- Tapestry needle

GAUGE
Rnd 1 = 1½ inches

PATTERN NOTES
Weave in ends as work progresses.

Join rounds with a slip stitch unless otherwise stated.

Chain-3 at beginning of double crochet row or round counts as first double crochet unless otherwise stated.

Instructions

Rnd 1 (RS): Ch 4, join in first ch to form ring, **ch 3** *(see Pattern Notes)*, 11 dc in ring, join in 3rd ch of beg ch-3. *(12 dc)*

Rnd 2: Ch 3, dc in same ch, 2 dc in each of next 2 dc, *ch 3, 2 dc in each of next 3 dc, rep from *

twice, ch 1, join with hdc in 3rd ch of beg ch-3. *(24 dc)*

Rnd 3: Ch 1, sc in sp formed by joining hdc, *ch 5, sk next 2 dc, **dc dec** *(see Stitch Guide)* in next 2 dc, ch 5, sk next 2 dc, sc in next ch-3 sp, rep from * twice, ch 5, sk next 2 dc, dc dec in next 2 dc, ch 5, join in first sc. *(8 ch-5 sps)*

Rnd 4: Sl st in first ch-5 sp, ch 3, 5 dc in same sp, 6 dc in each rem ch-5 sp, join in 3rd ch of beg ch-3. *(48 dc)*

Rnd 5: Ch 3, dc in next dc, ch 7, sk next 2 dc, *dc dec in next 2 dc, ch 7, sk next 2 dc, rep from * around, join in 3rd ch of beg ch-3. *(12 ch-7 sps)*

Rnd 6: Sl st in first ch-7 sp, ch 3, 8 dc in same sp, 9 dc in next ch-7 sp, (4 dc, ch 3, 4 dc) in next ch-7 sp, *9 dc in each of next 2 ch-7 sps, (4 dc, ch 3, 4 dc) in next ch-7 sp, rep from * twice, join in 3rd ch of beg ch-3. *(104 dc and 4 ch-3 sps)*

Rnd 7: Ch 9 *(counts as first dc, ch-6 sp)*, sk next 3 dc, sc in next dc, ch 6, sk next 3 dc, dc dec in next 2 dc, ch 6, sk next 3 dc, sc in next dc, ch 6, sk next 3 dc, dc dec in next 2 dc, ch 4, [sc, ch 4] twice in next ch-3 sp, *sk next 3 dc, dc dec in next 2 dc, [ch 6, sk next 3 dc, sc in next dc, ch 6, sk next 3 dc, dc dec in next 2 dc] twice, ch 4, [sc, ch 4] twice in next ch-3 sp,

CONTINUED ON PAGE 41

Harvest Rug

DESIGN BY ELAINE BARTLETT

SKILL LEVEL

EASY

FINISHED SIZE
27½ x 19½ inches

MATERIALS
- Red Heart Super Saver medium (worsted) weight yarn (7 oz/364 yds/ 198g per skein):
    2 skeins #336 warm brown
    1 skein #320 cornmeal
- Size N/13/9mm crochet hook or size needed to obtain gauge
- Tapestry needle

GAUGE
Working in pattern with 2 strands held tog: 6 sc and 5 ch-1 sps = 4 inches; 12 pattern st rows = 4 inches

PATTERN NOTES
Weave in ends as work progresses.

Join rounds with a slip stitch unless otherwise stated.

Work with 2 strands of yarn held together throughout unless otherwise stated.

Instructions

CENTER
Row 1 (RS): With warm brown, ch 70 loosely, sc in 2nd ch from hook, sc in each rem ch across, turn. *(69 sc)*

Row 2: Ch 1, sc in first sc, *ch 1, sk next sc, sc in next sc, rep from * across, turn. *(35 sc, 34 ch-1 sps)*

Row 3: Ch 1, sc in first sc, sc in next ch-1 sp, *ch 1, sc in next ch-1 sp, rep from * across to last sc, sc in last sc, turn. *(36 sc, 33 ch-1 sps)*

Row 4: Ch 1, sc in first sc, *ch 1, sc in next ch-1 sp, rep from * across to last sc, ch 1, sc in last sc, turn. *(35 sc, 34 ch-1 sps)*

Row 5: Rep row 3. Fasten off.

Row 6: With cornmeal, make slip knot on hook and join with sc in

first sc, *ch 1, sc in next ch-1 sp, rep from * across to last sc, ch 1, sc in last sc, turn. *(35 sc, 34 ch-1 sps)*

Row 7: Rep row 3. Fasten off.

Row 8: With warm brown, rep row 6.

Rows 9–12: [Rep rows 3 and 4 alternately] twice.

Row 13: Rep row 3. Fasten off.

Rows 14–45: [Rep rows 6–13 consecutively] 4 times. Fasten off.

CONTINUED ON PAGE 41

Spring Green Rug

AN ANNIE ORIGINAL DESIGN

SKILL LEVEL
EASY

FINISHED SIZE
54 inches from side to side

MATERIALS
- Red Heart Super Saver medium (worsted) weight yarn (7 oz/364 yds/198g per skein): 5 skeins #631 light sage
- Size Q/16mm crochet hook or size needed to obtain gauge
- Tapestry needle

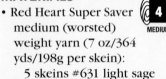

GAUGE
Rnds 1 & 2 = 6 inches in diameter

PATTERN NOTES
Weave in ends as work progresses.

Rug is worked with 3 strands held together throughout.

Join rounds with a slip stitch unless otherwise stated.

Chain-3 at beginning of double crochet round counts as first double crochet unless otherwise stated.

SPECIAL STITCHES
Beginning shell (beg shell): Ch 3, (dc, ch 2, 2 dc) in sp indicated.

Shell: (2 dc, ch 2, 2 dc) in sp indicated.

V-st: (Dc, ch 1, dc) in st indicated.

Instructions

Rnd 1 (RS): Ch 4, join in 4th ch from hook to form ring, **ch 3** *(see Pattern Notes)*, 11 dc in ring, join in 3rd ch of beg ch-3. *(12 dc)*

Rnd 2: Ch 4 *(counts as first dc, ch-1 sp)*, *dc in next dc, ch 1, rep from * around, join in 3rd ch of beg ch-4. *(12 dc, 12 ch-1 sps)*

Rnd 3: Sl st in next ch-1 sp, **beg shell** *(see Special Stitches)* in same sp, ch 1, sk next ch-1 sp, *shell *(see Special Stitches)* in next ch-1 sp, ch 1, sk next ch-1 sp, rep from * 4 times, join in 3rd ch of beg ch-3. *(6 shells)*

Rnd 4: Sl st in next dc and in next ch-2 sp, beg shell in same sp, ch 1, dc in next ch-1 sp, ch 1, *shell in ch-2 sp of next shell, ch 1, dc in next ch-1 sp, ch 1, rep from * 4 times, join in 3rd ch of beg ch-3. *(6 shells, 6 dc, 12 ch-1 sps)*

Rnd 5: Sl st in next dc and in next ch-2 sp, beg shell in same sp, ch 1, dc in next ch-1 sp, ch 1, V-st *(see Special Stitches)* in next st, ch 1, dc in next ch-1 sp, ch 1, *shell in ch-2 sp of next shell, ch 1, dc in next ch-1 sp, ch 1, V-st in next st, ch 1, dc in next ch-1 sp, ch 1, rep from * 4 times, join in 3rd ch of beg ch-3. *(6 shells, 6 V-sts, 12 dc, 24 ch-1 sps)*

Rnd 6: Sl st in next dc and in next ch-2 sp, beg shell in same sp, ch 1, sk next ch-1 sp, V-st in next st, ch 1, V-st in ch-1 sp of next V-st, ch 1, sk next ch-1 sp, V-st in next st, ch 1, *shell in ch-2 sp of next shell, ch 1, sk next ch-1 sp, V-st in next st, ch 1, V-st in ch-1 sp of next V-st, ch 1, sk next ch-1 sp, V-st in next st, ch 1, rep from * 4 times, join in 3rd ch of beg ch-3. *(6 shells, 18 V-sts, 24 ch-1 sps)*

Rnd 7: Sl st in next dc and in next ch-2 sp, beg shell in same sp, ch 1, dc in next ch-1 sp, ch 1, [V-st in ch-1 sp of next V-st, ch 1] 3 times, dc in next ch-1 sp, ch 1, *shell in ch-2 sp of next shell, ch 1, dc in next ch-1 sp, ch 1, [V-st in ch-1 sp of next V-st, ch 1] 3 times, dc in next ch-1 sp, ch 1, rep from * 4 times, join in 3rd ch of beg ch-3. *(6 shells, 18 V-sts, 12 dc, 36 ch-1 sps)*

Rnd 8: Sl st in next dc and in next ch-2 sp, beg shell in same sp, ch 1, sk next ch-1 sp, V-st in next st, ch 1, [V-st in ch-1 sp of next V-st, ch 1] 3 times, sk next ch-1 sp, V-st in next st, ch 1, *shell in ch-2 sp of next shell, ch 1, sk next ch-1 sp, V-st in next st, ch 1, [V-st in ch-1 sp of next V-st, ch 1] 3 times, sk next ch-1 sp, V-st in next st, ch 1, rep from * 4 times, join in 3rd ch of beg ch-3. *(6 shells, 30 V-sts, 24 ch-1 sps)*

Rnd 9: Sl st in next dc and in next ch-2 sp, beg shell in same sp, ch 1, dc in next ch-1 sp, ch 1, [V-st in ch-1 sp of next V-st, ch 1] 5 times, dc in next ch-1 sp, ch 1, *shell in ch-2 sp of next shell, ch 1, dc in next ch-1 sp, ch 1, [V-st in

ch-1 sp of next V-st, ch 1] 5 times, dc in next ch-1 sp, ch 1, rep from * 4 times, join in 3rd ch of beg ch-3. *(6 shells, 30 V-sts, 12 dc, 48 ch-1 sps)*

Rnd 10: Sl st in next dc and in next ch-2 sp, beg shell in same sp, ch 1, sk next ch-1 sp, V-st in next st, ch 1, [V-st in ch-1 sp of next V-st, ch 1] 5 times, sk next ch-1 sp, V-st in next st, ch 1, *shell in ch-2 sp of next shell, ch 1, sk next ch-1 sp, V-st in next st, ch 1, [V-st in ch-1 sp of next V-st, ch 1] 5 times, sk next ch-1 sp, V-st in next st, ch 1, rep from * 4 times, join in 3rd ch of beg ch-3. *(6 shells, 42 V-sts, 48 ch-1 sps)*

Rnd 11: Sl st in next dc and in next ch-2 sp, beg shell in same sp, ch 1, dc in next ch-1 sp, ch 1, [V-st in ch-1 sp of next V-st, ch 1] 7 times, dc in next ch-1 sp, ch 1, *shell in ch-2 sp of next shell, ch 1, dc in next ch-1 sp, ch 1, [V-st in ch-1 sp of next V-st, ch 1] 7 times, dc in next ch-1 sp, ch 1, rep from * 4 times, join in 3rd ch of beg ch-3. *(6 shells, 42 V-sts, 12 dc, 60 ch-1 sps)*

Rnd 12: Sl st in next dc and in next ch-2 sp, beg shell in same sp, ch 1, sk next ch-1 sp, V-st in next st, ch 1, [V-st in ch-1 sp of next V-st, ch 1] 7 times, sk next ch-1 sp, V-st in next st, ch 1, *shell in ch-2 sp of next shell, ch 1, sk next ch-1 sp, V-st in

next st, ch 1, [V-st in ch-1 sp of next V-st, ch 1] 7 times, sk next ch-1 sp, V-st in next st, ch 1, rep from * 4 times, join in 3rd ch of beg ch-3. *(6 shells, 54 V-sts, 60 ch-1 sps)*

Rnd 13: Sl st in next dc and in next ch-2 sp, beg shell in same sp, ch 1, dc in next ch-1 sp, ch 1, [V-st in ch-1 sp of next V-st, ch 1] 9 times, dc in next ch-1 sp, ch 1, *shell in ch-2 sp of next shell, ch 1, dc in next ch-1 sp, ch 1, [V-st in ch-1 sp of next V-st, ch 1] 9 times, dc in next ch-1 sp, ch 1, rep from * 4 times, join in 3rd ch of beg ch-3. *(6 shells, 54 V-sts, 12 dc, 72 ch-1 sps)*

CONTINUED ON PAGE 42

Richly Textured Pillow

DESIGN BY MICHELE WILCOX

SKILL LEVEL

EASY

FINISHED SIZE
8 x 16 inches, excluding Tassels

MATERIALS

- Bernat Satin medium (worsted) weight yarn (3½ oz/163 yds/100g per ball):
    1 ball each #04430 bordeaux, #04236 evergreen, #04010 camel, #04011 sable
- Size G/6/4mm crochet hook or size needed to obtain gauge
- Tapestry needle
- Polyester fiberfill
- 6-inch square piece of cardboard

GAUGE
4 sc = 1 inch; 4 sc rows = 1 inch

PATTERN NOTE
Weave in ends as work progresses.

Instructions

SIDE
Make 2.
Row 1 (RS): With evergreen, ch 32, sc in 2nd ch from hook and in each ch across, turn. *(31 sc)*

Rows 2–6: Ch 1, working in **back lps** *(see Stitch Guide)* only,

sc in each sc across, **changing color** *(see Stitch Guide)* to bordeaux in last sc of row 6, turn.

Row 7: Ch 1, sc in each sc across, turn.

Row 8: Ch 1, sc in first sc, *tr in next sc, sc in next sc, rep from * across, turn.

Rows 9–12: [Rep rows 7 and 8 alternately] twice.

Row 13: Ch 1, sc in each sc across, changing color to camel in last sc, turn.

Rows 14–16: Ch 1, sc in each sc across, changing color to sable in last sc of row 16, turn.

Rows 17 & 18: Rep rows 7 and 8 alternately once.

Row 19: Ch 1, sc in each sc across, changing color to camel

in last sc, turn.

Rows 20–22: Ch 1, sc in each sc across, changing color to evergreen in last sc of row 22, turn.

Row 23: Ch 1, sc in each sc across, turn.

Rows 24–26: Ch 1, working in back lps only, sc in each sc across, changing color to bordeaux in last sc of row 26, turn.

Rows 27–32: [Rep rows 7 and 8 alternately] 3 times.

Row 33: Ch 1, sc in each sc across, changing color to evergreen in last sc, turn.

Rows 34–37: Ch 1, working in back lps only, sc in each sc across, changing color to camel in last sc of row 37, turn.

Rows 38–40: Ch 1, sc in each sc

across, changing color to sable in last sc of row 40, turn.

Rows 41 & 42: Rep rows 7 and 8 alternately once.

Row 43: Ch 1, sc in each sc across, changing color to camel in last sc, turn.

Rows 44–46: Ch 1, sc in each sc across, changing color to bordeaux in last sc of row 46, turn.

Rows 47–52: [Rep rows 7 and 8 alternately] 3 times.

Row 53: Ch 1, sc in each sc across, changing color to evergreen in last sc, turn.

Row 54: Ch 1, sc in each sc across, turn.

Rows 55–59: Ch 1, working in back lps only, sc in each sc across, turn. At end of row 59, fasten off.

FINISHING
Hold pieces with WS tog, with tapestry needle and evergreen, sew edges tog, stuffing firmly with fiberfill before closing.

TASSEL
Make 4.
Wrap bordeaux around 6-inch cardboard square 30 times. Tie a separate strand of yarn around center of all strands *(Step 1)*. Cut

ends and remove from cardboard. Tie another strand about 1 inch below center *(Step 2)*.

Sew 1 Tassel to each corner of Pillow. ∎

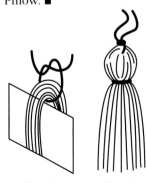

Step 1   Step 2
Tassel
Richly Textured Pillow

Midnight Blue Pillow

DESIGN BY ALICE HEIM

SKILL LEVEL

■■□□
EASY

FINISHED SIZE
16 x 16 inches

MATERIALS

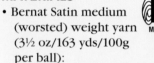

4
MEDIUM

- Bernat Satin medium (worsted) weight yarn (3½ oz/163 yds/100g per ball):
   3 balls #04110 admiral
- Size J/10/6mm crochet hook or size needed to obtain gauge
- Tapestry needle
- 16-inch square pillow form

GAUGE

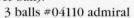

4 sts = 1½ inches

PATTERN NOTES
Weave in ends as work progresses.

Chain-3 at beginning of double crochet row or round counts as first double crochet unless otherwise stated.

SPECIAL STITCH
Puff stitch (puff st): [Yo, insert hook from right to left around **post** *(see Stitch Guide)* of st indicated on 2nd row below, yo, draw through, pulling lp up to height of working row] twice, yo, pull through 4 lps on hook, yo, pull through 2 lps on hook.

Instructions

FIRST SIDE
Row 1 (RS): Ch 44, sc in 2nd ch from hook, sc in each rem ch across, turn. *(43 sc)*

Row 2: Ch 1, sc in each sc across, turn.

Row 3: Ch 3 *(see Pattern Notes)*, dc in each of next 2 sc,***puff st** *(see Special Stitch)* around next sc on 2nd row below, sk sc behind puff st on working row, dc in each of next 3 sc, rep from * 9 times, turn. *(10 puff sts)*

Row 4: Ch 3, dc in each st across, turn.

Row 5: Ch 3, [puff st around next st on 2nd row below, dc in each of next 3 sts] 10 times, puff st around next st on 2nd row below, dc in last st, turn. *(11 puff sts)*

Row 6: Ch 3, dc in each st across, turn.

Rows 7–30: [Rep rows 3–6 consecutively] 6 times. At end of row 30, fasten off.

2ND SIDE
Row 1 (RS): Ch 44, sc in 2nd ch from hook, *dc in next ch, sc in next ch, rep from * across, turn. *(43 sts)*

Row 2: Ch 3 *(see Pattern Notes)*, *sc in next dc, dc in next sc, rep from * across, turn.

Row 3: Ch 1, sc in first st, *dc in next sc, sc in next dc, rep from * across, turn.

Rep rows 2 and 3 until piece measures same as First Side. At end of last row, fasten off.

FINISHING
Hold pieces with WS facing and working through both thicknesses in ends of rows, sts and chs, make slip knot on hook and join with sc in any st, sc in each st, 2 sc in end of each row and sc in each ch around, inserting pillow form before joining last side, join in first sc, fasten off.

TASSEL
Make 4.
Cut 26 pieces of yarn, each 8 inches long. Hold all pieces tog and fold in half, tie another piece of yarn around folded pieces 1 inch from fold. Rep for other Tassels. With tapestry needle, sew folded ends to corners of pillow. ■

Sea Breeze Table Runner

DESIGN BY MARTY MILLER

SKILL LEVEL

■■□□ **EASY**

FINISHED SIZE
15 x 44 inches, excluding Fringe

MATERIALS

- TLC Cotton Plus medium (worsted) weight yarn (3½ oz/178 yds/ 100g per skein):
    2 skeins each #3811 medium blue, #3100 cream and #3645 mint
- Size H/8/5mm crochet hook or size needed to obtain gauge
- Tapestry needle

GAUGE
19 sc = 4 inches; 21 rows = 4 inches

PATTERN NOTES
Two methods for beginning this table runner are given—the first method uses the traditional chain and first row of single crochet. The second method uses a foundation single crochet, which creates the chain and first row at the same time. Use either method.

SPECIAL STITCH
Foundation single crochet (foundation sc): Ch 2, insert hook in 2nd ch from hook, yo, draw up a lp, yo, draw through 1 lp on hook (*1 ch*), yo, draw through 2 lps on hook (*foundation sc*), insert hook under 2 lps of ch made in first foundation sc, yo, draw up a lp, yo, draw through 1 lp (*1 ch*), yo, draw through 2 lps. (*2 foundation sc*)

Continue in this manner for number of foundation sc needed.

Instructions

Method 1
Row 1 (WS): With medium blue, ch 201, sc in 2nd ch from hook, sc in each rem ch across. Fasten off, leaving an 8-inch end. (*200 sc*)

Method 2
Row 1 (WS): With medium blue, work 200 **foundation sc** (*see Special Stitch*). Fasten off, leaving an 8-inch end. (*200 foundation sc*)

Both Methods
Row 2 (RS): With RS facing and leaving an 8-inch end, attach cream with sl st in first sc, ch 1, sc in same sc, ch 1, sk next sc, *sc in next sc, ch 1, rep from * across to last 2 sc, sc in each of last 2 sc.

Fasten off, leaving an 8-inch end. Turn.

Row 3: Leaving an 8-inch end, attach mint with sl st in first st, ch 1, sc in first sc, ch 1, *sk next sc, sc in next ch-1 sp, ch 1, rep from * across to last ch-1 sp, sc in last ch-1 sp, sc in last sc. Fasten off, leaving an 8-inch end. Turn.

Rows 4–78: Rep row 3 in following color sequence: 1 row medium blue, 1 row cream, 1 row mint.

Row 79: Leaving an 8-inch end, attach medium blue with sl st in first sc, ch 1, sc in first sc, sc in each rem sc and in each ch-1 sp across, turn. (*200 sc*)

Row 80: Sl st in each st across. Fasten off, leaving an 8-inch end.

Edging
For piece started with Method 1, hold piece with RS facing and beg ch at top, attach medium blue with sl st in unused lp of first ch, sl st in each rem unused lp of beg ch. Fasten off, leaving an 8-inch end.

FRINGE
Trim long yarn ends at ends of each row to 6 inches. ■

TV Time Accessories

AN ANNIE'S ORIGINAL DESIGN

Remote Holder

SKILL LEVEL
EASY

FINISHED SIZE
8½ x 20½ inches

MATERIALS
- Medium (worsted) weight yarn:
  3½ oz/175 yds/99g green
- Size G/6/4mm crochet hook or size needed to obtain gauge
- Tapestry needle
- Sewing needle
- 7½ x 10¼ piece of dark green felt (optional for pocket lining)
- Matching sewing thread

GAUGE
Rnds 1 & 2 = 2½ inches across
Motif = 3¾ x 3¾ inches square

PATTERN NOTES
Weave in ends as work progresses.

Join rounds with a slip stitch unless otherwise stated.

Chain-3 at beginning of double crochet row or round counts as first double crochet unless otherwise stated.

Instructions

MOTIF
Make 12.
Rnd 1 (RS): Ch 4, join in first ch to form a ring, **ch 3** *(see Pattern Notes)*, 2 dc in ring, ch 3, [3 dc in ring, ch 3] 3 times, join in 3rd ch of beg ch-3. *(12 dc, 4 ch-3 sps)*

Rnds 2 & 3: Ch 3, dc in each st around and (2 dc, ch 3, 2 dc) in each ch-3 sp, join in 3rd ch of beg ch-3. At end of rnd 3, fasten off. *(28 dc, 4 ch-3 sps)*

ASSEMBLY
Holding 2 Motifs WS tog and matching sts, sew tog through **back lps** *(see Stitch Guide)* only of 1 edge (forming seam at top of 1st Motif and at bottom of 2nd Motif), rep to join 1 Motif to top of 2nd, 3rd, and 4th Motifs (forming strip of 5 Motifs), rep once for 2nd strip of 5 Motifs. Holding strips WS tog, matching sts on 1 long edge of each strip, sew tog through back lps only.

For **pocket**, holding last 2 Motifs with WS tog and matching sts, sew tog through back lps only across 1 side.

Top edge of pocket
Row 1 (RS): Working across 1 long edge of pocket, join in top right-hand ch-3 sp, ch 3, dc in same sp, dc in each of next 11 dc, dc in each of next 2 ch-3 sps, dc in each of next 11 dc, 2 dc in next ch-3 sp, turn, leaving rem sts unworked. *(28 dc)*

Rows 2 & 3: Ch 3, dc in each st across, turn. At end of row 3, **do not turn**.

Row 4: Ch 1, working left to right work **reverse sc** *(see illustration)* in each st across, fasten off.

EDGING
Holding pocket with WS facing

RS of back on one end, matching sts and working through both thicknesses of pocket and back on 3 sides and working through back sts only along top edge of pocket, join in any st, work reverse sc in each st and ch sp around and 3 reverse sc in each corner ch-3 sp, join in first reverse sc, fasten off.

FINISHING
If lining pocket, fold felt in half crosswise RS tog to measure 5⅛ x 7½ inches. Sew ¼-inch side seams, leaving top open. Turn lining RS out. Place felt inside pocket. Tack in place to top edge of pocket and to back of Holder.

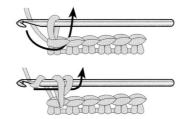

Reverse Single Crochet

Tissue Box Cover

SKILL LEVEL
EASY

FINISHED SIZE
Fits boutique-style tissue box

MATERIALS
- Medium (worsted) weight yarn: 3½ oz/175 yds/99g variegated
- Size G/6/4mm crochet hook or size needed to obtain gauge
- Tapestry needle

4
MEDIUM

GAUGE
Rnds 1–3 = 4¾ inches across
7 sts = 2 inches; 6 rows = 2 inches

PATTERN NOTES
Weave in ends as work progresses.

Join rounds with a slip stitch unless otherwise stated.

Chain-3 at beginning of double crochet row or round counts as first double crochet unless otherwise stated.

Instructions

Rnd 1 (RS): Starting at top, ch 24, join in first ch to form a ring, **ch 3** *(see Pattern Notes)*, 2 dc in same ch, dc in each of next 5 chs, *3 dc in next ch, dc in each of next 5 chs, rep from * twice, join in 3rd ch of beg ch-3. *(32 dc)*

Rnd 2: Ch 3, 5 dc in next dc, [dc in each of next 7 dc, 5 dc in next dc] 3 times, dc in each of last 6 dc, join in 3rd ch of beg ch-3. *(48 dc)*

Rnd 3: Ch 1, sc in each of first 3 dc, 3 sc in next dc, [sc in each of next 11 dc, 3 sc in next dc] 3 times, sc in each of last 8 dc, join in first sc. *(56 sc)*

Rnd 4: Ch 3, working in **back lps** *(see Stitch Guide)*, sc in next st, *dc in next st, sc in next st, rep from * around, join in 3rd ch of beg ch-3.

Rnd 5: Ch 1, sc in first st, dc in next st, *sc in next st, dc in next st, rep from * around, join in first sc.

Rnds 6–17: [Rep rnds 4 and 5 alternately] 6 times.

Rnd 18: Rep rnd 4.

Rnd 19: Ch 1, working left to right, work reverse sc *(see illustration above)* in each sc, join in first reverse sc, fasten off.

Coaster Set

SKILL LEVEL

EASY

FINSHED SIZES
Basket: 3 inches deep x 4½ inches square
Coaster: 4¼ inches across

MATERIALS
• Medium (worsted) weight yarn:
  2 oz/100yds/56g variegated
  10 yds each green, red, tan
• Size G/6/4mm crochet hook or size needed to obtain gauge
• Tapestry needle

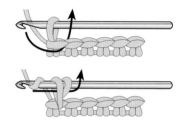

4
MEDIUM

GAUGE
Rnds 1 & 2 = 2½ inches across

PATTERN NOTES
Weave in ends as work progresses.

Join rounds with a slip stitch unless otherwise stated.

Chain-3 at beginning of double crochet row or round counts as first double crochet unless otherwise stated.

Instructions

BASKET
Rnd 1 (RS): Starting at bottom with variegated, ch 4, join in first ch to form a ring, **ch 3** *(see Pattern Notes)*, 2 dc in ring, ch 3, [3 dc in ring, ch 3] 3 times, join in 3rd ch of beg ch-3. *(12 dc, 4 ch-3 sps)*

Rnd 2: Ch 3, dc in each of next 2 dc, (2 dc, ch 3, 2 dc) in next ch-3 sp *(corner)*, *dc in each of next 3 dc, corner in next ch-3 sp, rep from * twice, join in 3rd ch of beg ch-3. *(28 dc, 4 ch-3 sps)*

Rnd 3: Ch 3, dc in each of next 4 dc, corner in next corner ch-3 sp, *dc in each of next 7 dc, corner in next corner ch-3 sp, rep from * twice, dc in next 2 dc, join in 3rd ch of beg ch-3. *(44 dc, 4 ch-3 sps)*

Rnd 4: Ch 1, sc in each of first 7 dc, 3 sc in next corner ch-3 sp *(sc corner)*, *sc in each of next 11 dc, sc corner in next corner ch-3 sp, rep from * twice, sc in next 4 dc, join in first sc. *(56 sc)*

Rnd 5: Ch 1, working in **back lps** *(see Stitch Guide)* only, sc in first sc, dc in next sc, *sc in next sc, dc in next sc, rep from * around, join in first sc.

Rnd 6: Ch 3, sc in next st, *dc in next st, sc in next st, rep from * around, join in 3rd ch of beg ch-3.

Rnd 7: Ch 1, sc in first st, dc in next st, *sc in next st, dc in next st, rep from * around, join in first sc.

Rnds 8–11: [Rep rnds 6 and 7 alternately] twice.

Rnd 12: Rep rnd 6.

Rnd 13: Ch 1, working left to right, work reverse sc *(see illustration)* in each st around, join in first sc, fasten off.

Reverse Single Crochet

COASTER
Make 1 each of variegated, green, red and tan.
Rnd 1 (RS): Ch 4, join in first ch to form a ring, ch 3, 2 dc in ring, [3 dc in ring, ch 3] 3 times, join in 3rd ch of beg ch-3. *(12 dc, 4 ch-3 sps)*

Rnd 2: Ch 3, dc in each of next 2 dc, (2 dc, ch 3, 2 dc) in next ch-3 sp *(corner)*, *dc in each of next 3 dc, corner in next ch-3 sp, rep from * twice, join in 3rd ch of beg ch-3. *(28 dc, 4 ch-3 sps)*

Rnd 3: Ch 3, dc in each of next 4 dc, corner in next corner ch-3 sp, *dc in each of next 7 dc, corner in next corner ch-3 sp, rep from * twice, dc in next 2 dc, join in 3rd ch of beg ch-3, fasten off. *(44 dc, 4 ch-3 sps)* ∎

Clutter Keepers

DESIGNS BY MARTY MILLER

SKILL LEVEL ■■□□ EASY

FINISHED SIZES
Basket #1: 4 x 4 x 4½ inches
Basket #2: 6 x 6 x 6 inches
Basket #3: 9 x 12 x 3 inches

MATERIALS
- TLC Cotton Plus medium (worsted) weight yarn (3½ oz/178 yds/100g per skein): **MEDIUM**
  4 skeins #3533 periwinkle
  3 skeins each #3252 tangerine and #3303 tan
- Size H/8/5mm and K/10½/6.5mm crochet hook or size needed to obtain gauge
- Tapestry needle
- Stitch markers

GAUGE
Size K hook and 3 strands held tog: 8 sc = 3 inches; 9 rows = 3 inches

PATTERN NOTES
Weave in ends as work progresses.

Two methods for beginning these baskets are given—the first method uses the traditional chain and first row of single crochet. The second method uses a foundation single crochet, which creates the chain and first row at the same time. Use either method.

Use 3 strands of yarn held together throughout and K hook, unless otherwise directed.

Sides of the baskets are worked from the bottom to the top.

SPECIAL STITCH
Foundation single crochet (foundation sc): Ch 2, insert hook in 2nd ch from hook, yo, draw up a lp, yo, draw through 1 lp on hook (*1 ch*), yo, draw through 2 lps on hook (*foundation sc*), insert hook under 2 lps of ch made in first foundation sc, yo, draw up a lp, yo, draw through 1 lp (*1 ch*), yo, draw through 2 lps. (*2 foundation sc*)

Continue in this manner for number of foundation sc needed.

Instructions

BASKET #1
Bottom
Method 1
Row 1 (RS): With K hook and 3 strands of tan held tog, ch 9, sc in 2nd ch from hook, sc in each rem ch across, turn. (*8 sc*)

Method 2
Row 1 (RS): With K hook and 3 strands of tan, work 8 **foundation sc** (*see Special Stitch*), turn. (*8 foundation sc*)

Both Methods
Row 2: Ch 1, sc in each sc across, turn.

Rows 3–9: Rep row 2. At end of row 9, **do not turn.**

Edging
Ch 1, 2 sc in same sp as last sc on row 9, place marker in first of these 2 sc, working along next side in ends of rows, sk row 9, sc in each of next 7 rows, working along next side, 2 sc in bottom of first sc of row 1, place marker in first of these 2 sc, sc in bottom of each of next 6 sc, 2 sc in bottom of last sc, place marker in last of these 2 sc, working along next side in ends of rows, sk row 1, sc in next 8 rows, join in first sc of row 9, place marker in joining sl st, fasten off. (*35 sc, 1 sl st*)

Side
Make 4.
Method 1
Row 1 (RS): With K hook and 3 strands of tan held tog, ch 9, sc in 2nd ch from hook, sc in each rem ch across, turn. (*8 sc*)

Method 2
Row 1 (RS): With K hook and 3 strands of tan, work 8 foundation sc, turn. (*8 foundation sc*)

Both Methods
Row 2: Ch 1, sc in each sc across, turn.

Rows 3–11: Rep row 2. At end of row 11, **do not turn.**

Edging
Ch 1, 2 sc in same sp as last sc on row 11, place marker in first of these 2 sc, working along next side in ends of rows, sk row 11, sc in each of next 9 rows, working along next side, 2 sc in bottom of

first sc of row 1, place marker in first of these 2 sc, sc in bottom of each of next 6 sc, 2 sc in bottom of last sc, place marker in last of these 2 sc, working along next side in ends of rows, sk row 1, sc in each of next 10 rows, join in first sc of row 11, place marker in joining sl st, fasten off. *(39 sc, 1 sl st)*

ASSEMBLY
With RS facing, pin Sides tog at marked sts. With H hook and 1 strand tan, starting at bottom of any 2 Sides, sc in **back lps** *(see Stitch Guide)* only of corresponding sts across Sides. Fasten off. Rep on rem Sides.

Pin Bottom to bottom edges of Sides. With H hook and 1 strand of tan, working through both thicknesses of Sides and bottom and in back lps only, sc evenly spaced around, working 1 sc

connecting corner of Bottom to 1 adjacent Side, then working another sc in same corner of Bottom and corner of next adjacent Side, join in first sc. Fasten off.

TOP EDGING
With K hook and 3 strands of tan, sc in each sc around top edge of Basket, join in first sc, fasten off.

BASKET #2
Bottom/Sides
Make 5.
Method 1
Row 1 (RS): With K hook and 3 strands of tangerine, ch 17, sc in 2nd ch from hook, sc in each rem ch across, turn. *(16 sc)*

Method 2
Row 1 (RS): With K hook and 3 strands of tangerine, work 16 **foundation sc** *(see Special Stitch)*, turn. *(16 foundation sc)*

Both Methods
Row 2: Ch 1, sc in each sc across, turn.

Rows 3–17: Rep row 2. At end of row 17, **do not turn**.

Edging
Ch 1, 2 sc in same sp as last sc on row 17, place marker in first of these 2 sc, working along next side in ends of rows, sk row 17, sc in each of next 15 rows, working along next side, 2 sc in bottom of first sc of row 1, place marker in first of these 2 sc, sc in bottom of each of next 14 sc, 2 sc in bottom of last sc, place marker in last of these 2 sc, working along next side in ends of rows, sk row 1, sc in each of next 16 rows, join in first sc of row 17, place marker in joining sl st, fasten off. *(67 sc, 1 sl st)*

CONTINUED ON PAGE 42

Autumn Lace

DESIGN BY ELIZABETH ANN WHITE

SKILL LEVEL

FINISHED SIZE
13 x 50 inches, excluding
Tassels

MATERIALS
- Aunt Lydia's Fashion Crochet
  size 3 crochet cotton (150
  yds per ball):
    9 balls #377 tan
- Size 0/2.50mm steel crochet
  hook or size needed to
  obtain gauge
- 8-inch square piece of
  cardboard

GAUGE
5 cls = 1¾ inches; 3 cl rows =
1 inch

SPECIAL STITCH
Cluster (cl): Holding back
last lp on hook, 3 dc as
indicated, yo, pull through
all lps on hook.

Instructions

RUNNER
Row 1: Ch 78, **cl** *(see Special Stitch)* in 4th ch from hook *(first 3 chs count as ch sp)*, [ch 1, sk

next ch, cl in next ch] across, turn. *(38 cls)*

Row 2: Ch 4 *(counts as ch sp)*, [cl in next ch sp, ch 1] across, cl in last ch sp, turn.

Next rows: Rep row 2 until Runner measures 50 inches. At end of last row, fasten off.

TASSEL
Make 4.
Wrap crochet cotton around

cardboard 100 times. Tie separate 12-inch strand around center of all strands at 1 end of cardboard, cut ends at other end of cardboard.

Wrap separate 18-inch strand 12 times around all strands 1 inch below 12-inch strand. Secure end.

Attach 1 Tassel to each corner of Runner. ■

Vintage Fan

DESIGN BY ISABELLE WOLTERS

SKILL LEVEL
INTERMEDIATE

FINISHED SIZE
10 x 18 inches

MATERIALS
- Aunt Lydia's Classic Crochet-Special Value size 10 crochet cotton (1000 yds per ball): 1 ball #226 natural
- Size 7/1.65 steel crochet hook or size needed to obtain gauge
- Straight pins
- Pinning board
- Starch

GAUGE
2 tr rows = 1 inch

PATTERN NOTES
Weave in ends as work progresses.

Join rounds with a slip stitch unless otherwise stated.

Chain-4 at beginning of treble crochet row or round counts as first treble crochet unless otherwise stated.

SPECIAL STITCHES
Shell: (2 tr, ch 2, 2 tr) in indicated sp.

Double shell: (2 tr, ch 2, 2 tr, ch 2, 2 tr) in indicated sp.

Picot: Ch 5, sl st in first ch of ch-5.

Instructions

Rnd 1 (WS): Ch 8, join in first ch to form a ring, ch 1, 18 sc in ring, join in first sc. *(18 sc)*

Rnd 2: Ch 3 *(counts as first dc)*, dc in same st as beg ch-3, 2 dc in each rem sc, join in 3rd ch of beg ch-3. *(36 dc)*

***Note:** Remainder of doily is worked in rows.*

Row 3 (WS): [Ch 2, sl st in next dc] 20 times, **ch 4** *(see Pattern Notes)*, tr in each of next 15 dc, turn, leaving rem sts unworked. *(16 tr)*

Row 4 (RS): Ch 4, tr in same st as beg ch-4, tr in each of next 14 tr, 2 tr in last tr, turn. *(18 tr)*

Row 5: Ch 4, tr in each of next 2 tr, [ch 1, tr in next tr] 12 times, ch 1, tr in each of next 3 tr, turn. *(18 tr, 18 ch sps)*

Row 6: Ch 4, tr in each of next 2 tr, [ch 2, tr in next tr] 12 times, ch 2, tr in each of next 3 tr, turn.

Row 7: Ch 4, tr in each of next 2 tr, [ch 3, tr in next tr] 12 times, ch 3, tr in each of next 3 tr, turn.

Row 8: Ch 4, tr in each of next 2 tr, [ch 4, tr in next tr] 12 times, ch 4, tr in each of next 3 tr, turn.

Row 9: Ch 4, tr in each of next 2 tr, [ch 5, tr in next tr] 12 times, ch 5, tr in each of next 3 tr, turn.

Row 10: Ch 4, tr in each of next 2 tr, [ch 6, tr in next tr] 12 times, ch 6, tr in each of next 3 tr, turn.

Row 11: Ch 4, tr in each of next 2 tr, [ch 7, tr in next tr] 12 times, ch 7, tr in each of next 3 tr, turn.

Row 12: Ch 4, tr in each of next 2 tr, [ch 5, (2 sc, ch 3, 2 sc) in next ch-7 sp] 13 times, ch 5, tr in each of next 3 tr, turn. *(58 sts)*

Row 13: Ch 4, tr in each of next 2 tr, [ch 6, (sc, ch 3, sc) in next ch-3 sp] 13 times, ch 6, tr in each of next 3 tr, turn. *(32 sts)*

Row 14: Ch 4, tr in each of next 2 tr, ch 4, **shell** *(see Special Stitches)* in next ch-3 sp, [ch 4, 7 tr in next ch-3 sp, ch 4, shell in next ch-3 sp] 6 times, ch 4, tr in each of next 3 tr, turn. *(7 shells, 48 tr)*

Row 15: Ch 4, tr in each of next 2 tr, ch 4, shell in ch-2 sp of next shell, *ch 4, tr in first tr of next 7-tr group, [ch 1, tr in next tr] 6 times, ch 4, shell in ch-2 sp of next shell, rep from * 5 times, ch 4, sk next ch-4 sp, tr in each of last 3 tr, turn.

Row 16: Ch 4, tr in each of next 2 tr, ch 4, **double shell** *(see*

Special Stitches) in ch-2 sp of next shell, *ch 4, sc in next ch-1 sp, [ch 6, sc in next ch-1 sp] 5 times, ch 4, double shell in ch-2 sp of next shell, rep from * 5 times, ch 4, sk next ch-4 sp, tr in each of next 3 tr, turn. *(7 double shells, 42 sts)*

Row 17: Ch 4, tr in each of next 2 tr, ch 4, shell in ch-2 sp of each of next 2 shells, *ch 4, sc in next ch-6 sp, [ch 6, sc in next ch-6 sp] 4 times, ch 4, shell in ch-2 sp of each of next 2 shells, rep from * 5 times, ch 4, sk next ch-4 sp, tr in each of next 3 tr, turn. *(14 shells, 36 sts)*

Row 18: Ch 4, tr in each of next 2 tr, ch 4, shell in ch-2 sp of next shell, ch 5, shell in ch-2 sp of next shell, *ch 4, sc in next ch-6 sp, [ch 6, sc in next ch-6 sp] 3 times, ch 4, shell in ch-2 sp of next shell, ch 5, shell in ch-2 sp of next shell, rep from * 5 times, ch 4, sk next ch-4 sp, tr in each of next 3 tr, turn. *(14 shells, 30 sts)*

Row 19: Ch 4, tr in each of next 2 tr, ch 4, shell in ch-2 sp of next shell, ch 3, shell in 3rd ch of next ch-5 sp, ch 3, shell in ch-2 sp of next shell, *ch 4, sc in next ch-6 sp, [ch 6, sc in next ch-6 sp] twice, ch 4, shell in ch-2 sp of next shell, ch 3, shell in 3rd ch of next ch-5 sp, ch 3, shell in ch-2 so of next shell, rep from * 5 times, ch 4, sk next ch-4 sp, tr in each of next 3 tr, turn. *(21 shells, 24 sts)*

Row 20: Ch 4, tr in each of next 2 tr, ch 4, shell in ch-2 sp of next shell, ch 4, tr in ch-2 of next shell, [ch 1, tr] 4 times in same ch-2 sp, ch 4, shell in ch-2 sp of next shell, *ch 4, sc in next ch-6 sp, ch 7, sl st in 5th ch from hook, ch 3, sc in next ch-6 sp, ch 4, shell in ch-2 sp of next shell, ch 4, tr in next ch-2 sp of shell, [ch 1, tr] 4 times in same ch-2 sp, ch 4, shell in ch-2 sp of next shell, rep from * 5 times, ch 4, sk next ch-4 sp, tr in each of next 3 tr, turn. *(14 shells, 53 sts)*

Row 21: Ch 4, tr in each of next

2 tr, ch 4, shell in ch-2 sp of next shell, ch 4, sk next ch-4 sp, tr in next tr, [ch 1, tr in next ch-1 sp, ch 1, tr in next tr] 4 times, ch 4, shell in ch-2 sp of next shell, *ch 1, shell in next shell, ch 4, sk next ch-4 sp, tr in next tr, [ch 1, tr in next ch-1 sp, ch 1, tr in next tr] 4 times, ch 4, shell in ch-2 sp of next shell, rep from * 5 times, ch 4, sk next ch-4 sp, tr in each of next 3 tr, turn. *(14 shells, 69 sts)*

Row 22: Ch 4, tr in each of next 2 tr, ch 4, [2 tr, **picot** *(see Special Stitches)*, 2 tr) in ch-2 sp of next shell, *ch 4, [(tr, picot, tr) in next ch-1 sp] 8 times, ch 4, 2 tr in ch-2 sp of next shell, picot, 2 tr in ch-2 sp of next shell, rep from * 5 times, ch 4, [(tr, picot, tr) in next ch-1 sp] 8 times, ch 4, (2 tr, picot, 2 tr) in ch-2 sp of next shell, ch 4, sk next ch-4 sp, tr in each of next 3 tr, fasten off. *(150 sts)*

Starch doily; pin to blocking board. Allow to dry completely. ■

Mocha & Cream

DESIGN BY LORI ZELLER

SKILL LEVEL
EASY

FINISHED SIZE
9½ inches in diameter

MATERIALS
• Size 5 crochet cotton:
  100 yds cream
• Size 10 crochet cotton:
  50 yds linen
• Size B/1/2.25mm crochet
  hook or size needed to
  obtain gauge
• Tapestry needle

GAUGE
Rnds 1–3 = 1¾ inches

PATTERN NOTES
Weave in ends as work progresses.

Join rounds with a slip stitch
unless otherwise stated.

Instructions

Rnd 1 (RS): With cream, ch 6,
join in first ch to form a ring, ch
4 *(counts as first dc, ch-1 sp)*, [dc
in ring, ch 1] 15 times, join in 3rd
ch of beg ch-4. *(16 dc)*

Rnd 2: Sl st in next ch-1 sp, ch
1, sc in same sp, ch 3, *sc in next
ch-1 sp, ch 3, rep from * around,
join in first sc. *(16 sc)*

Rnd 3: Sl st in next ch-1 sp, ch
1, sc in same sp, ch 3, *sc in next
ch-3 sp, ch 3, rep from * around,
join in first sc. *(16 sc)*

Rnd 4: Sl st in next ch-3 sp, ch
1, sc in same sp, ch 2, [tr, ch 1] 3
times in next ch-3 sp, tr in same
sp, ch 2, *sc in next ch-3 sp, ch
2, [tr, ch 1] 3 times in next ch-3
sp, tr in same sp, ch 2, rep from *
around, join in first sc. *(8 sc, 32 tr)*

Rnd 5: Sl st in each of next 2
chs, in next tr and in next ch-1
sp, ch 1, sc in same sp, [ch 3, sc
in next ch-1 sp] twice, ch 5, *sc
in next ch-1 sp, [ch 3, sc in next
ch-1 sp] twice, ch 5, rep from *
around, join in first sc. *(24 sc)*

Rnd 6: Sl st in next ch-3 sp, ch
1, sc in same sp, ch 3, sc in next
ch-3 sp, [tr, ch 1] 3 times in 3rd
ch of next ch-5 sp, tr in same st,
ch 2, sc in next ch-3 sp, ch 3, sc
in next ch-3 sp, [tr, ch 1] 3 times
in 3rd ch of next ch-5 sp, tr in
same st, ch 2, rep from * around,
join in first sc. *(16 sc, 32 tr)*

Rnd 7: Sl st in next ch-3 sp, ch 1,
sc in same sp, ch 5, sc in next ch-1
sp, [ch 3, sc in next ch-1 sp] twice,
ch 5, *sc in next ch-3 sp, ch 5, sc
in next ch-1 sp, [ch 3, sc in next
ch-1 sp] twice, ch 5, rep from *
around, join in first sc. *(32 sc)*

Rnd 8: Sl st in each of first 3 chs
of first ch-5 sp, ch 1, sc in same
ch as last sl st, ch 4, sc in next
ch-3 sp, ch 3, sc in next ch-3 sp,
ch 4, sc in 3rd ch of next ch-5 sp,
ch 5, *sc in 3rd ch of next ch-5
sp, ch 4, sc in next ch-3 sp, ch 3,
sc in next ch-3 sp, ch 4, sc in 3rd
ch of next ch-5 sp, ch 5, rep from
* around, join in first sc. *(32 sc)*

Rnd 9: Sl st in next ch-4 sp, ch 1,
sc in same sp, ch 7, sk next ch-3
sp, sc in next ch-4 sp, ch 2, [tr,
ch 1] 4 times in 3rd ch of next
ch-5 sp, tr in same st, ch 2, *sc in
next ch-4 sp, ch 7, sk next ch-3
sp, sc in next ch-4 sp, ch 2, [tr,
ch 1] 4 times in 3rd ch of next
ch-5 sp, tr in same st, ch 2, rep
from * around, join in first sc.
(16 sc, 40 tr)

Rnd 10: Sl st in each of first 4
chs of next ch-7 sp, ch 1, (sc, ch
5, sc) in same st as last sl st, ch
4, sc in next ch-1 sp, [ch 3, sc in
next ch-1 sp] 3 times, ch 4, *(sc,
ch 5, sc) in 4th ch of next ch-7
sp, ch 4, sc in next ch-1 sp, [ch
3, sc in next ch-1 sp] 3 times, ch
4, rep from * around, join in first
sc. *(47 sc)*

Rnd 11: Sl st in next ch-5 sp, ch
5 *(counts as first tr, ch-1 sp)*, [tr
in same sp, ch 1] 4 times, tr in
same sp, ch 2, sc in next ch-3 sp,
ch 3, (sc, ch 5, sc) in next ch-3
sp, ch 3, sc in next ch-3 sp, ch
2, *tr in next ch-5 sp, [ch 1, tr
in same sp] 5 times, ch 2, sc in
next ch-3 sp, ch 3, (sc, ch 5, sc)
in next ch-3 sp, ch 3, sc in next
ch-3 sp, ch 2, rep from * around,
join in first sc. *(32 sc, 48 tr)*

Rnd 12: Sl st in next ch-1 sp, ch
1, sc in same sp, [ch 3, sc in next
ch-1 sp] 4 times, ch 2, tr in next
ch-5 sp, [ch 1, tr in same sp] 5
times, ch 2, *sc in next ch-3 sp,
[ch 3, sc in next ch-1 sp] 4 times,
ch 2, tr in next ch-5 sp, [ch 1,
tr in same sp] 5 times, ch 2,

rep from * around, join in first sc. *(40 sc, 40 tr)*

Rnd 13: Sl st in next ch-3 sp, ch 1, sc in same sp, ch 3, sc in next ch-3 sp, ch 5, [sc in next ch-3 sp, ch 3] twice, [sc in next ch-3 sp, ch 3] 5 times, *sc in next ch-3 sp, ch 3, sc in next ch-3 sp, ch 5, [sc in next ch-3 sp, ch 3] twice, [sc in next ch-3 sp, ch 3] 5 times, rep from * around, join in first sc, turn. *(72 sc)*

Rnd 14: Sl st in last ch-3 sp made on previous rnd, turn, ch 1, sc in same sp, ch 2, tr in next ch-5 sp, [ch 1, tr in same sp] 6 times, ch 2, sk next ch-3 sp, sc in next ch-3 sp, [ch 3, sc in next ch-3 sp] twice, ch 5, [sc in next ch-3 sp,

ch 3] twice, *sc in next ch-3 sp, ch 2, tr in next ch-5 sp, [ch 1, tr in same sp] 6 times, ch 2, sk next ch-3 sp, sc in next ch-3 sp, [ch 3, sc in next ch-3 sp] twice, ch 5, [sc in next ch-3 sp, ch 3] twice, rep from * around, join in first sc. *(56 tr, 48 sc)*

Rnd 15: Sl st in each of next 2 chs, in next tr and in next ch-1 sp, ch 1, sc in same sp, [ch 3, sc in next ch-1 sp] 5 times, ch 3, sk next ch-2 sp, sc in next ch-3 sp, ch 2, sk next ch-3 sp, tr in next ch-5 sp, [ch 1, tr in same sp] 6 times, ch 2, sk next ch-3 sp, sc in next ch-3 sp, ch 3, *sc in next ch-1 sp, [ch 3, sc in next ch-1 sp] 5 times, ch 3, sk next ch-2 sp, sc in next ch-3 sp, ch 2, sk next ch-3

sp, tr in next ch-5 sp, [ch 1, tr in same sp] 6 times, ch 2, sk next ch-3 sp, sc in next ch-3 sp, ch 3, rep from * around, join in first sc, fasten off. *(64 sc, 56 tr)*

Rnd 16: With linen, make slip knot on hook and join with sc in any ch-sp, ch 3, *sc in next ch-sp, ch 3, rep from * around, join in first sc. *(120 sc)*

Rnd 17: Sl st in next ch-3 sp, ch 1, sc in same sp, ch 3, *sc in next ch-3 sp, ch 3, rep from * around, join in first sc. *(120 sc)*

Rnd 18: Sl st in next ch-3 sp, ch 1, (sc, ch 2, sc) in same sp, (sc, ch 2, sc) in each rem ch-3 sp, join in first sc, fasten off. *(240 sc)* ∎

Candle Mat Doily

DESIGN BY ZELDA WORKMAN

FINISHED SIZE
12 inches in diameter

MATERIALS
• Elmore-Pisgah America's Best
  size 10 crochet cotton (350
  yds per ball):
     100 yds each #3 cream
     and #485 coral
• Size 7/1.65mm steel crochet
  hook or size needed to
  obtain gauge
• Tapestry needle
• Stitch markers
• Starch

GAUGE
Motif = 3 x 4½ inches

PATTERN NOTES
Weave in ends as work
progresses.

Join rounds with a slip stitch
unless otherwise stated.

SPECIAL STITCHES
2-dc cluster (2-dc cl): [Yo,
insert hook in indicated sp, yo,
draw up a lp, yo, draw through
2 lps on hook] twice, yo, draw
through all 3 lps on hook.

Picot: Ch 4, sl st in 4th ch
from hook.

Instructions

MOTIF
Make 6.
Rnd 1 (RS): With cream, ch 12,
join in first ch to form a ring, ch
1, 4 sc in ring, ch 3, 8 sc in ring,
ch 3, 4 sc in ring, join in first sc.
(16 sc, 2 ch-3 sps)

Rnd 2: Ch 4 *(counts as first dc,
ch-1 sp)*, [dc in next sc, ch 1] 3
times, (dc, ch 3, dc) in next ch-3
sp, [ch 1, dc in next sc] 8 times,
ch 1, (dc, ch 3, dc) in next ch-3
sp, [ch 1, dc in next sc] 4 times,
ch 1, join in 3rd ch of beg ch-4.
(20 dc, 17 ch-1 sps, 2 ch-3 sps)

Rnd 3: Ch 1, sc in next ch-1 sp,
[ch 3, sc in next ch-1 sp] 3 times,
ch 3, (sc, ch 3, sc) in next ch-3

sp, [ch 3, sc in next ch-1 sp] 9
times, ch 3, (sc, ch 3, sc) in next
ch-3 sp, [ch 3, sc in next ch-1
sp] 5 times, ch 3, join in first sc,
fasten off. *(22 ch-3 sps)*

Rnd 4: Attach coral in last ch-3
sp of previous rnd, ch 1, (sc, ch
2, dc) in same sp *(cl)*, [ch 3, **2-dc
cl** *(see Special Stitches)* in next
ch-3 sp] 4 times, ch 3, (2-dc cl,
ch 5, 2-dc cl) in next ch-3 sp,
[ch 3, 2-dc cl in next ch-3 sp]
10 times, ch 3, (2-dc cl, ch 5,
2-dc cl) in next ch-3 sp, [ch 3,
2-dc cl in next ch-3 sp] 5 times,
ch 3, join in top of beg cl, fasten
off. *(24 cls)*

Rnd 5: Attach cream in last
ch-3 sp of previous rnd, ch 1, sc
in same sp, **picot** *(see Special*

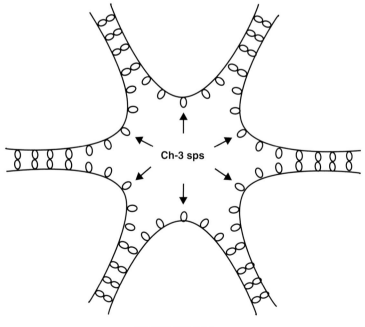

Candle Mat Doily
Fig. 1

Stitches), [ch 1, sc in next ch-3 sp, picot] 5 times, ch 1, (sc, ch 5, sc) in next ch-5 sp, picot, [ch 1, sc in next ch-3 sp, picot] 11 times, ch 1, (sc, ch 5, sc) in next ch-5 sp, picot, [ch 1, sc in next ch-3 sp, picot] 5 times, ch 1, join in first sc. *(24 picots)*

Rnd 6: Ch 6 *(counts as first dc, ch-3 sp)*, [dc in next sc, ch 3] 4 times, tr in next sc, ch 3, [tr, ch 3, tr, ch 5, tr, ch 3, tr] in next ch-5 sp, ch 3, sk next sc, tr in next sc, [ch 3, dc in next sc] 9 times, ch 3, tr in next sc, ch 3, [tr, ch 3, tr, ch 5, tr, ch 3, tr] in next ch-5 sp, ch 3, sk

next sc, tr in next sc, [ch 3, dc in next sc] 4 times, ch 3, join in 3rd ch of beg ch-6, fasten off. *(30 sts)*

Rnd 7: Attach coral in 3rd ch of beg ch-6 of previous rnd, ch 1, sc in same st, picot, [ch 1, sc in next dc, picot] 4 times, [ch 1, sc in next tr, picot] 3 times, ch 1, (sc, ch 3, sc) in 3rd ch of next ch-5 sp, picot, [ch 1, sc in next tr, picot] 3 times, [ch 1, sc in next dc, picot] 9 times, [ch 1, sc in next tr, picot] 3 times, ch 1, (sc, ch 3, sc) in 3rd ch of next ch-5 sp, picot, [ch 1, sc in next tr, picot] 3 times, [ch 1, sc in next dc, picot] 4 times, ch 1,

join in first sc, fasten off. *(36 sts, 32 picots)*

Work rem Motifs in same manner except for picot joining on last rnd. Using Fig. 1 as a guide, ch-3 sp and 2 picots on each side of ch-3 sp rem free and next 4 picots are joined to 4 corresponding picots on previous Motif. To join 4 picots to previous Motif, ch 2, sc in corresponding picot on previous Motif, ch 1, sl st in first ch of ch-2 just made. On last Motif, join to previous and first Motif.

Starch lightly and press. ■

Hot Pot Mates CONTINUED FROM PAGE 8

Row 18: Ch 1, working in front lps only, sc in each sc across, turn.

Rows 19–28: Ch 1, sc in each sc across, turn.

Edging
Working around outer edge, ch 1, sc in each st and in end of each row and work 2 sc in each corner, join in first sc, fasten off.

ASSEMBLY
Fold each end over to WS at row 18, matching sts, working in **back lps** *(see Stitch Guide)* only, sew 12 rows on each side tog forming a pocket at each end.

Pot Holder

DESIGN BY CONNIE FOLSE

SKILL LEVEL
EASY

FINISHED SIZE
8¼ inches in diameter

MATERIALS
- Medium (worsted) weight cotton yarn: 1½ oz/75 yds/42g each chocolate and variegated
- Size G/6/4mm crochet hook or size needed to obtain gauge
- Tapestry needle

GAUGE
Rnds 1 & 2 = 2½ inches

PATTERN NOTES
Weave in ends as work progresses.

Join rounds with a slip stitch unless otherwise stated.

Chain-3 at beginning of double crochet row or round counts as

first double crochet unless otherwise stated.

SPECIAL STITCHES
Beginning shell (beg shell): Ch 3, (2 dc, ch 2, 3 dc) in indicated st.

Shell: (3 dc, ch 2, 3 dc) in indicated st.

Instructions

FRONT
Rnd 1 (RS): With variegated, ch 3, join in first ch to form ring, **ch 3** *(see Pattern Notes)*, 11 dc in ring, join in 3rd ch of beg ch-3. *(12 dc)*

Rnd 2: Ch 3, dc in same st, 2 dc in each rem dc around, join in 3rd ch of beg ch-3. *(24 dc)*

Rnd 3: Beg shell *(see Special Stitches)* in same st as joining, sk next 2 dc, *shell *(see Special Stitches)* in next dc, sk next 2 dc, rep from * 6 times, join in 3rd ch of beg ch-3. *(8 shells)*

Rnd 4: Ch 1, sc between last shell made on previous rnd and first shell made, shell in ch-2 sp of first shell, *sc between same shell and next shell, shell in ch-2 sp of next shell, rep from * 6 times, join in first sc. *(8 shells, 8 sc)*

Rnd 5: Ch 1, sc in same sc as joining, (6 dc, ch 2, 6 dc) in ch-2 sp of next shell, *sc in next sc, (6 dc, ch 2, 6 dc) in ch-2 sp of next shell, shell in ch-2 sp of next shell, rep from * 6 times, join in first sc, fasten off. *(96 dc, 8 sc)*

BACK
Rnds 1–5: With chocolate, rep rnds 1–5 of Front. At end of last rnd, do not fasten off.

Rnd 6: With WS of Back and WS of Front held tog and carefully matching sts of rnd 5 on both, sl st in each of next 4 dc on Back, ch 1, working through both thicknesses, sc in next st on Back and 10th st on rnd 5 of Front, sc in each of next 2 sts on Back, (sc, ch 2, sc) in next ch-2 sp, sc in each of next 2 sts, sk next 7 sts on Front, working through both thicknesses, sc in next st, sc in each of next 2 sts of Front, (sc, ch 2, sc) in next ch-2 sp, sc in each of next 2 sts, sk next 7 sts on Back, *working through both thicknesses, sc in next sc, sc in each of next 2 sts on Back, (sc, ch 2, sc) in next ch-2 sp, sc in each of next 2 sts, sk next 7 sts on Front, working through both thicknesses, sc in next st, sc in each of next 2 sts of Front, (sc, ch 2, sc) in next ch-2 sp, sc in each of next 2 sts, sk next 7 sts on Back, rep from * around, join in first sc, fasten off. *(112 sts)* ∎

Charger Place Mat CONTINUED FROM PAGE 16

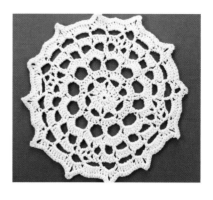

rep from * twice, sk next 3 dc, dc in last dc, join in 3rd ch of beg ch-9. *(13 dc, 12 sc, 12 ch-6 sps, 12 ch-4 sps)*

Rnd 8: Sl st in first ch-6 sp, ch 3, 4 dc in same sp, 5 dc in each of next 3 ch-6 sps, 2 dc in next ch-4 sp, (dc, ch 3, dc) in next ch-4 sp, 2 dc in next ch-4 sp, *5 dc in each of next 4 ch-6 sps, 2 dc in next ch-4 sp, (dc, ch 3, dc) in next ch-4 sp, 2 dc in next ch-4 sp, rep from * twice, join in 3rd ch of beg ch-3. *(104 dc, 4 ch-3 sps)*

Rnd 9: Ch 8 *(counts as first dc, ch-5 sp)*, sk next 4 dc, dc

between last sk dc and next dc, [ch 5, sk next 5 dc, dc between last sk dc and next dc] 3 times, ch 5, sc in next ch-3 sp, ch 5, sk next 3 dc, dc between last sk dc and next dc, *[ch 5, sk next 5 dc, dc between last sk dc and next dc] 4 times, ch 5, sc in next ch-3 sp, ch 5, sk next 3 dc, dc between last sk dc and next dc, rep from * twice, join in 3rd ch of beg ch-8. *(24 ch-5 sps)*

Rnd 10: Sl st in first ch-5 sp, ch 3, (2 dc, ch 3, 3 dc) in same sp, 7 dc in next ch-5 sp, *(3 dc, ch 3, 3 dc) in next ch-5 sp, 7 dc in next ch-5 sp, rep from * around, join

in 3rd ch of beg ch-3, **turn**. *(156 dc, 12 ch-3 sps)*

Rnd 11 (WS): Ch 1, sc in same ch, sc in each dc and (2 sc, ch 3, 2 sc) in each ch-3 sp around, join in first sc, fasten off. *(204 sc, 12 ch-3 sps)* ∎

Harvest Rug CONTINUED FROM PAGE 17

Rows 46 & 47: Rep rows 6 and 7. Fasten off.

Row 48: With warm brown, rep row 6.

Rows 49 & 50: Rep rows 3 and 4.

Row 51: Rep row 3.

Row 52: Ch 1, sc in first sc, *sc in next ch-1 sp, sc in next sc, rep from * across. Fasten off. *(69 sc)*

EDGING

Rnd 1 (RS): Hold piece with RS facing, working across opposite side of foundation ch with cornmeal, join with sc in first ch, *ch 1, sk next ch, sc in next ch, rep from * to last ch, (sc, ch 2,

sc) in last ch *(corner)*, continuing along next side, **ch 1, sk next row, sc in end of next row, rep from ** across side, work (sc, ch 2, sc) *(corner)* in first sc of row 52, ***ch 1, sk next sc, sc in next sc, rep from *** to last sc, (sc, ch 2, sc) in last sc *(corner)*, continuing along next side, ****ch 1, sk next row, sc in end of next row, rep from **** across side to first sc, sc in same ch as first sc, ch 2, join in first sc. *(124 sc, 120 ch-1 sps, 4 ch-2 sps)*

Rnd 2: Sl st in next ch-1 sp, ch 1, sc in same ch-1 sp, *ch 1, sc in next ch-1 sp, rep from * around, working (sc, ch 2, sc) in each ch-2 corner sp, ch 1, join in first sc. Fasten off. *(128 sc, 124 ch-1 sps, 4 ch-2 sps)*

Rnd 3: With warm brown, join with sc in any ch-1 sp, *ch 1, sc in next ch-1 sp, rep from * around, working (sc, ch 2, sc) in each ch-2 corner sp, ch 1, join in first sc. Fasten off. *(132 sc, 128 ch-1 sps, 4 ch-2 sps)* ∎

Spring Green Rug CONTINUED FROM PAGE 19

Rnd 14: Sl st in next dc and in next ch-2 sp, beg shell in same sp, ch 1, sk next ch-1 sp, V-st in next st, ch 1, [V-st in ch-1 sp of next V-st, ch 1] 9 times, sk next ch-1 sp, V-st in next st, ch 1, *shell in ch-2 sp of next shell, ch 1, sk next ch-1 sp, V-st in next st, ch 1, [V-st in ch-1 sp of next V-st, ch 1] 9 times, sk next ch-1 sp, V-st in next st, ch 1, rep from * 4 times, join in 3rd ch of beg ch-3, turn. *(6 shells, 66 V-sts, 72 ch-1 sps)*

Rnd 15: Sl st in next dc and in next ch-1 sp, turn, ch 1, sc in same ch-1 sp as last sl st, ch 1, 10 tr in ch-2 sp of next shell, ch 1, sc in ch-1 sp of next V-st, [ch 3, sc in next V-st] 10 times, ch 1, *10 tr in next shell, ch 1, sc in next V-st, [ch 3, sc in next V-st] 10 times, ch 1, rep from * 3 times, 10 tr in next shell, ch 1, sc in next V-st, [ch 3, sc in next V-st] 9 times, ch 1, join with hdc in first sc. *(60 tr, 66 sc, 60 ch-3 sps, 12 ch-1 sps)*

Rnd 16: Ch 1, sc in sp formed by joining hdc, ch 1, [dc in next tr, ch 1] 10 times, sc in next ch-3 sp, [ch 3, sc in next ch-3 sp] 9 times, ch 1, *[dc in next tr, ch 1] 10 times, sc in next ch-3 sp, [ch 3, sc in next ch-3 sp] 9 times, ch 1, rep from * 3 times, [dc in next tr, ch 1] 10 times, sc in next ch-3 sp, [ch 3, sc in next ch-3 sp] 8 times, ch 1, join with hdc in first sc. *(60 dc, 60 sc, 54 ch-3 sps, 66 ch-1 sps)*

Rnd 17: Ch 1, sc in sp formed by joining hdc, ch 1, *dc in next dc, ch 1, [dc in next ch-1 sp, ch 1, dc in next dc, ch 1] 9 times, sc in next ch-3 sp, [ch 3, sc in next ch-3 sp] 8 times, ch 1, rep from * 4 times, dc in next dc, ch 1, [dc in next ch-1 sp, ch 1, dc in next dc, ch 1] 9 times, sc in next ch-3 sp, [ch 3, sc in next ch-3 sp] 7 times, ch 1, join with hdc in first sc. *(114 dc, 54 sc, 48 ch-3 sps, 120 ch-1 sps)*

Rnd 18: Ch 1, sc in sp formed by joining hdc, ch 1, *sc in next dc, [ch 3, sk next dc, sc in next dc] 9 times, ch 1, [sc in next ch-3 sp, ch 1] 8 times, rep from * 4 times, sc in next dc, [ch 3, sk next dc, sc in next dc] 9 times, ch 1, [sc in next ch-3 sp, ch 1] 7 times, join in first sc. *(108 sc, 54 ch-3 sps, 54 ch-1 sps)*

Rnd 19: Ch 1, sc in first st, *(3 sc, ch 3, 3 sc) in each of next 9 ch-3 sps, [sc in next st, ch 1] 7 times, sc in next st, rep from * 4 times, (3 sc, ch 3, 3 sc) in each of next 9 ch-3 sps, [sc in next st, ch 1] 7 times, join in first sc, fasten off. *(372 sc, 54 ch-3 sps, 42 ch-1 sps)* ■

Clutter Keepers CONTINUED FROM PAGE 31

ASSEMBLY
With tangerine, work same as Assembly for Basket #1.

TOP EDGING
With tangerine, work same as Top Edging of Basket #1.

BASKET #3
Bottom
Method 1
Row 1 (RS): With K hook and 3 strands of periwinkle, ch 33, sc in 2nd ch from hook, sc in each rem ch across, turn. *(32 sc)*

Method 2
Row 1 (RS): With K hook and 3 strands of periwinkle, work 32 **foundation sc** *(see Special Stitch)*, turn. *(32 foundation sc)*

Both Methods
Row 2: Ch 1, sc in each sc across, turn.

Rows 3–27: Rep row 2. At end of row 27, **do not turn**.

Edging
Ch 1, 2 sc in same sp as last sc on row 27, place marker in first of these 2 sc, working along next side in ends of rows, sk row 27, sc in each of next 25 rows, working along next side, 2 sc in bottom of first sc of row 1, place marker in first of these 2 sc, sc in bottom of each of next 30 sc, 2 sc in bottom of last sc, place marker in last of these 2 sc, working along next side in ends of rows, sk row 1, sc in each of next 26 rows, join in first sc of row 27, place marker in joining sl st, fasten off. *(119 sc, 1 sl st)*

Short Side
Make 2.
Method 1
Row 1 (RS): With K hook and 3 strands of periwinkle, ch 27, sc in 2nd ch from hook, sc in each rem ch across, turn. *(26 sc)*

Method 2
Row 1 (RS): With K hook and 3 strands of periwinkle, work 26 foundation sc, turn. *(26 foundation sc)*

Both Methods
Row 2: Ch 1, sc in each sc across, turn.

Rows 3–5: Rep row 2. At end of row 5, **do not turn.**

Edging
Ch 1, 2 sc in same sp as last sc on row 5, place marker in first of these 2 sc, working along next side in ends of rows, sk row 5, sc in each of next 3 rows, working along next side, 2 sc in bottom of first sc of row 1, place marker in first of these 2 sc, sc in bottom of each of next 24 sc, 2 sc in bottom of last sc, place marker in last of these 2 sc, working along next side in ends of rows, sk row 1, sc in each of next 4 rows, join in first sc of row 5, place marker in joining sl st, fasten off. *(63 sc, 1 sl st)*

Long Side
Make 2.
Method 1
Row 1 (RS): With K hook and 3 strands of periwinkle, ch 33, sc in 2nd ch from hook, sc in each rem ch across, turn. *(32 sc)*

Method 2
Row 1 (RS): With K hook and 3 strands of periwinkle, work 32 **foundation sc** *(see Special Stitch)*, turn. *(32 foundation sc)*

Both Methods
Row 2: Ch 1, sc in each sc across, turn.

Rows 3–5: Rep row 2. At end of row 5, **do not turn.**

Edging
Ch 1, 2 sc in same sp as last sc on row 5, place marker in first of these 2 sc, working along next side in ends of rows, sk row 5, sc in each of next 3 rows, working along next side, 2 sc in bottom of first sc of row 1, place marker in first of these 2 sc, sc in bottom of each of next 30 sc, 2 sc in bottom of last sc, place marker in last of these 2 sc, working along next side in ends of rows, sk row 1, sc in each of next 4 rows, join in first sc of row 5, place marker in joining sl st, fasten off. *(75 sc, 1 sl st)*

ASSEMBLY
With periwinkle, work same as Assembly for Basket #1.

TOP EDGING
With periwinkle, work same as Top Edging of Basket #1. ■

2

Little Ones

These quick-to-stitch
infant and toddler designs
are just what you need
for that Little One.

Bootie Bouquet

Bouquet of Booties

DESIGNS BY ANN WHITE

SKILL LEVEL ◼◼◻◻
EASY

FINISHED SIZES
Instructions given fit infant's
sizes 0–2

**FINISHED GARMENT
MEASUREMENTS**
Length: 3⅔ inches [4⅖ inches]
Height (base of heel to top
of cuff):
    Soft Lilac and Yellow:
      3¾ inches
    Blue, Pink and Green:
      3½ inches

MATERIALS
- Bernat Baby super
  fine (fingering)
  weight yarn (1¾ oz/286 yds/
  50g per ball):
    1 skein each #00451
    baby blue, #00469
    pink, #21185 soft lilac,
    #00436 yellow, #00444
    baby green
- Size B/1/2.25mm and
  C/2/2.75mm crochet
  hooks or sizes needed to
  obtain gauge
- Tapestry needle
- 4 yds white satin ribbon

GAUGE
Size B hook (for sizes 0 & 1):
6 dc = 1 inch; 3 dc rows =
1 inch

Size C hook (for size 2): 4 dc =
1 inch; 5 dc rows = 2 inches

PATTERN NOTES
Weave in ends as work progresses.

Join rounds with a slip stitch
unless otherwise stated.

Chain-3 at beginning of double
crochet round counts as first
double crochet unless otherwise
stated.

For an unusual baby shower
centerpiece, use silk leaves and
floral wire to create a bouquet
of Booties. Fold Bootie to form
flower and use floral tape to
secure it to the wire and leaves.

SPECIAL STITCHES
Shell: 5 dc in indicated st or sp.

Popcorn (pc): 5 dc in indicated
st, drop lp from hook, insert hook
in first dc of 5-dc group, pull
dropped lp through.

Instructions

BLUE BOOTIE
Make 2.
Foot
Rnd 1 (RS): With baby blue, ch
4, 11 dc in 4th ch from hook *(beg
3 sk chs count as a dc)*, join in
3rd ch of beg 3 sk chs. *(12 dc)*

Rnd 2: Ch 3 *(see Pattern Notes)*,
dc in same st, 2 dc in each rem
st around, join in 3rd ch of beg
ch-3. *(24 dc)*

Rnds 3–5: Ch 3, dc in each dc
around, join in 3rd ch of beg ch-3.
At end of last rnd, fasten off.

Row 6: Now working in rows, sk
first 12 dc, join baby blue in next
dc, ch 3, dc in each dc and in
each sk st, turn. *(24 dc)*

Rows 7–11: Ch 3, dc in each st
across, turn.

For **heel**, fold row 11 of piece in
half; matching sts and working
through both thicknesses, sl st
in each st across, fasten off.

Cuff
Rnd 1: Working around top
opening of Foot, with baby blue,
make slip knot on hook and join
with sc in end of row by heel
seam, work 35 additional sc
evenly spaced around opening,
join in first sc. *(36 sc)*

Rnd 2: Ch 4 *(counts as first dc
and ch-1 sp)*, sk next sc, *dc in
next sc, ch 1, sk next sc, rep from
* around, join in 3rd ch of beg
ch-4. *(18 ch-1 sps)*

Rnd 3: Sl st in first ch-1 sp, ch 1,
sc in same sp, *ch 4, sc in next
ch-1 sp, rep from * around, ch 2,
join with hdc in first sc.

Rnd 4: Ch 1, sc in sp formed by
joining hdc, *ch 4, sc in next ch-4
sp, rep from * around, ch 2, join
with hdc in first sc.

Rnd 5: Ch 1, sc in sp formed by
joining hdc, **shell** *(see Special
Stitches)* in next ch-4 sp, *sc in
next ch-4 sp, shell in next ch-4
sp, rep from * around, join in first
sc, fasten off.

FINISHING
Cut 1-yd length of ribbon in half, weave 1 piece of ribbon through rnd 2 of each Cuff.

SOFT LILAC/PINK BOOTIE
Make 2.
Foot
With soft lilac/pink, work same as Foot for Blue Bootie.

Cuff
Rnds 1 & 2: With soft lilac/pink, rep rnds 1 and 2 of Cuff of Blue Bootie.

Rnd 3: Ch 3, dc in each ch-1 sp and in each dc around, join in 3rd ch of beg ch-3. *(36 dc)*

Rnd 4: Ch 2, **fpdc** *(see Stitch Guide)* around next dc, ***bpdc** (see Stitch Guide) around next dc, fpdc around next dc, rep from * around, join in 2nd ch of beg ch-2.

Rnds 5 & 6: Ch 2, fpdc around next st, bpdc around next st, fpdc around next st, rep from * around, join in 2nd ch of beg ch-2. At end of last rnd, fasten off.

FINISHING
Cut 1-yd length of ribbon in half, weave 1 piece of ribbon through rnd 2 of each Cuff.

YELLOW BOOTIE
Make 2.
Foot
With yellow, work same as Foot for Blue Bootie.

Cuff
Rnds 1 & 2: With yellow, rep rnds 1 and 2 of Cuff of Blue Bootie.

Rnd 3: Sl st in first ch-1 sp, ch 1, sc in same sp, **shell** *(see Special Stitches)* in next ch-1 sp, *sc in next ch-1 sp, shell in next ch-1 sp, rep from * around, join in first sc. *(9 shells)*

Rnds 4 & 5: Sl st in each of next 3 dc, ch 1, sc in same dc, shell in next sc, *sc in 3rd dc of next shell, shell in next sc, rep from * around, join in first sc. At end of last rnd, fasten off.

FINISHING
Cut 1-yd length of ribbon in half, weave 1 piece of ribbon through rnd 2 of each Cuff.

GREEN BOOTIE
Make 2.
Foot
With baby green, work same as Foot for Blue Bootie.

Cuff
Rnds 1 & 2: With baby green, rep rnds 1 and 2 of Cuff of Blue Bootie.

Rnd 3: Ch 3, dc in each ch-1 sp and in each dc around, join in 3rd ch of beg ch-3. *(36 dc)*

Rnd 4: Ch 3, dc in next dc, **pc** *(see Special Stitches)* in next dc, *dc in each of next 2 dc, pc in next dc, rep from * around, join in 3rd ch of beg ch-3. *(12 pc, 24 dc)*

Rnd 5: Ch 3, dc in each st around, join in 3rd ch of beg ch-3. *(36 dc)*

Rnd 6: Ch 1, working from left to right, **reverse sc** *(see Fig. 1)* in each dc around, join in first reverse sc, fasten off.

FINISHING
Cut rem ribbon in half, weave 1 piece of ribbon through rnd 2 of each Cuff.

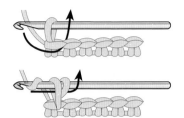

**Reverse Single Crochet
Fig. 1**

Bootie Vase
DESIGN BY COLLEEN SULLIVAN

SKILL LEVEL **INTERMEDIATE**

FINISHED SIZE
6 inches tall x 7 inches long, excluding trim

MATERIALS
• Medium (worsted) weight yarn: 3 oz/150 yds/85g white
• Size G/6/4mm crochet hook or size needed to obtain gauge
• Tapestry needle
• 5 x 8-inch piece plastic canvas
• 14 oz vegetable can
• 2¾-inch diameter round piece of plastic foam
• 1½-inch square piece of cardboard
• Polyester fiberfill

4 MEDIUM

GAUGE
4 hdc = 1 inch; 3 hdc rows = 1 inch

PATTERN NOTES
Weave in ends as work progresses.

Join rounds with a slip stitch unless otherwise stated.

Chain-2 at beginning of half double crochet row or round counts as first half double crochet unless otherwise stated.

Instructions

SOLE

Rnd 1 (RS): Ch 13, sc in 2nd ch from hook, sc in each of next 6 sc, hdc in next ch, dc in each of next 3 chs, 5 dc in last ch—*toe*, working in unused lps on opposite side of foundation ch, dc in each of next 3 chs, hdc in next ch, sc in each of next 6 chs, 2 sc in last ch, join in first sc. *(28 sts)*

Rnd 2: Ch 1, 2 sc in first sc, sc in each of next 6 sc, hdc in each of next 3 sts, dc in next st, 2 dc in each of next 2 sts, 3 dc in next st, 2 dc in each of next 2 sts, dc in next st, hdc in each of next 3 sts, sc in each of next 6 sts, 2 sc in each of last 2 sts, join in first sc. *(37 sts)*

Rnd 3: Ch 2 *(see Pattern Notes)*, hdc in same st, 2 hdc in next st, hdc in each of next 8 sts, dc in each of next 3 sts, 2 dc in each of next 9 sts, dc in each of next 3 sts, hdc in each of next 8 sts, 2 hdc in each of last 4 sts, join in 2nd ch of beg ch-2. *(52 sts)*

Rnd 4: Ch 2, hdc in same st, 2 hdc in each of next 2 sts, hdc in each of next 15 sts, dc in each of next 3 sts, [2 dc in next st, dc in next st] 5 times, dc in each of next 3 sts, hdc in each of next 15 sts, 2 hdc in each of last 3 sts, join in 2nd ch of beg ch-2. *(63 sts)*

Rnd 5: Ch 1, 2 sc in first st, sc in each st to last st, 2 sc in last st, join in first sc. *(65 sc)*

Rnd 6: Ch 2, working in **back lps** *(see Stitch Guide)* only, hdc in each st around, join in 2nd ch of beg ch-2.

Rnds 7 & 8: Ch 2, hdc in each st, join in 2nd ch of beg ch-2. At end of last rnd, fasten off.

Using sole as pattern, cut a piece of plastic canvas ⅛-inch smaller on all edges. Insert plastic canvas piece into crocheted piece.

VAMP

Row 1: With front of Sole facing and working in back lps only of 12 center sts on rnd 8 at end of toe, make slip knot on hook and join with sc in first st, sc in each of next 11 sts, turn. *(12 sc)*

Row 2: Ch 1, **sc dec** *(see Stitch Guide)* in first 2 sc, ch 1, [sc dec in next 2 sc, ch 1] 4 times, sc dec in last 2 sc, turn. *(6 sc)*

Rows 3–10: Ch 1, sc dec in first sc and in next ch-1 sp, ch 1, *sc dec in next sc and in next ch-1 sp, ch 1, rep from * to last sc, sc in last sc, turn.

Row 11: Ch 1, sc in each sc and in each ch-1 sp across, fasten off. *(11 sc)*

Easing to fit, sew ends of rows 1–11 on each side of Instep to back lps of next 10 sc on each side of toe.

CUFF

Rnd 1 (RS): Working in rem unused sts on rnd 8 and in sts on row 11 of Instep, make slip knot on hook and join with sc in first st on rnd 8 on 1 side, 2 sc in same st, sc in each st around, join in first sc. *(46 sc)*

Rnd 2: Ch 4 *(counts as first dc and ch-1 sp)*, sk next sc, *dc in next sc, ch 1, sk next sc, rep from * around, join in 3rd ch of beg ch-4. *(23 dc)*

Rnd 3: Ch 1, sc in each sc and in each ch around, join in first sc. *(46 sc)*

Rnd 4: Ch 1, sc dec in first 2 sc, ch 1, *sc dec in next 2 sc, ch 1, rep from * around, join in first sc. *(23 sc)*

Rnds 5–16: Ch 1, sc dec in first sc and in next ch-1 sp, *sc dec in next sc and in next ch-1 sp, ch 1, rep from * around, join in first sc.

Trim

Rnd 17: Ch 1, sc in first sc, 3 hdc in next ch-1 sp, *sc in next sc, 3 hdc in next ch-1 sp, rep from * around, join in first sc, fasten off.

Vamp Edging

Working in **front lps** *(see Stitch Guide)* only of rnd 8, join in first st at Cuff, sl st in each st around Vamp, fasten off.

Sole Trim

Rnd 1: With Cuff facing and working in front lps of rnd 5 on Sole, make slip knot on hook and join with sc in any st, sc dec in next 2 sts, sc in each rem st around, join in first sc. *(64 sc)*

Rnd 2: Ch 1, sc in first sc, 3 hdc in next sc, *sc in next sc, 3 hdc in next sc, rep from * around, join in first sc, fasten off.

POMPOM

Make 2.
Wrap yarn around 1½-inch piece of cardboard 60 times, slide lps off cardboard. Tie separate 6-inch strand tightly around center of all lps, cut lps. Trim ends to 1 inch.

For **tie**, ch 110, fasten off. Weave tie through rnd 2 of Cuff and tie in bow at front. Sew pompom to each end of tie.

FINISHING

Insert plastic foam into can. Create Bootie flowers as stated in Bouquet of Booties Pattern Notes, and push ends of wires into plastic foam. Stuff toe of Bootie Vase with fiberfill. Insert can into Bootie Vase. ■

Sweet Pea Gown

DESIGN BY DONNA PIGLOWSKI

SKILL LEVEL ■■□□
EASY

FINISHED SIZES
Instructions given fit child's size 0–3 months; changes for size 6–9 months are in [ ].

MATERIALS

- Bernat Baby super fine (fingering) yarn (Sparkles: 1½ oz/205 yds/42g per ball):
  4 balls #00576 white sparkle
- Size 10 crochet cotton: 420 yds white
- Size 0/2.50mm steel crochet hook
- Size F/5/3.75mm crochet hook or size needed to obtain gauge
- Tapestry needle

GAUGE
Size F hook: Dc, sk st, shell = 1 inch; 2 shell/dc rows = 1 inch

PATTERN NOTES
Weave in ends as work progresses.

Join rounds with a slip stitch unless otherwise stated.

Chain-2 at beginning of half double crochet round counts as first half double crochet unless otherwise stated.

Chain-3 at beginning of double crochet row or round counts as first double crochet unless otherwise stated.

SPECIAL STITCHES
Cross-stitch (cross-st): Sk indicated st, dc in next st, working behind dc just made, dc in sk st.

V-stitch (V-st): (Dc, ch 1, dc) in indicated st.

Shell: 5 dc in indicated st.

Instructions

YOKE
Row 1 (RS): Starting at neckline with size F hook and white sparkle, ch 53 [57] loosely, dc in 4th ch from hook *(beg 3 sk chs count as a dc)*, dc in each ch across, turn. *(51 [55] dc)*

Row 2: Ch 3 *(see Pattern Notes)*, 2 dc in each dc to last 2 dc, sk next dc, dc in last dc, turn. *(98 [106] dc)*

Row 3: Ch 3, **cross-st** *(see Special Stitches)* in next 2 dc, rep from * across to last dc, dc in last dc, turn. *(50 [54] sts)*

Row 4: Ch 3, *dc in each of next 14 [16] sts, 2 dc in next st, ch 1, 2 dc in next st, rep from * once, dc in each of next 32 sts, **2 dc in next st, ch 1, 2 dc in next st, dc in each of next 14 [16] sts, rep from ** once, dc in last st, turn. *(106 [114] dc)*

Row 5: For **left front**, ch 3, 8 [9] cross-sts, **V-st** *(see Special Stitches)* in next ch-1 sp, for **sleeve**, 9 [10] cross-sts, V-st in next ch-1 sp, for **back**, 18 cross-sts, V-st in next ch-1 sp, for **sleeve**, 9 [10] cross-sts, V-st in next ch-1 sp, for **right front**, 8 [9] cross-sts, dc in last st, turn. *(52 [56] cross-sts, 4 V-sts)*

Row 6: Ch 3, dc in each of next 17 [19] sts, V-st in ch-1 sp of next V-st, dc in each of next 20 [22] sts, V-st in ch-1 sp of next V-st, dc in each of next 38 sts, V-st in ch-1 sp of next V-st, dc in each of next 20 [22] sts, V-st in ch-1 sp of next V-st, dc in each of next 17 [19] sts, dc in last st, turn. *(122 [130] sts)*

Row 7: Ch 3, 9 [10] cross-sts, V-st in ch-1 sp of next V-st, 11 [12] cross-sts, V-st in ch-1 sp of next V-st, 20 cross-sts, V-st in ch-1 sp of next V-st, 11 [12] cross-sts, V-st in ch-1 sp of next V-st, 9 [10] cross-sts, dc in last st, turn. *(60 [64] cross-sts, 4 V-sts)*

Row 8: Ch 3, dc in each of next 19 [21] sts, V-st in ch-1 sp of next V-st, dc in each of next 24 [26] sts, V-st in ch-1 sp of next V-st, dc in each of next 42 sts, V-st in ch-1 sp of next V-st, dc in each of next 24 [26] sts, V-st in ch-1 sp of next V-st, dc in each of next 19 [21] sts, dc in last st, turn. *(138 [146] sts)*

Row 9: Ch 3, 10 [11] cross-sts, V-st in ch-1 sp of next V-st, 13 [14] cross-sts, V-st in ch-1 sp of next V-st, 22 cross-sts, V-st in ch-1 sp of next V-st, 13 [14] cross-sts, V-st in ch-1 sp of next V-st, 10 [11] cross-sts, dc in last st, fasten off. *(68 [72] cross-sts)*

CONTINUED ON PAGE 70

Nursery Notions

DESIGNS BY DEBI YORSTON

SKILL LEVEL ■■☐▢
EASY

FINISHED SIZES
Shoulder Protector: 8¼ x
21¼ inches

Bottle Cover: 3½ inches across
x 6½ inches long

MATERIALS

• TLC Baby Amore
  medium (worsted)
  weight yarn (5 oz/286 yds/
  140g per ball):
    1 skein each #9001 white
    and #9256 yellow
• Size H/8/5mm crochet
  hook or size needed to
  obtain gauge
• Tapestry needle
• 30-inch length of ¼-inch
  white ribbon

GAUGE
7 hdc = 2 inches; 11 hdc rows =
4½ inches

PATTERN NOTES
Weave in ends as work
progresses.

Join rounds with a slip stitch
unless otherwise stated.

Instructions

SHOULDER PROTECTOR
Row 1 (RS): With yellow, ch
26, hdc in 3rd ch from hook
and in each rem ch across, turn.
(24 hdc)

Rows 2–15: Ch 2, hdc in first
hdc, hdc in each st across, turn.

Row 16: Ch 2, **hdc dec** *(see
Stitch Guide)* in first 2 hdc, hdc
in each st across to last 2 hdc,
hdc dec in last 2 hdc, turn.
(22 hdc)

Rows 17–21: Rep row 16.
(12 hdc at end of last row)

Rows 22–27: Rep row 2.

Row 28: Ch 2, 2 hdc in first hdc,
hdc in each st across to last hdc,
2 hdc in last hdc, turn. *(14 hdc)*

Rows 29–33: Rep row 28.
(24 hdc at end of last row)

Rows 34–48: Rep row 2. At end
of last row, fasten off.

Edging
Rnd 1: Hold piece with RS facing
and row 48 at top, with white,
make slip knot on hook and join
with sc in first hdc of row 48, 2
sc in same st, sc in each of next
22 hdc, 3 sc in last hdc, working
across next side in ends of rows,
sc in first row, 2 sc in next row,

CONTINUED ON PAGE 71

Filet Ripple Afghan

DESIGN BY ELAINE BARTLETT

FINISHED SIZE
33 x 45 inches

MATERIALS
- Red Heart Soft Yarn medium (worsted) weight yarn (5 oz/256 yds/140g per ball):
  5 balls #4600 white
- Size H/8/5mm crochet hook or size needed to obtain gauge
- Tapestry needle

GAUGE
4 dc = 1 inch

PATTERN NOTE
Weave in ends as work progresses.

SPECIAL STITCH
V-stitch (V-st): (Dc, ch 2, dc) in indicated st.

Instructions

Row 1 (RS): Ch 134, working in back bar of chs, dc in 3rd ch from hook, dc in each of next 7 chs, ***V-st** (see Special Stitch) in next ch, dc in each of next 8 chs, sk next 2 chs, dc in each of next 8 chs, rep from * 5 times, V-st in next ch, dc in each of next 7 chs, **dc dec** (see Stitch Guide) in last 2 chs, turn. (112 dc, 7 V-sts)

Row 2: Ch 2, dc in next dc, dc in each of next 7 dc, *V-st in ch-2

sp of next V-st, dc in each of next 8 dc, sk next 2 dc, dc in each of next 8 dc, rep from * 5 times, V-st in ch-2 sp of next V-st, dc in each of next 7 dc, dc dec in last 2 dc, turn. (112 dc, 7 V-sts)

Row 3: Rep row 2.

Row 4: Ch 2, dc in next dc, *[ch 1, sk next dc, dc in next dc] 3 times, ch 1, sk next dc, V-st in ch-2 sp of next V-st, [ch 1, sk next dc, dc in next dc] 4 times, sk next dc, dc in next dc, rep from * 5 times, [ch 1, sk next dc, dc in next dc] 3 times, ch 1, sk next dc, V-st in ch-2 sp of next V-st, [ch 1, sk next dc, dc in next dc] 3 times, ch 1, sk next dc, dc dec in last 2 dc, turn.

(56 dc, 56 ch-1 sps, 7 V-sts)

Row 5: Ch 2, dc in next ch-1 sp, *[dc in next dc, dc in next ch-1 sp] 3 times, dc in next dc, V-st in ch-2 sp of next V-st, [dc in next dc, dc in next ch-1 sp] 4 times, sk next 2 dc, dc in next ch-1 sp, rep from * 5 times, [dc in next dc, dc in next ch-1 sp] 3 times, dc in next dc, V-st in ch-2 sp of next V-st, [dc in next dc, dc in next ch-1 sp] 3 times, dc in next dc, dc dec in last 2 dc, turn. *(112 dc, 7 V-sts)*

Rows 6 & 7: Rep row 2.

Rows 8–79: [Rep rows 4–7 consecutively] 18 times. At end of last row, fasten off. ■

Baby Pocket Afghan

DESIGN BY DEBORA GARDNER

SKILL LEVEL ■■□□
EASY

FINISHED SIZE
30 x 36 inches

MATERIALS
- Red Heart Baby Econo medium (worsted) weight yarn (7 oz/ 675 yds/198g per skein):
  2 skeins #1 white
  1 skein #1680 pastel green
- Size D/3/3.25mm and K/10½/6.5 crochet hooks or size needed to obtain gauge
- Tapestry needle

GAUGE
Size K hook: 3 sts = 1 inch; 11 rows = 4¾ inches

PATTERN NOTES
Weave in ends as work progresses.

Join rounds with a slip stitch unless otherwise stated.

SPECIAL STITCH
V-stitch (V-st): (Sc, ch 1, sc) in indicated st.

Instructions

CENTER
Row 1 (WS): With K hook and white, ch 99, sc in 2nd ch from hook, dc in next ch, *sc in next ch, dc in next ch, rep from * across, turn. *(98 sts)*

Row 2 (RS): Ch 1, sc in each dc and dc in each sc across. At end of last row, fasten off.

Rows 3–76: Rep row 2. At end of last row, fasten off.

Border
Rnd 1 (RS): With RS facing and with size K hook and pastel green, make slip knot on hook and join with sc in last st made on row 76, ch 4, working across next side in ends of sc rows only, sc in next sc row, *ch 4, sc in next sc row, rep from * across, working across next side in unused lps of foundation ch, (sc, ch 4, sc) in first ch *(corner)*, ch 4, sk next 2 chs, **sc in next ch, ch 4, sk next ch, rep from ** to last ch, (sc, ch 4, sc) in last ch *(corner)*, ch 4, working across next side in ends of sc rows only, ***sc in next sc row, ch 4, rep from *** across, working across row 76, (sc, ch 4, sc) in first st *(corner)*, ch 4, sk next 2 sts, ****sc in next st, ch 4, sk next 2 sts, rep

CONTINUED ON PAGE 71

Baby Antoinette

DESIGNS BY HOLLY FIELDS

FINISHED SIZE
Instructions given fit child's
size 6 months

**FINISHED GARMENT
MEASUREMENTS**
Chest: 20 inches
Bonnet: 16 inches in
circumference

MATERIALS
- Red Heart Luster-
  Sheen fine (sport)
  weight yarn (4 oz/335 yds/
  113g per skein):
  2 skeins #0821 spa blue
  1 skein #0001 white
- Size E/4/3.5mm crochet
  hook or size needed to
  obtain gauge
- Tapestry needle
- Sewing needle
- Sewing thread
- 2½ yds ½-inch-wide pink
  satin ribbon
- 15 pink ribbon roses,
  ½-inch wide excluding
  leaves

GAUGE
6 dc = 1 inch; 3 dc rows =
1 inch

PATTERN NOTES
Weave in ends as work
progresses.

Join rounds with a slip stitch
unless otherwise stated.

Chain-3 at beginning of double
crochet row or round counts as
first double crochet unless otherwise stated.

SPECIAL STITCH
Shell: (Sc, ch 3, 2 dc) in st
indicated.

Instructions

SWEATER
Body
Right Front
Row 1 (WS): Starting at shoulder
and with spa blue, ch 19, dc in 5th
ch from hook *(beg 4 sk chs count
as first dc)*, dc in each rem ch
across, turn. *(16 dc)*

Row 2 (RS): Ch 3 *(see Pattern
Notes)*, dc in each dc across and
in 4th ch of beg 4 sk chs, turn.

Row 3: Ch 3, dc in first dc and
in each dc across, turn. *(17 dc)*

Rows 4–11: [Rep rows 2 and 3
alternately] 4 times. *(21 dc at end
of last row)*

Row 12: Rep row 2.

Row 13: Ch 3, **dc dec** *(see Stitch
Guide)* in next 2 dc, dc in each dc
across, turn. *(20 dc)*

Row 14: Ch 3, dc in each dc
to last 2 dc, dc dec in last 2 dc,
turn. *(19 dc)*

Rows 15–24: [Rep rows 13 and
14 alternately] 5 times. *(9 dc at*

end of last row) At end of last row,
fasten off, leaving an 8-inch end.

Left Front
Work same as Right Front, but
mark row 1 as RS row.

Back
Row 1 (WS): Starting at neck
edge and with spa blue, ch 58, dc
in 5th ch from hook *(beg 4 sk chs
count as a dc)*, dc in each rem
ch across, turn. *(55 dc)*

Row 2 (RS): Ch 3, dc in each dc
across, turn.

Rows 3–24: Rep row 2. At end
of last row, fasten off.

ASSEMBLY
Sew shoulder seams. Sew side
seams to within 3½ inches from
shoulders.

Edging
Rnd 1: With RS facing, join spa
blue at bottom of Left Front, sc
evenly spaced around entire
piece, working 3 sc in each of 2
front corners, 2 sc in end of each
row, and 23 sc along back of neck
opening, join in **front lp** *(see
Stitch Guide)* of first sc. *(196 sc)*

Rnd 2: Ch 3, 3 dc in same lp as
joining, working in front lps only,
*sk next 3 sc, **shell** *(see Special
Stitch)* in next sc, rep from *
around, sc in same lp as beg ch-3,
join in bottom of beg ch-3, fasten
off. *(48 shells)*

CONTINUED ON PAGE 72

Sunshine "t" Top

DESIGN BY MARGARET HUBERT

SKILL LEVEL
BEGINNER

FINISHED SIZES
Instructions given fit child's size 6 months; changes for sizes 12 months, 18 months and 24 months are in [ ].

FINISHED GARMENT MEASUREMENTS
Chest size: 21 [22, 23, 24] inches

MATERIALS
- Plymouth Encore Chunky bulky (chunky) weight yarn (3½ oz/ 143 yds/100g per ball): 2 [2, 3, 3] balls #1382 yellow
- Sizes K/10½/6.5mm and P/15mm crochet hooks or size needed to obtain gauge
- Tapestry needle

GAUGE
Size P hook: 2 sts = 1 inch

PATTERN NOTES
Weave in ends as work progresses.

Front and Back are worked lengthwise.

Instructions

FRONT/BACK
Make 2.
Row 1 (RS): Starting at side edge with P hook, ch 26 [27, 28, 29], sc in 2nd ch from hook and in each rem ch across, turn. *(25 [26, 27, 28] sc)*

Row 2: Working in **back lps** *(see Stitch Guide)* only, ch 1 *(counts as first sc)*, sk first sc, sc in each rem sc across, turn.

Rep row 2 until piece measures 10½ [11, 11½, 12] inches from beg. At end of last row, fasten off.

SLEEVE
Make 2.
Row 1: With K hook, ch 26 [27, 28, 29], sc in 2nd ch from hook and in each rem ch across, turn. *(25 [26, 27, 28] sc)*

Row 2: Ch 1 *(counts as first sc)*, sk first sc, sc in each rem sc across, turn.

Row 3: Rep row 2.

Row 4: With P hook and working in back lps only, ch 1, sk first sc, sc in each rem sc across, turn.

Rep row 4 until piece measures 6 [6½, 7, 7½] inches from beg. At end of last row, fasten off.

ASSEMBLY
Hold Front and Back with RS tog. Pin shoulders 3 [3, 3¼, 3½] inches from each outside edge, leaving 4½ [5, 5, 5] opening for neck. Sew shoulder seams. Mark Front and Back 5 [5½, 6, 6½] inches down from shoulder seam to determine sleeve placement. Fold 1 Sleeve in half, pin center to shoulder seam. Pin Sleeves in place, having ends meet marked places on Front and Back. Sew in Sleeves. Sew Sleeve seams and side seams. ∎

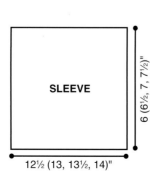

SLEEVE

6 (6½, 7, 7½)"

12½ (13, 13½, 14)"

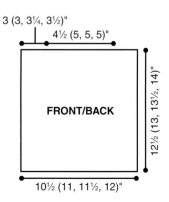

3 (3, 3¼, 3½)"

4½ (5, 5, 5)"

FRONT/BACK

12½ (13, 13½, 14)"

10½ (11, 11½, 12)"

Hooded Beach Towel

DESIGN BY MARGARET HUBERT

SKILL LEVEL ◼◼◻◻
EASY

FINISHED SIZE
32 x 33 inches, including Hood

MATERIALS

- Lion Brand Cotton-Ease medium (worsted) weight yarn (3½ oz/207 yds/100g per ball): 4 balls #194 lime
- Sizes H/8/5mm and I/9/5.5mm crochet hooks or size needed to obtain gauge
- Tapestry needle

GAUGE
Size I hook: 13½ sts = 3¾ inches

PATTERN NOTES
Weave in ends as work progresses.

Join rounds with a slip stitch unless otherwise stated.

Chain-3 at beginning of double crochet row or round counts as first double crochet unless otherwise stated.

SPECIAL STITCHES
Cross-stitch (cross-st): Sk indicated st, dc in next st, working over dc just made, dc in sk st.

V-stitch (V-st): (Dc, ch 1, dc) in indicated st.

Shell: 5 dc in indicated st.

Instructions

CENTER
Row 1 (RS): Starting at bottom with I hook, ch 110, sc in 4th ch from hook *(beg 3 sk chs count as first sc and ch-1)*, *ch 1, sk next ch, sc in next ch, rep from * 52 times, turn. *(55 sc, 54 ch-1 sps)*

Row 2: Ch 1, sc in first sc, sc in next ch-1 sp, *ch 1, sk next sc, sc in next ch-1 sp, rep from * 52 times, sc in 2nd ch of beg 4 sk chs, turn. *(56 sc, 53 ch-1 sps)*

Row 3: Ch 1, sc in first sc, *ch 1, sk next sc, sc in next ch-1 sp, rep from * 52 times, ch 1, sk next sc, sc in last sc, turn. *(55 sc, 54 ch-1 sps)*

Row 4: Ch 1, sc in first sc, sc in next ch-1 sp, *ch 1, sk next sc, sc in next ch-1 sp, rep from * 52 times, sc in last sc, turn. *(56 sc, 53 ch-1 sps)*

Rep rows 3 and 4 until piece measures 23 inches from beg, ending with a RS row. At end of last row, fasten off.

HOOD
Row 1: With WS facing, sk first 35 sts of last row, join in next st, ch 1, sc in same sc, sc in next ch-1 sp, *ch 1, sk next sc, sc in next ch-1 sp, rep from * 17 times, sc in next sc, turn, leaving rem sts unworked. *(21 sc, 18 ch-1 sps)*

Row 2: Ch 1, sc in first sc, *ch 1, sk next sc, sc in next ch-1 sp, rep from * 17 times, ch 1, sk next sc, sc in last sc, turn. *(20 sc, 17 ch-1 sps)*

Row 3: Ch 1, sc in first sc, sc in next ch-1 sp, *ch 1, sk next sc, sc in next ch-1 sp, rep from * 17 times, sc in last sc, turn. *(21 sc, 18 ch-1 sps)*

Rep rows 2 and 3 until Hood measures 9 inches from beg. At end of last row, fasten off.

ASSEMBLY
Fold Hood in half, sew top tog.

BORDER
Rnd 1 (RS): Hold piece with RS facing and foundation ch at top, join in unused lp of center ch of foundation ch, ch 1, sc in same ch and in each ch to last ch, 3 sc in last ch *(corner)*, working across next side in ends of rows, work 66 sc evenly spaced to last row, 3 sc in last row *(corner)*, working across next side, work 35 sc to Hood, working in ends of rows of Hood, work 32 sc evenly spaced to top of Hood and 32 sc evenly spaced down next side of Hood, work 35 sc across to next corner; working across next side in ends of rows, 3 sc in end of first row *(corner)*, work 66 sc evenly spaced to next corner; working across next side in unused lps of foundation ch, 3 sc in first ch *(corner)*, sc in each rem ch around to first sc, join in beg sc.

Rnd 2: Ch 3 *(see Pattern Notes)*, *cross-st *(see Special Stitches)* in next 2 sc, rep from * to 2nd sc of next corner, 3 dc in 2nd sc *(dc corner)*, **cross-st in next 2 sc, rep from ** to 2nd sc of next corner,

3 dc in 2nd sc *(dc corner)*, ***cross-st in next 2 sc, rep from *** to 2nd sc of next corner, 3 dc in 2nd sc *(dc corner)*, ****cross-st in next 2 sc, rep from **** to 2nd sc of next corner, 3 dc in 2nd sc *(dc corner)*; *****cross-st in next 2 sc, rep from ***** to beg ch-3, join in 3rd ch of beg ch-3.

Rnd 3: Ch 1, sc in each st to 2nd dc of next dc corner, 3 sc in 2nd dc *(corner)*, sc in each st to 2nd dc of next corner, 3 sc in 2nd dc *(corner)*, sc in each st to last cross-st before Hood edge, sk cross-st, working around Hood, sc in each dc, working across next side, sk next cross-st, sc in each st to 2nd dc of next corner, 3 sc in 2nd dc *(corner)*, sc in each st to 2nd dc of next corner, 3 sc in 2nd dc *(corner)*, sc in each st to first sc, join in first sc, fasten off. ■

Buttercup Jacket

DESIGN BY CATHY COSTA

SKILL LEVEL
BEGINNER

FINISHED SIZES
Instructions given fit child's size 6 months; changes for 12 months and 18 months are in [ ].

FINISHED GARMENT MEASUREMENTS
Chest size: 19 [20, 21½] inches

MATERIALS

- Bernat Baby Coordinates light (light worsted) weight yarn (6 oz/431 yds/160g per skein):
  2 skeins #09612 daisy yellow
- Patons CiCi super bulky (super chunky) weight yarn (1¾ oz/37 yds/50g per ball):
  1 ball #64132 rio and red
- Size K/10½/6.5mm crochet hook or size needed to obtain gauge
- Tapestry needle
- Sewing needle
- Sewing thread
- Stitch markers
- 2 red ⅞-inch buttons

GAUGE
With 2 strands daisy yellow held tog: 10 hdc = 4 inches; 9 hdc rows = 4 inches

PATTERN NOTES
Weave in ends as work progresses.

Sweater is worked with 2 strands of daisy yellow held together.

SPECIAL STITCH
Top chain stitch (top ch st): Insert hook between indicated sts, yo, draw lp through, insert hook around next st from front to back, yo, draw yo through piece and through both lps on hook.

Instructions

BODY
Row 1 (RS): Ch 49 [51, 56], hdc in 2nd ch from hook, hdc in each rem ch across, turn. *(48 [50, 55] hdc)*

Rows 2–17 [2–17, 2–18]: Ch 1, hdc in each hdc across, turn.

Mark each side for underarm.

FIRST FRONT
For 6 Month & 12 Month Sizes Only
Row 1 (WS): Ch 1, hdc in each of first 12 hdc, turn, leaving rem sts unworked. *(12 hdc)*

Row 2 (RS): Ch 1, hdc in each hdc, turn.

Rows 3 & 4: Rep row 2.

Row 5: Sl st in each of first 3 hdc, ch 1, hdc in each of next 9 hdc, turn. *(9 hdc)*

Row 6: Rep row 2.

Row 7: Ch 1, **hdc dec** *(see Stitch Guide)* in first 2 hdc, hdc in each rem hdc across, turn. *(8 hdc)*

Rows 8 & 9 [8–11]: Rep row 2. At end of last row, fasten off.

For 18 Month Size Only
Row 1 (RS): Ch 1, hdc in each of first 14 hdc, turn, leaving rem sts unworked. *(14 hdc)*

Row 2: Ch 1, hdc in each hdc across, turn.

Rows 3 & 4: Rep row 2.

Row 5: Sl st in each of first 3 hdc, ch 1, hdc in each of next 11 hdc, turn. *(11 hdc)*

Row 6: Rep row 2.

Row 7: Ch 1, **hdc dec** *(see Stitch Guide)* in first 2 hdc, hdc dec in next 2 hdc, hdc in each rem hdc across, turn. *(9 hdc)*

Rows 8 & 9 [8–11]: Rep row 2. At end of last row, fasten off.

BACK
For all sizes
Row 1: Join daisy yellow in next unused hdc on row 17 [17, 18] from First Front, ch 1, hdc in same hdc, hdc in each of next 23 [25, 26] hdc, turn, leaving rem sts unworked. *(24 [26, 27] hdc)*

Row 2: Ch 1, hdc in each hdc across, turn.

Rows 3–7: Rep row 2.

CONTINUED ON PAGE 74

Bare Necessities

Poke Bonnet

DESIGN BY BEVERLY STUDY

SKILL LEVEL
INTERMEDIATE

FINISHED SIZE
Instructions given fit child's
size 6–12 months

MATERIALS
- Bernat Baby super
  fine (fingering)
  weight yarn (1¾ oz/
  286 yds/50g per ball):
  2 balls #00469 pink
- Size C/2/2.75mm crochet
  hook or size needed to
  obtain gauge
- Tapestry needle
- Sewing needle
- Sewing thread
- 1 yd ⅝-inch-wide white
  ribbon

GAUGE
3 split puff sts = 1 inch; 10
split puff rows = 3 inches;
6 sc = 1 inch

PATTERN NOTES
Weave in ends as work
progresses.

Join rounds with a slip stitch
unless otherwise stated.

Chain-3 at beginning of double
crochet round counts as first
double crochet unless otherwise
stated.

SPECIAL STITCHES
Puff stitch (puff st): Yo, insert
hook in indicated sp, yo, pull up
long lp, yo, insert hook in same
sp, yo, pull up long lp, yo, pull
through all 5 lps on hook.

**Beginning split puff stitch
(beg split puff st):** Yo, insert
hook in indicated sp, yo, pull up
long lp, insert hook in next sp, yo,
pull up long lp, yo, pull through
all 5 lps on hook.

Split puff stitch (split puff st):
Yo, insert hook in same sp as last
st made, yo, pull up long lp, yo,
insert hook in next sp, yo, pull up
long lp, yo, pull through all 5 lps
on hook.

Instructions

BONNET

Rnd 1 (RS): Ch 6, join in first ch to form ring, **ch 3** *(see Pattern Notes)*, [**puff st** *(see Special Stitches)* in ring] 9 times, join in 3rd ch of beg ch-3. *(9 puff sts, 1 dc)*

Rnd 2: Ch 3, working in sps between sts, **beg split puff st** *(see Special Stitches)* in first 2 sps, dc in same sp as last st made, ***split puff st** *(see Special Stitches)* in same sp and in next sp, dc in same sp as last st made, rep from * around, join in 3rd ch of beg ch-3. *(9 split puff sts, 10 dc)*

Rnd 3: Ch 3, beg split puff st in first 2 sps, split puff st in rem sps, join in 3rd ch of beg ch-3. *(18 split puff sts, 1 dc)*

Rnd 4: Ch 3, beg split puff st in first 2 sps, [split puff st, dc in same sp as last st made] 15 times, split puff st in each of next 2 sps, join in 3rd ch of beg ch-3. *(18 split puff sts, 16 dc)*

Rnd 5: Ch 3, beg split puff st in first 2 sps, split puff st in each rem sp, join in 3rd ch of beg ch-3. *(33 split puff sts, 1 dc)*

Rnd 6: Ch 3, beg split puff st in first 2 sps, (split puff st, dc) in next sp, [split puff st in next sp, (split puff st, dc) in next sp] 14 times, split puff st in each of next 3 sps, join in 3rd ch of beg ch-3. *(33 split puff sts, 16 dc)*

Rnd 7: Rep rnd 3. *(48 split puff sts, 1 dc)*

Rnd 8: Ch 3, beg split puff st in first 2 sps, split puff st in next sp,

CONTINUED ON PAGE 75

Sweet Baby Edgings

Little Boy Blue Edging

DESIGN BY JUDY CROW

SKILL LEVEL ■■□□ **EASY**

FINISHED SIZE
½ inch x desired length

MATERIALS
- Medium (worsted) weight yarn: 2 oz/100 yds/56g blue
- Size G/6/4mm crochet hook or size needed to obtain gauge
- Tapestry needle
- 1 yd fleece

GAUGE
Gauge not important to this project.

PATTERN NOTES
Weave in ends as work progresses.

To prepare blanket, cut fleece into a 30 x 30-inch square, rounding corners.

With tapestry needle and yarn, work blanket stitch around edges, spacing stitches ¼ inch apart.

Instructions

Rnd 1 (RS): Make slip knot on hook and join with sc in any sp, sc in each sp around, join in first sc.

Rnd 2: Ch 1, sc in same sc as joining, work reverse sc (see Fig. 1) in each st around, join in first sc, fasten off.

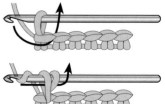

**Reverse Single Crochet
Fig. 1**

Baby Love Edging
DESIGN BY ANN WHITE

SKILL LEVEL
EASY

FINISHED SIZE
1 inch x desired length

MATERIALS
- Size 10 crochet cotton:
  350 yds shaded pink
- Size 7/1.65mm steel crochet
  hook or size needed to
  obtain gauge
- Tapestry needle
- Purchased baby blanket

GAUGE
Gauge not important to
this project.

PATTERN NOTE
Weave in ends as work progresses.

SPECIAL STITCHES
Love knot: Draw up lp on hook
½ inch, yo and draw through lp
just made, insert hook in lp on
left side (not through beg ½-inch
lp) yo and draw through, yo and
draw through 2 lps on hook.

Double love knot: [Draw up
lp on hook ½ inch yo and draw
through lp just made, insert hook
in lp on left side (not through beg
½-inch lp) yo and draw through,
yo and draw through 2 lps on
hook] twice.

Instructions

Rnd 1 (RS): Working through
edge of blanket and spacing sts
¼ inch apart, make slip knot on
hook and join with sc in 1 corner,
ch 3, *sc in edge, ch 3, rep from
*around, join in first sc.

Rnd 2: Sl st in next ch-3 sp, ch 1,
in same sp work {sc, **double love
knot** *(see Special Stitches)* in

same sp and in each rem ch-3 sp,
join in first sc.

Rnd 3: Love knot *(see Special
Stitches)* in same sc as joining,
(sc, double love knot) in center
of next double love knot and in
center of each rem double love
knot, join in first st.

Rnd 4: Rep rnd 3. At end of rnd,
fasten off.

Sweet Dreams Edging
DESIGN BY JUDY CROW

SKILL LEVEL
EASY

FINISHED SIZE
½ inch x desired length

MATERIALS
- Super fine (fingering)
  weight yarn:
  3 oz/510 yds/84g yellow
- Size 6/1.80mm steel crochet
  hook or size needed to
  obtain gauge
- Tapestry needle
- Purchased baby blanket

GAUGE
Gauge not important to
this project.

PATTERN NOTE
Weave in ends as work progresses.

Instructions

Rnd 1 (RS): Working through
edge of blanket and spacing sts
½ inch apart, make slip knot on
hook and join with sc in 1 corner,
ch 2, *sc in edge, ch 2, rep from
* around ending with an even
number of ch-2 sps, join in first sc.

Rnd 2: Sl st in next ch-2 sp, ch 1, sc
in same sp, (3 dc, ch 2, 3 dc) in next

ch-2 sp, *sc in next ch-2 sp, (3 dc, ch
2, 3 dc) in next ch-2 sp, repeat from
* around, join in first sc.

Rnd 3: Ch 1, sc in same sc as
joining, ch 3, (sc, ch 3, sc) in next
ch-2 sp, ch 3, *sc in next sc, ch 3,
(sc, ch 3, sc) in next ch-2 sp, ch 3,
rep from * around, join in first sc,
fasten off.

Lavender Lace Edging
DESIGN BY JUDY CROW

SKILL LEVEL
EASY

FINISHED SIZE
1¼ inches x desired length

MATERIALS
- Super fine (fingering)
  weight yarn:
  3 oz/510 yds/84g
  lavender
- Size 6/1.80mm steel crochet
  hook or size needed to
  obtain gauge
- Tapestry needle
- Purchased baby blanket

GAUGE
Gauge not important to
this project.

PATTERN NOTE
Weave in ends as work
progresses.

Instructions

Rnd 1 (RS): Working through
edge of blanket and spacing
sts ½ inch apart, make slip knot
on hook and join with sc in 1
corner, ch 2, *sc in edge, ch 2,
rep from * around ending with
an even number of ch-2 sps, join
in first sc.

CONTINUED ON PAGE 77

Baby Shells Afghan

DESIGN BY CINDY HARRIS

SKILL LEVEL
EASY

FINISHED SIZE
36 x 39 inches

MATERIALS
- Light (light worsted) weight yarn: 30 oz/2700 yds/850g variegated
- Size J/10/6mm crochet hook or size needed to obtain gauge
- Tapestry needle

GAUGE
7 dc = 2 inches

PATTERN NOTES
Weave in ends as work progresses.

Chain-3 at beginning of double crochet row counts as first double crochet unless otherwise stated.

SPECIAL STITCH
Shell: 5 dc in indicated st.

Instructions

CENTER
Row 1 (RS): Ch 129, dc in 4th ch from hook *(beg 3 sk chs count as a dc)*, dc in each rem ch across, turn. *(127 dc)*

Row 2: Ch 3 *(see Pattern Notes)*, dc in each dc across, turn.

Row 3: Ch 3, dc in each of next 4 dc, *sk next 2 dc, **shell** *(see Special Stitch)* in next dc, ch 2, sk next 3 dc, dc in each of next 5 chs, rep from * 9 times, sk next 2 dc, shell in next dc, ch 2, sk next 2 dc, dc in each of next 5 dc, turn. *(115 dc)*

Row 4: Ch 3, dc in each of next 4 dc, *sk next ch-2 sp, shell in next dc, ch 2, sk next 4 dc, dc in each of next 5 dc, rep from * 10 times, turn.

Rows 5–56: Rep row 4.

Row 57: Ch 3, dc in each dc and in each ch across, turn. *(137 dc)*

Row 58: Rep row 2.

BORDER
Ch 1, 2 sc in first dc, sc in each dc to last dc, 3 sc in last dc, working across next side in sps formed by edge sts of rows, 2 sc in each sp, working across next side in unused lps of foundation ch, 3 sc in first ch, sc in each ch to last ch, 3 sc in last ch, working across next side in sps formed by edge sts, 2 sc in each sp, sc in same dc as beg 2 sc, join in first sc, fasten off. ■

Sweet Pea Gown CONTINUED FROM PAGE 50

Edging

Row 1: With RS facing and with size 0 steel hook, join white sparkle in end of row 9 on right front, working in ends of rows and in unused lps of foundation ch, ch 3, dc in same sp, [sc in next row, 3 dc in next row] 4 times, sc in each ch of foundation ch, working across left front, [3 dc in next row, sc in next row] 4 times, 2 dc in last row, fasten off. *(87 [91] sts)*

Row 2: With size 0 steel hook and white, make slip knot on hook and join with sc in first st, *ch 1, sc in next st, rep from * across, turn.

Row 3: Ch 2 *(see Pattern Notes)*, hdc in same sc, sl st in next sc, *3 hdc in next st, sl st in next st, rep from * across with 2 hdc in last st, fasten off.

BODY

Rnd 1 (RS): Starting at left front edging, with size F hook and white sparkle, make slip knot on hook and join with sc in end of row 1 of edging, 2 sc in same row, sc in each of next 22 [24] sts on row 9 of Yoke, sc in next ch-1 sp, for armhole, ch 4 [6], sk next 28 [30] sts, sc in next ch-1 sp, sc in each of next 46 sts, sc in next ch-1 sp, for armhole, ch 4 [6], sk next 28 [30] sts, sc in next ch-1 sp, sc in each of next 22 [24] sts, 3 sc in opposite end of row 1 on edging of right front, join in first sc. *(100 [104] sts and 2 ch-4 [ch-6] sps)*

Rnd 2: Ch 3, *sk next st, **shell** *(see Special Stitches)* in next st, sk next st, dc in next st, rep from * 25 [27] times, sk next st, shell in next st, sk last st, join in 3rd ch of beg ch-3, turn. *(27 [29] shells and 28 dc)*

Rnds 3–44 [3–48]: Ch 3, shell in 3rd dc of next shell, *dc in next dc, shell in 3rd dc of next shell, rep from * around, join in 3rd ch of beg ch-3, turn. At end of last rnd, fasten off.

Rnd 45 [49]: With size 0 steel hook and white, make slip knot on hook and join in first sc, ch 1, *sc in next st, ch 1, rep from * around, join in first sc, turn. *(162 [174] sts)*

Rnd 46 [50]: Ch 2, hdc in same sc, sl st in next sc, *3 hdc in next sc, sl st in next sc, rep from * around, join in 2nd ch of beg ch-2, fasten off.

SLEEVE

Rnd 1 (RS): With size F hook and white sparkle, make slip knot on hook and join with sc in first sc of 1 armhole, sc in each ch and in each st around armhole, join in first sc. *(32 [36] sc)*

Rnd 2: Ch 3, *sk next st, shell in next st, sk next st, dc in next st, rep from * around, sk last st, join in 3rd ch of beg ch-3, turn. *(8 [9] shells, 9 [10] dc)*

Rnds 3–15 [3–17]: Ch 3, shell in 3rd dc of next shell, *dc in next dc, shell in 3rd dc of next shell, rep from * around, join in 3rd ch of beg ch-3, turn. At end of last rnd, fasten off.

Rnd 16 [18]: With size 0 steel hook and white, make slip knot on hook and join in 3rd ch of beg ch-3, ch 1, *sc in next st, ch 1, rep from * around, join in first sc, turn.

Rnd 17 [19]: Ch 2, hdc in same sc, sl st in next sc, *3 hdc in next sc, sl st in next sc, rep from * around, join in 2nd ch of beg ch-2, fasten off. *(23 [26] hdc, 8 [9] sl sts)*

Rep on other armhole.

TIES

Neck Tie
Row 1: With size F hook and white sparkle, ch 175 loosely, fasten off.

Row 2: Working in back bar of chs, with size 0 steel hook and white, make slip knot on hook and join in first ch, *ch 1, sc in next ch, rep from * across, fasten off.

Wrist Tie
Make 2.
Row 1: With size F hook and white sparkle, ch 82 loosely, fasten off.

Row 2: Working in back bar of chs, with size 0 steel hook and white, make slip knot on hook and join in first ch, *ch 1, sc in next ch, rep from * across, fasten off.

Bottom Tie
Row 1: With size F hook and white sparkle, ch 200 loosely, fasten off.

Row 2: Working in back bar of chs, with size 0 steel hook and white, make slip knot on hook and join in first ch, *ch 1, sc in next ch, rep from * across, fasten off.

FINISHING

Weave Neck Tie through sts of row 1 of Yoke. Weave Wrist Tie through sts of rnd 11 [15] on each Sleeve. Weave Bottom Tie through sts of rnd 38 [42] of Body. ■

Nursery Notions CONTINUED FROM PAGE 52

*sc in next row, 2 sc in next row, rep from * across, working across next side in unused lps of foundation ch, 3 sc in first ch, sc in each of next 22 chs, 3 sc in next ch, working across next side in ends of rows, sc in first row, 2 sc in next row, **sc in next row, 2 sc in next row, rep from ** to first sc, join in first sc. *(200 sc)*

Rnd 2: Sl st in next sc, ch 1, sc in same sc, ch 3, sk next sc, *sc in next sc, ch 3, sk next sc, rep from * around, join in first sc, fasten off.

BOTTLE COVER
Rnd 1 (RS): With white, ch 4, 12 dc in 4th ch from hook, join in first dc. *(12 dc)*

Rnd 2: Ch 1, 2 sc in each dc, join in first sc. *(24 sc)*

Rnd 3: Working in **back lps** *(see Stitch Guide)* only, ch 2, hdc in each sc, join in first sc.

Rnds 4–16: Ch 2, hdc in each hdc, join in first hdc. At end of last rnd, fasten off.

Rnd 17: With yellow, make slip knot on hook and join with sc in first hdc, ch 3, sk next hdc, *sc in next hdc, ch 3, sk next hdc, rep from * around, join in first sc, fasten off.

FINISHING
Weave ribbon through every 2 sts on rnd 17. Pull ends even. Tie in bow. ■

Baby Pocket Afghan CONTINUED FROM PAGE 54

from **** to first sc, ch 4, sc in same st as joining sc made, ch 1, join with dc in first sc *(corner)*. *(178 sc, 170 ch-4 sps, 4 corner sps)*

Rnds 2 & 3: Sc in sp formed by joining dc, ch 4, *sc in next ch-4 sp, ch 4, rep from * to next ch-4 corner sp, corner in ch-4 corner sp, **sc in next ch-4 sp, ch 4, rep from ** to next ch-4 corner sp, corner in ch-4 corner sp, ***sc in next ch-4 sp, ch 4, rep from *** to next ch-4 corner sp, corner in ch-4 corner sp, ****sc in next ch-4 sp, ch 4, rep from **** to next ch-4 corner sp, sc in joining sp, ch 1, join with dc in first sc.

Rnd 4: Ch 1, (2 sc, ch 2, 2 sc) in sp formed by joining dc and in each ch-4 sp around, join in first sc, fasten off. *(696 sc)*

POCKET
Row 1 (WS): With K hook and white, ch 29, sc in 2nd ch from hook, dc in next ch, *sc in next ch, dc in next ch, rep from * across, turn. *(28 sts)*

Row 2 (RS): Ch 1, sc in each dc

and dc in each sc across. At end of last row, fasten off.

Rows 3–26: Rep row 2. At end of last row, fasten off.

Border
Rnd 1 (RS): With RS facing, with size K hook and pastel green, make slip knot on hook and join with sc in last st made on row 26, ch 4, working across next side in ends of sc rows only, sc in next sc row, *ch 4, sc in next sc row, rep from * across, working across next side in opposite side of foundation ch, (sc, ch 4, sc) in first ch *(corner)*, ch 4, sk next 2 chs, **sc in next ch, ch 4, sk next ch, rep from ** to last ch, (sc, ch 4, sc) in last ch *(corner)*, ch 4, working across next side in ends of sc rows only, ***sc in next sc row, ch 4, rep from *** across, working across row 26, (sc, ch 4, sc) in first st *(corner)*, ch 4, sk next 2 sts, ****sc in next st, ch 4, sk next 2 sts, rep from **** to first sc, ch 4, sc in same st as joining sc, ch 1, join with dc in first sc *(corner)*. *(58 sc, 50 ch-4 sps, 4 corner sps)*

Rnds 2–4: Rep rnds 2–4 of Center Border. *(216 sc at end of last rnd)*

RIBBON
Row 1: With size D hook and pastel green, ch 3, **V-st** *(see Special Stitch)* in 3rd ch from hook, turn.

Row 2: Ch 2, shell in ch-2 sp of shell, turn.

Rep row 2 until piece measures approximately 5 feet long. At end of last row, fasten off.

FINISHING

Sew Ribbon to Pocket on RS about 1½ inches in from edges *(see Pocket Finisher illustration)*. Tie Ribbon ends in a bow at top edge. Fold afghan according to Afghan Assembly illustration. Matching corners, place Pocket on folded Afghan, mark where all 4 Front corners touch. Unfold Afghan, position Pocket with WS facing on Afghan, matching corners to marks, fold Border to inside *(see Pocket Assembly illustration)*, and sew edges of Front to Afghan (matching dotted lines on both illustrations).

For Pillow, fold Afghan again, fold Pocket over Afghan (Pocket Border and Ribbon are on outside). ■

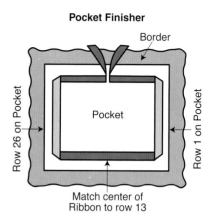

Pocket Finisher

Border

Row 26 on Pocket

Pocket

Row 1 on Pocket

Match center of Ribbon to row 13

Afghan Assembly

1: Fold in thirds.

2: Fold ends to center, then fold again at center.

3: Sew Pocket, wrong side facing out, in place along dotted lines.

Pocket Assembly

Leave top edge of Pocket free or unattached

Border

Wrong side of Pocket

Fold Border to inside. Sew three edges of Pocket to Afghan (see dotted lines on both Pocket and Afghan Assembly illustrations)

Baby Antoinette CONTINUED FROM PAGE 56

Rnd 3: With WS facing and working in unused lps of rnd 2, with white make slip knot on hook and join with sc in unused lp of same sc as beg ch-3 of previous rnd made, sc in each rem lp, join in first sc, turn. *(196 sc)*

Rnd 4: Ch 3, 3 dc in first sc, *sk next 3 sc, shell in next sc, rep from * around, sc in same sc as beg ch-3 made, join in bottom of beg ch-3, turn. *(48 shells)*

Rnd 5: Ch 3, 3 dc in first sc, *shell in ch-3 sp of next shell, rep from * around, join in sp formed by beg ch-3, fasten off.

Sleeve
Make 2.
Row 1 (RS): With spa blue, ch 23, dc in 5th ch from hook *(beg 4 sk chs count as a dc)*, dc in each rem ch across, turn. *(20 dc)*

Row 2: Ch 3, dc in each dc, turn.

Rows 3–18: Rep row 2. At end of last row, fasten off, leaving an 8-inch end.

ASSEMBLY
Sew sleeve seams. Sew sleeves into armholes.

Sleeve Edging
Rnd 1: With RS facing and with spa blue, make slip knot on hook and join with sc near seam, work 35 sc evenly spaced around sleeve edge, join in first sc. *(36 sc)*

Rnd 2: Ch 5 *(counts as first dc and ch-2 sp)*, sk next 2 sc, dc in next sc, *ch 2, sk next 2 sc, dc in next sc, rep from * to last 2 sc, ch 2, sk last 2 sc, join in 3rd ch of beg ch-5. *(12 ch-2 sps)*

Rnd 3: Ch 1, sc in same ch as joining, 2 sc in next ch-2 sp, *2 sc in next ch-2 sp, sc in next dc, rep from * around, join in front lp of first sc. *(36 sc)*

Rnd 4: Ch 3, 3 dc in same lp as joining, working in front lps only, *sk next 3 sc, shell in next sc, rep from * to last sc, sc in last sc, join in bottom of beg ch-3, fasten off. *(8 shells)*

Rnd 5: With WS facing and working in unused lps of rnd 4, with white make slip knot on hook and join with sc in unused lp of same sc as beg ch-3 of previous rnd, sc in each rem lp, join in first sc, turn.

Rnd 6: Ch 3, 3 dc in first sc, *sk next 3 sc, shell in next sc, rep from * to last sc, sc in last sc, join in bottom of beg ch-3, turn.

Rnd 7: Ch 3, 3 dc in first sc, *shell in ch-3 sp of next shell, rep from * to last sc, sc in last sc, join in 3rd ch of beg ch-3, turn.

Rnds 8 & 9: Rep rnd 7. At end of last rnd, fasten off.

FINISHING
Referring to photo for placement and with sewing needle and matching thread, sew 8 ribbon roses along front opening.

Cut 2 lengths of ribbon, each 18 inches long. Weave 1 length through ch-2 sps of rnd 2 on 1 Sleeve Edging. Tie in bow and trim ends. Rep with rem length.

Cut 24-inch length of ribbon. Referring to photo for placement, weave through shells at front opening, tie in bow and trim ends.

BONNET
Back
Row 1 (WS): With spa blue, ch 23, dc in 5th ch from hook *(beg 4 sk chs count as a dc)*, dc in each rem ch across, turn. *(20 dc)*

Row 2 (RS): Ch 3 *(see Pattern Notes)*, dc in each dc across, turn.

Rows 3–12: Rep row 2. At end of last row, fasten off.

Top & Sides
Row 1 (WS): With spa blue, ch 73, dc in 5th ch from hook *(beg 4 sk chs count as a dc)*, dc in each rem ch across, turn. *(70 dc)*

Row 2 (RS): Ch 3, dc in each dc across, turn.

Rows 3–10: Rep row 2. At end of last row, fasten off, leaving an 8-inch end.

ASSEMBLY
Holding Back vertically rather than horizontally, sew Top and Sides to 3 sides of Back, gathering as needed.

Edging
Rnd 1 (RS): With RS facing and working first along bottom edge of Bonnet, with spa blue make slip knot on hook and join with sc in end of first row of side, sc evenly spaced in ends of rows (about 2 sc per row) and in each sc around, working 3 sc in each front corner, join in first sc.

Rnd 2: Ch 5 *(counts as first dc and ch-2 sp)*, sk next 2 sc, dc in next sc, *ch 2, sk 2 sc, dc in next sc, rep from * across, working across front opening in front lps only, ch 3, 3 dc in same sc, **sk next 3 sc, shell in next sc, rep from * around, join in 3rd ch of beg ch-5.

Row 3: Now working in rows, ch 1, *2 sc in next ch-2 sp, sc in next dc, rep from * across, sl st in ch-3 sp of first shell, fasten off.

Row 4: With WS facing and bottom edge to right, with white make slip knot on hook and join with a sc in unused lp of rnd 1 at base of first shell made on rnd 3, sc in each rem unused lp of rnd 1, turn.

Row 5: Ch 3, 3 dc in first sc, *sk next 3 sc, shell in next sc, rep from * to last sc, sc in last sc, turn.

Row 6: Ch 3, 3 dc in first sc, *shell in ch-3 sp of next shell, rep from * to last ch-3 sp, sc in last ch-3 sp, fasten off.

FINISHING
Referring to photo for placement and with sewing needle and matching thread, sew 7 ribbon roses along front of Bonnet.

Weave rem length of ribbon through rnd 2 of bottom edge of Bonnet; tie in bow and trim ends. ■

Buttercup Jacket CONTINUED FROM PAGE 62

First Shoulder
Row 8: Ch 1, hdc in each of first 8 [8, 9] hdc, turn, leaving rem sts unworked. *(8 [8, 9] hdc)*

Row(s) 9 [9–11, 9–11]: Ch 1, hdc in each hdc across, turn. At end of last row, fasten off.

2nd Shoulder
Row 8: Sk next 8 [10, 9] unworked hdc from First Shoulder, join daisy yellow in next hdc, ch 1, hdc in same hdc, hdc in each rem hdc across, turn.

Row(s) 9 [9–11, 9–11]: Ch 1, hdc in each hdc across, turn. At end of last row, fasten off.

2ND FRONT
For 6 Month & 12 Month Sizes Only
Row 1 (WS): Join daisy yellow in next unused hdc from Back, ch 1, hdc in same hdc, hdc in each rem hdc across, turn. *(12 hdc)*

Row 2 (RS): Ch 1, hdc in each hdc, turn.

Rows 3 & 4: Rep row 2.

Row 5: Ch 1, hdc in each of next 9 hdc, turn, leaving rem sts unworked. *(9 hdc)*

Row 6: Rep row 2.

Row 7: Ch 1, hdc in each of first 8 hdc, turn, leaving rem st unworked. *(8 hdc)*

Rows 8 & 9 [8–11]: Rep row 2. At end of last row, fasten off.

For 18 Month Size Only
Row 1 (RS): Ch 1, hdc in each of first 14 hdc, turn, leaving rem sts unworked. *(14 hdc)*

Row 2: Ch 1, hdc in each hdc across, turn.

Rows 3 & 4: Rep row 2.

Row 5: Sl st in each of first 3 hdc, ch 1, hdc in each of next 11 hdc, turn. *(11 hdc)*

Row 6: Rep row 2.

Row 7: Ch 1, **hdc dec** *(see Stitch Guide)* in first 2 hdc, hdc dec in next 2 hdc, hdc in each rem hdc across, turn. *(9 hdc)*

Rows 8–11: Rep row 2. At end of last row, fasten off.

ASSEMBLY
For all sizes
Sew shoulder seams.

Body Edging
With RS facing and lower edge at top, join daisy yellow in first st in right-hand corner, sc evenly spaced around edge of piece, working 2 sc in each corner st where Fronts meet for neck shaping, join in first sc, fasten off.

COLLAR
Row 1 (RS): With WS facing and neck edge at top, join daisy yellow in left front neck edge, ch 1, working in back lps only, work 35 [38, 38] hdc around neck edge, turn.

Rows 2–4: Ch 1, hdc in each hdc across, turn, fasten off.

SLEEVES
First Sleeve
Rnd 1 (RS): Join daisy yellow at underarm where previously marked, ch 1, work 20 [24, 24] hdc evenly spaced around armhole, join in first hdc. *(20 [24, 24] hdc)*

Rnds 2–10: Ch 1, hdc in each hdc, turn.

Rnd 11: Ch 1, **hdc dec** *(see Stitch Guide)* in first 2 hdc, hdc in each of next 7 [9, 9] hdc, hdc dec in

next 2 hdc, hdc in each of next 7 [9, 9] hdc, hdc dec in last 2 hdc, turn. *(17 [21, 21] hdc)*

Rnds 12 & 13 [12–14, 12–15]: Rep rnd 2. At end of last rnd, fasten off.

TRIMS
Note: Rio and red yarn has nubby sections that need to be pushed through to RS for full effect of yarn to be visible on RS of Jacket.

Body Trim
With RS facing and holding 1 strand of rio and red on WS of Body, join rio and red with sl st by inserting hook from front to back around **post** *(see Stitch Guide)* of first hdc of row 1 at right front, work **top ch st** *(see Special Stitch)* by inserting hook in sp between first and 2nd hdc and around 2nd hdc, work top ch st around each rem hdc across row.

Work trim in same manner on row 3 of Body.

Collar Trim
With RS facing and holding 1 strand of rio and red on WS of Collar, join rio and red around post of first hdc of row 4 of Collar, work top ch st by inserting hook in sp between first and 2nd hdc and around 2nd hdc, work top ch st around each rem hdc across row.

Work trim in same manner on row 3 of Collar.

Sleeve Trim

With RS facing and holding 1 strand of rio and red on WS of 1 Sleeve, join rio and red around post of first hdc of row 1 of Sleeve, work top ch st by inserting hook in sp between first and 2nd hdc and around 2nd

hdc, work top ch st around each rem hdc across row.

Work trim in same manner on row 2 of Sleeve.

Rep on other Sleeve.

FINISHING

Referring to photo for placement

and with sewing needle and matching thread, sew on buttons on front.

BUTTON LOOP

Join 2 strands of daisy yellow in right front edge across from button on left front edge, ch 6, join in same sp on right front edge, fasten off. ∎

Bare Necessities CONTINUED FROM PAGE 65

in next sp work (split puff st, dc), [split puff st in each of next 2 sps, (split puff st, dc) in next sp] 14 times, split puff st in each of next 3 sps, join in 3rd ch of beg ch-3. *(48 split puff sts, 16 dc)*

Rnds 9 & 10: Rep rnd 3. *(63 split puff sts, 1 dc at end of last rnd)*

Rnd 11: Ch 3, beg split puff st in first 2 sps, split puff st in next sp, (split puff st, dc) in next sp, [split puff st in each of next 3 sps, (split puff st, dc) in next sp] 15 times, split puff st in each of next 3 sps, join in 3rd ch of beg ch-3. *(48 split puff sts, 16 dc)*

Rnds 12 & 13: Rep rnd 3. *(76 split puff sts, 1 dc at end of last rnd)*

Rnd 14: Ch 3, beg split puff st in first 2 sps, split puff st in each of next 2 sps, (split puff st, dc) in next sp, [split puff st in each of next 4 sps, (split puff st, dc) in next sp] 14 times, split puff st in each of next 4 sps, join in 3rd ch of beg ch-3. *(78 split puff sts, 16 dc)*

Rnds 15 & 16: Rep rnd 3. *(93 split puff sts, 1 dc at end of last rnd)*

Rnd 17: Ch 3, beg split puff st in first 2 sps, split puff st in each of next 2 sps, (split puff st, dc) in next sp, [split puff st in each of next 5

sps, (split puff st, dc) in next sp] 14 times, split puff st in each of next 5 sps, join in 3rd ch of beg ch-3. *(93 split puff sts, 16 dc)*

Rnd 18: Rep rnd 3. *(108 split puff sts, 1 dc)*

Rnd 19: Ch 1, sc in each st around, join in first sc.

Rnd 20: Ch 1, sc in each of first 5 sc, sk next 2 sc, [sc in each of next 5 sts, sk next sc] 17 times, join in first sc, fasten off. *(90 sc)*

Note: Mark first sc of previous rnd as center back.

Row 21: Now working in rows, make slip knot on hook and join with sc in 15th st from center back, sc in each of next 61 sts, fasten off, leaving rem sts unworked. *(62 sc)*

Row 22: Make slip knot on hook and join with sc in 14th st from center back, sc in each of next 63 sts, fasten off, leaving rem sts unworked. *(64 sc)*

Row 23: Make slip knot on hook and join with sc in 13th st from center back, sc in each of next 65 sts, fasten off, leaving rem sts unworked. *(66 sc)*

Rnd 24: Now working in rnds, make slip knot on hook and join

with sc in center back, sc in each sc around, join in first sc, fasten off.

Brim

Note: On following row, work puff st and split puff st in sc instead of sps.

Row 1: With RS facing, make slip knot on hook and join with sc in 20th sc from center back, puff st in next sc, [split puff st in same sc as last st made and in next sc] 50 times, sc in next sc, fasten off, leaving rem sts unworked, fasten off. *(2 sc, 1 puff st, 50 split puff sts)*

Row 2: Make slip knot on hook and join with sc in 19th st from center back, dc in next sc, beg split puff st in next 2 sps, split puff st in each sp to last sc, dc in last sc, sc in next st on rnd 24, fasten off. *(2 sc, 2 dc, 51 split puff sts)*

Row 3: Make slip knot on hook and join with sc in 18th st from center back, dc in next sc, beg split puff st in next 2 sps, split puff st in each sp to last sc, dc in last sc, sc in next st on rnd 24, fasten off. *(2 sc, 2 dc, 52 split puff sts)*

Row 4: Make slip knot on hook and join with sc in 17th st from center back, dc in next sc, beg split puff st in next 2 sps, split puff st in each sp to last sc, dc in last sc, sc in next st on rnd 24, fasten off. *(2 sc, 2 dc, 53 split puff sts)*

Row 5: Make slip knot on hook and join with sc in 16th st from center back, dc in next sc, beg split puff st in next 2 sps, split puff st in each sp to last sc, dc in last sc, sc in next st on rnd 24, fasten off. *(2 sc, 2 dc, 54 split puff sts)*

Row 6: Make slip knot on hook and join with sc in 15th st from center back, dc in next sc, beg split puff st in next 2 sps, split puff st in each sp to last sc, dc in last sc, sc in next st on rnd 24, fasten off. *(2 sc, 2 dc, 55 split puff sts)*

Row 7: Make slip knot on hook and join with sc in 14th st from center back, dc in next sc, beg split puff st in next 2 sps, split puff st in each sp to last sc, dc in last sc, sc in next st on rnd 24, fasten off. *(2 sc, 2 dc, 56 split puff sts)*

Rnd 8: Now working in rnds, make slip knot on hook and join with sc in center back sc, evenly spacing sc so piece lays flat, sc in sts and in ch sps around, join in first sc, fasten off.

FINISHING

Cut ribbon in half. Fold 1 end of 1 piece ¼ inch to back; with sewing needle and matching thread, tack fold to Bonnet on 1 side of Brim. Rep on other side of Brim with rem piece of ribbon.

Fancy Pants

DESIGN BY AMANDA CUNARD

SKILL LEVEL
EASY

FINISHED SIZES
Instructions given fit child's size 6 months; changes for 12 months are in [ ].

FINISHED GARMENT MEASUREMENTS
Waist: 21-inches in circumference [22½-inches in circumference]

MATERIALS
- Bernat Baby super fine (fingering) weight yarn (1¾ oz/ 286 yds/50g per skein): 2 skeins #00469 pink
- Size E/4/3.5mm crochet hook or size needed to obtain gauge
- Tapestry needle
- Sewing needle
- Sewing thread
- 2⅓ yds ¼-inch-wide white ribbon
- Matching sewing thread

GAUGE
5 dc = 1 inch; 3 dc rows = 1 inch

PATTERN NOTES
Weave in ends as work progresses.

Join rounds with a slip stitch unless otherwise stated.

Chain-3 at beginning of double crochet row or round does not count as first double crochet unless otherwise stated.

Work even-numbered rows in **front lps** *(see Stitch Guide)* and odd-numbered rows in **back lps** *(see Stitch Guide)* unless otherwise specified.

SPECIAL STITCH
Shell: 5 dc in indicated st.

Instructions

SIDE
Make 2.
Row 1 (WS): Ch 54 [58], dc in 4th ch from hook *(beg 3 sk chs count as first dc)*, dc in each rem ch across, turn. *(52 [56] dc)*

Row 2 (RS): Ch 3 *(see Pattern Notes)*, dc in each sc across, turn.

Row 3: Ch 3, dc in each dc across, turn.

Rows 4–10 [4–12]: Rep row 3.

Row 11 [13]: Sl st in each of first 0 [3] dc, ch 3, [**dc dec** *(see Stitch Guide)* in next 2 dc] twice, dc in each of next 42 dc, [dc dec in next 2 dc] twice, dc in next dc, turn, leaving rem 0 [2] sts unworked. *(48 sts)*

Rows 12–18 [14–20]: Ch 3, [dc dec in next 2 sts] twice, dc in each st to last 5 sts, [dc dec in next 2 sts] 2 times, dc in last st, turn. *(20 sts at end of last row)*

Rows 19–21 [21–23]: Ch 3, dc in each st across, turn. At end of last row, fasten off.

ASSEMBLY
With WS tog and matching sts, sew ends of rows 1-11 [1–13] tog for side seams. Sew crotch seam.

RUFFLES
With waist facing and working in unused lps of row 4 [6], make slip knot on hook and join with sc in side seam, sk next st, **shell** *(see*

Special Stitch) in next st, sk next st, *sc in next st, sk next st, shell in next st, sk next st, rep from * around, skipping other seam, join in first sc, fasten off.

Rep in rem unused lps of rows 6 [8], 8 [10] and 10 [12].

Working on 1 side of piece in unused lps of row 12 [14], make slip knot on hook and join with sc in first st, shell in next st, sk next st, sc in next st, *sk next st, shell in next st, sk next st, sc in next st, rep from * across, fasten off.

Rep in unused lps on other side of piece.

TRIMS
Waist Trim
Hold piece with RS facing and foundation ch at top, working in unused lps of foundation ch, make slip knot on hook and join with sc in any ch, ch 5, sk next ch, *sc in next ch, ch 5, sk next

ch, rep from * around, join in first sc, fasten off.

Leg Trim
Rnd 1 (RS): Working around leg opening, make slip knot on hook and join with sc in end of any row of leg opening, sc in same row, 2 sc in end of each rem row and sc in each st around, join in first sc.

Rnd 2: Ch 1, sc in first sc, ch 5, sk next sc, *sc in next sc, ch 5, sk next sc, rep from * around, join in first sc, fasten off.

Rep on other leg opening

FINISHING
Cut 36-inch length of ribbon; weave through ch-5 sps of Waist Trim. Tie ends in bow at front.

Cut rem ribbon in half, weave 1 piece through ch-5 sps of each Leg Trim. Tie ends in bow at top. ■

Sweet Baby Edgings CONTINUED FROM PAGE 67

Rnd 2: Sl st in next ch-2 sp, ch 3 *(counts as first dc)*, 2 dc in same sp, ch 2, sk next ch-2 sp, *3 dc in next ch-2 sp, ch 2, sk next ch-2 sp, rep from * around, join in 3rd ch of beg ch-3.

Rnd 3: Sl st in next dc, ch 1, sc in same dc, 5 dc in next ch-2 sp, *sc in 2nd dc of next 3-dc group, 5 dc in next ch-2 sp, rep from *

around, join in first sc.

Rnd 4: Ch 1, sc in same sc as joining, sc in each of next 2 dc, (sl st, ch 5, sl st, ch 7, sl st, ch 5, sl st) in next st, sc in each of next 2 dc, *sc in next sc, sc in each of next 2 dc, (sl st, ch 5, sl st, ch 7, sl st, ch 5, sl st) in next dc, sc in each of next 2 dc, rep from * around, join in first sc, fasten off. ■

3

Gifts to Share

Homemade gifts are as great to give as they are to receive, but with our busy schedules, it's not always easy to make something at the last minute. Share one of these gifts with a friend or relative. You'll find something for people of all ages.

Spoil Yourself Bath Set

DESIGNS BY KATHLEEN STUART

SKILL LEVEL ◼◼▢▢
EASY

FINISHED SIZES
Bath Mitt: Fits up to 3-inch wide palm
Washcloth: 9½ x 9½ inches
Soap Holder: 3 x 5½ inches
Back Scrubber: 4 x 23 inches, excluding handles
Bag: 10 x 10½ inches

MATERIALS

- TLC Cotton Plus medium (worsted) weight yarn (3½ oz/ 178 yds/100g per ball):
  4 balls #3100 cream
  1 ball #3503 spruce
- Size J/10/6mm crochet hook or size needed to obtain gauge
- Tapestry needle
- Stitch markers

GAUGE
18 sts = 4 inches

PATTERN NOTES
Weave in ends as work progresses.

Join rounds with a slip stitch unless otherwise stated.

SPECIAL STITCHES
Shell: 5 dc in indicated st or sp.

Popcorn (pc): 5 dc in indicated st, drop lp from hook, insert hook in first dc of 5-dc group, pull dropped lp through.

Instructions

BATH MITT
Note: Bath Mitt is worked lengthwise.

Row 1 (WS): With cream, ch 35, sc in 2nd ch from hook and in each rem ch across, turn. *(34 sc)*

Rows 2–31: Ch 1, *sc in **front lp** *(see Stitch Guide)* of next sc, sc in **back lp** *(see Stitch Guide)* of next sc, rep from * across, turn.

ASSEMBLY
Fold piece in half, matching row 31 to unused lps on opposite side of foundation ch, ch 1, working through both thicknesses, sl st in each of next 21 sts, sl st in each of next 5 sts on row 31 only, working through both thicknesses, sl st in each of last 8 sts, fasten off.

Turn piece RS out.

Bottom Edging
Note: Work edging around end closest to thumb opening. Work in continuous rnds, do not join unless specified. Mark beg of rnds.

Rnd 1 (RS): With spruce, make slip knot on hook and join with sc in end of any row, work 31 sc evenly spaced around edge. *(32 sc)*

Rnds 2–4: *Sc in front lp of next sc, sc in back lp of next sc, rep from * around. At end of last rnd, join in first sc, fasten off.

Top Edging
Note: Work in continuous rnds, do not join unless specified. Mark beg of rnds.

Rnd 1 (RS): With cream, make slip knot on hook and join with sl st in end of any row of top opening, ch 1, working in ends of rows, **sc dec** *(see Stitch Guide)* in same row and in next row, [sc dec in end of next 2 rows] 15 times. *(16 sc)*

Rnd 2: [Sc dec in next 2 sc] 8 times. *(8 sc)*

Rnd 3: [Sc dec in next 2 sc] 4 times, fasten off, leaving an 8-inch end. *(4 sc)*

Weave end through rnd 3 and pull to tighten. Secure end.

Thumb
Note: Work in continuous rnds, do not join unless specified. Mark beg of rnds.

Rnd 1 (RS): With spruce, make slip knot on hook and join with sc in side of thumb opening, work 11 sc evenly spaced around opening. *(12 sc)*

Rnds 2–9: *Sc in front lp of next sc, sc in back lp of next sc, rep from *around.

Rnd 10: [Sc dec in next 2 sc] 6 times, join in first sc, fasten off, leaving an 8-inch end for sewing. Weave end through sc of rnd 10 and pull to close opening. Secure end.

WASHCLOTH
Center
Row 1 (RS): With cream, ch 31, sc in 2nd ch from hook, sc in each rem ch across, turn. *(30 sc)*

Rows 2–29: Ch 1, sc in front lp of first sc, sc in back lp of next sc, *sc in front lp of next sc, sc in back lp of next sc, rep from * across, turn. At end of row 29, **do not turn or fasten off**. Change to spruce by drawing lp through.

Border
Note: Work in continuous rnds, do not join unless specified. Mark beg of rnds.

Rnd 1 (RS): Ch 1, working around Center in ends of rows, in unused lps of foundation ch and in sc, sc in end of row 28 and sc evenly spaced in ends of rows and in each st, working 3 sc in each corner.

Rnds 2–4: *Sc in front lp of next sc, sc in back lp of next sc, rep from * to 2nd sc of next corner, 3 sc in 2nd sc, continue working in front lp/back lp pattern as established across sides and working 3 sc in 2nd sc of each rem corner.

Note: When working rnds 3 and 4, be sure to work in same front or back lps as prior row. Adjust pattern as necessary near corners to retain established pattern by doing either 2 sts in front lp only or 2 sts in back lp only.

Fasten off at end of rnd 4.

BACK SCRUBBER
Row 1: With cream, ch 91, sc in 2nd ch from hook, sc in each rem ch across, turn. *(90 sc)*

Rows 2–29: Ch 1, sc in front lp of first sc, sc in back lp of next sc, *sc in front lp of next sc, sc in back lp of next sc, rep from * across, turn.

Row 30: Fold piece in half, matching row 29 to opposite side of foundation ch, ch 1, working through both thicknesses, sl st in each st across, fasten off.

Edging
Note: Work in continuous rnds, do not join unless specified. Mark beg of rnds.

Rnd 1: With spruce, make slip knot on hook and join with sc in end of any row on 1 side of Scrubber, working in ends of rows, work 29 sc evenly spaced around. *(30 sc)*

Rnds 2–4: Ch 1, sc in front lp of first sc, sc in back lp of next sc, *sc in front lp of next sc, sc in back lp of next sc, rep from * across, turn.

Rep on opposite end of Scrubber.

HANDLE
Fold Scrubber in half, ch 1, working through both thicknesses, sl st in next 15 sts, ch 50 (*Handle*), turn, sl st in first sl st made, ch 1, turn, sc in each ch across, sl st in last sl st of beg 15 sl sts, fasten off.

Rep on opposite Edging.

SOAP HOLDER
Note: Soap Holder is worked lengthwise.

Row 1 (WS): With cream, ch 19, sc in 2nd ch from hook, sc in each rem ch across, turn. (*18 sc*)

Rows 2–27: Ch 1, sc in front lp of first sc, sc in back lp of next sc, *sc in front lp of next sc, sc in back lp of next sc, rep from * across, turn.

ASSEMBLY
Fold piece in half, matching row 27 to unused lps on opposite side of foundation ch, ch 1, working through both thicknesses, sl st in each st across, working through

both thicknesses in ends of rows across next side, sl st in each row, fasten off.

Turn piece RS out.

Edging
Note: Work in continuous rnds, do not join unless specified. Mark beg of rnds.

Rnd 1 (RS): With RS facing and with cream, make slip knot on hook and join with sc in end of any row, working in ends of rows, work 27 sc evenly spaced around. (*28 sc*)

Rnd 2: [Sc in next sc, ch 1, sk next sc] 14 times, join in first sc, fasten off. (*14 sc*)

Rnd 3: With spruce, make slip knot on hook and join with sc in first sc, sc in each ch and rem sc around. (*28 sc*)

Rnds 4–6: [Sc in front lp of next st, sc in back lp of next st] around. At end of last rnd, join in first sc, fasten off.

TIE
With cream, ch 80, fasten off. Weave Tie through rnd 2 of Edging. Tie double knot at each end of Tie. Tie in bow.

BAG
Note: Bag is worked lengthwise.

Row 1 (WS): With cream, ch 41, sc in 2nd ch from hook, sc in each rem ch across, turn. (*40 sc*)

Rows 2–75: Ch 1, [sc in front lp of next st, sc in back lp of next st] across, turn.

ASSEMBLY
Fold piece in half, matching row 75 to unused lps on opposite side of foundation ch, ch 1, working through both thicknesses, sl st in each st across, working through both thicknesses in ends of rows across next side, sl st in each row, fasten off.

Turn piece RS out.

Edging
Note: Work in continuous rnds, do not join unless specified. Mark beg of rnds.

Rnd 1 (RS): With RS facing and with cream, make slip knot on hook and join with sc in end of any row, working in ends of rows, work 75 sc evenly spaced around. (*76 sc*)

Rnd 2: *Sc in next sc, ch 1, sk next sc, rep from * around, join in first sc, fasten off. (*38 sc*)

Rnd 3: With spruce, make slip knot on hook and join with sc in first sc, sc in each ch and rem sc around. (*76 sc*)

Rnds 4–7: [Sc in front lp of next st, sc in back lp of next st] around. At end of last rnd, join in first sc, fasten off.

TIE
Make 2.
With cream, ch 100, fasten off. Weave 1 Tie through half of ch-1 sps on rnd 2 of Edging, starting at seam side. Weave rem Tie through rem ch-1 sps on rnd 2, starting at seam side. Tie double knot at each end of Ties; knot ends of Ties tog on either side to form drawstring. ■

Golf Club Covers

DESIGN BY JOCELYN SASS

SKILL LEVEL ■■□□
EASY

FINISHED SIZE
9 inches long

MATERIALS
- Red Heart Super Saver medium (worsted) weight yarn (7 oz/ 364 yds/198g per skein): 2 oz/100 yds/56g each #256 carrot, #336 warm brown, #380 Windsor blue ½ oz/25 yds/14g #316 soft white
- Sizes F/5/3.75mm and G/6/4mm crochet hooks or size needed to obtain gauge
- Tapestry needle
- Stitch markers

GAUGE
4 sc = 1 inch; 9 sc rows = 1 inch

PATTERN NOTES
Weave in ends as work progresses.

Do not join rounds unless stated. Mark first stitch of each round.

Chain-3 at beginning of double crochet round counts as first double crochet unless otherwise stated.

Instructions

#1 COVER
Note: Work in continuous rnds, do not join unless specified. Mark beg of rnds.

Rnd 1 (RS): Starting at top with size G hook and warm brown, ch 5, 2 sc in 2nd ch from hook, sc in each of next 2 chs, 3 sc in last ch, working in unused lps on opposite side of foundation ch, sc in each of last 3 chs. *(10 sc)*

Rnd 2: 2 sc in each of first 2 sc, sc in each of next 2 sc, 2 sc in each of next 3 sc, sc in each of next 2 sc, 2 sc in last sc. *(16 sc)*

Rnd 3: 2 sc in each of first 3 sc, sc in each of next 5 sc, 2 sc in each of next 4 sc, sc in each of next 3 sc, 2 sc in last sc. *(24 sc)*

Rnd 4: Sc in first sc, 2 sc in each of next 3 sc, sc in each of next 9 sc, 2 sc in each of next 3 sc, sc in each of last 8 sc. *(30 sc)*

CONTINUED ON PAGE 112

Best Friends Treat Holders

DESIGNS BY SHEILA LESLIE

SKILL LEVEL ■■□
INTERMEDIATE

FINISHED SIZE
Fits 5¼-inch tall coffee can with 12½-inch circumference

MATERIALS

- Bernat Super Value medium (worsted) weight yarn (7 oz/ 382 yds/197g per skein):
  1 skein #07469 honey
  5 yds each #07391 white, #07513 scarlet, #07421 black, #00608 bright yellow
- Size H/6/5mm crochet hook or size needed to obtain gauge
- Tapestry needle
- Sewing needle
- Sewing thread
- Polyester fiberfill
- 14 mm black shank style buttons: 2
- Small piece black felt
- Hot glue or tacky craft glue
- Empty coffee can with plastic lid
- Stitch markers

GAUGE
4 sc = 1 inch

PATTERN NOTES
Weave in ends as work progresses.

Join rounds with a slip stitch unless otherwise stated.

Chain-2 at beginning of half double crochet round counts as first half double crochet unless otherwise stated.

Chain-3 at beginning of double crochet round counts as first double crochet unless otherwise stated.

Instructions

HEAD
Note: Work in continuous rnds, do not join unless specified. Mark beg of rnds.

Rnd 1 (RS): Starting at top with honey, ch 2, 6 sc in 2nd ch from hook. *(6 sc)*

Rnd 2: 2 sc in each sc. *(12 sc)*

Rnd 3: *Sc in next sc, 2 sc in next sc, rep from * around. *(18 sc)*

Rnd 4: Sc in each of next 2 sc, 2 sc in next sc, rep from * around. *(24 sc)*

Rnd 5: *2 sc in next sc, sc in each of next 3 sc, rep from * around. *(30 sc)*

Rnd 6: *Sc in each of next 4 sc, 2 sc in next sc, rep from * around. *(36 sc)*

Rnds 7 & 8: Sc in each sc around.

Rnd 9: *Sc in each of next 8 sc, 2 sc in next sc, rep from * around. *(40 sc)*

Rnds 10–17: Sc in each sc around.

Rnd 18: *Sc in each of next 3 sc, sc dec (see Stitch Guide) in next 2 sc, rep from * around. *(32 sc)*

Rnd 19: *Sc in each of next 6 sc, sc dec in next 2 sc, rep from * around. *(28 sc)*

Rnd 20: *Sc in each of next 2 sc, sc dec in next 2 sc, rep from * around. *(21 sc)*

Stuff Head with fiberfill.

Rnd 21: *Sc in next sc, sc dec in next 2 sc, rep from * around. *(14 sc)*

Rnd 22: [Sc dec in next 2 sc] 7 times, join in first sc, fasten off, leaving a 14-inch end. *(7 sc)*

MUZZLE
Rnds 1 & 2: With white, rep rnds 1 and 1 of Head.

Rnd 3: *2 sc in each of next 3 sc, sc in each of next 3 sc, rep from * around. *(18 sc)*

Rnd 4: *[Sc in next sc, 2 sc in next sc] 3 times, sc in each of next 3 sc, rep from * around. *(24 sc)*

Rnds 5 & 6: Sc in each sc around.

Rnd 7: Sc in each sc, join in first sc, fasten off, leaving 14-inch end.

Stuff Muzzle.

EYE PATCH
Row 1 (RS): With white, ch 9, sc

in 2nd ch from hook, sc in each of next 2 chs, 2 hdc in each of next 3 chs, sc in each of next 2 chs, turn. *(11 sts)*

Row 2: Ch 1, sc in each of first 6 sc, 2 hdc in each of next 3 sts, sc in next st, sl st in last st, fasten off, leaving a 12-inch end.

EAR
Make 2.
Row 1 (RS): With honey, ch 15, sc in 2nd ch from hook, sc in each of next 5 chs, hdc in each of next 4 chs, dc in each of next 3 chs, 3 dc in last ch, working in unused lps on opposite side of beg ch, 3 dc in first ch, dc in each of next 3 chs, hdc in each of next 4 chs, sc in each of next 6 chs, turn. *(32 sts)*

Row 2: Ch 1, sc in each of next 9 sts, hdc in each of next 4 sts, dc in next st, 2 dc in next st, 3 dc in each of next 2 sts, 2 dc in next st, dc in next st, hdc in each of next 4 sts, sc in each of next 9 sts, turn. *(38 sts)*

Row 3: Ch 1, sc in each of next 16 sts, 2 sc in next st, sc in each of next 4 sts, 2 sc in next st, sc in each of next 16 sts, fasten off, leaving a 12-inch end. *(40 sts)*

LID COVER
Rnd 1 (RS): With honey, ch 4, join with sl st in first ch to form a ring, **ch 3** *(see Pattern Notes)*, work 11 dc in ring, join in 3rd ch of beg ch-3. *(12 dc)*

Rnd 2: Ch 3, dc in same st, 2 dc in each rem dc around, join in 3rd ch of beg ch-3. *(24 dc)*

Rnd 3: Ch 3, 2 dc in next dc, *dc in next dc, 2 dc in next dc, rep from * around, join in 3rd ch of beg ch-3. *(36 dc)*

Rnd 4: Ch 2 *(see Pattern Notes)*, hdc in next dc, 2 hdc in next dc,

*hdc in each of next 2 dc, 2 hdc in next dc, rep from * around, join in 2nd ch of beg ch-2, fasten off. *(48 hdc)*

Rnd 5: Working in **back lps** *(see Stitch Guide)* only, join scarlet in any st, ch 3, dc in each rem st around, join in 3rd ch of beg ch-3, fasten off.

TAG
With bright yellow, ch 2, 6 sc in 2nd ch from hook, join in first sc, ch 5, fasten off.

BODY
Rnd 1 (RS): Starting at bottom with honey, ch 4, join in first ch to form a ring, **ch 3** *(see Pattern Notes)*, work 10 dc in ring, join in 3rd ch of beg ch-3. *(11 dc)*

Rnd 2: Ch 3, dc in same st, 2 dc in each rem dc around, join in 3rd ch of beg ch-3. *(22 dc)*

Rnd 3: Ch 3, 2 dc in next dc, *dc in next dc, 2 dc in next dc, rep from * around, join in 3rd ch of beg ch-3. *(33 dc)*

Rnd 4: Ch 3, dc in next dc, 2 dc in next dc, *dc in each of next 2 dc, 2 dc in next dc, rep from * around, join in 3rd ch of beg ch-3. *(44 dc)*

Rnds 5–14: Ch 3, dc in each dc around, join in 3rd ch of beg ch-3. At end of rnd 14, fasten off.

FEET
Make 2.
Note: Work in continuous rnds, do not join unless specified. Mark beg of rnds.

Rnd 1 (RS): With honey, ch 2, 12 sc in 2nd ch from hook. *(12 sc)*

Rnds 2 & 3: Sc in each sc around.

Rnd 4: *Sc in each of next 3 sc, 2

sc in next sc, rep from * around. *(15 sc)*

Rnd 5: Rep rnd 2.

Rnd 6: *Sc in each of next 4 sc, 2 sc in next sc, rep from * around. *(18 sc)*

Rnd 7: Rep rnd 2.

Rnd 8: *Sc in each of next 4 sc, **sc dec** *(see Stitch Guide)* in next 2 sc, rep from * around. *(15 sc)*

Rnd 9: *Sc in each of next 3 sc, sc dec in next 2 sc, rep from * around. *(12 sc)*

Rnd 10: *Sc in each of next 2 sc, sc dec in next 2 sc, rep from * around, join in first sc, fasten off, leaving a 14-inch end.

ARM
Make 2.
Note: Work in continuous rnds, do not join unless specified. Mark beg of rnds.

Rnds 1–3 (RS): Rep rnds 1–3 of Feet.

Rnds 4 & 5: Sc in each sc around.

Rnds 6–12: Rep rnds 4–10 of Feet.

Stuff Arms lightly.

TAIL
Note: Work in continuous rnds, do not join unless specified. Mark beg of rnds.

Rnd 1 (RS): With honey, ch 2, 6 sc in 2nd ch from hook. *(6 sc)*

Rnd 2: Sc in each sc around.

Rnd 3: [Sc in each of next 2 sc, 2 sc in next 3 sc] twice. *(8 sc)*

Rnds 4–9: Rep rnd 2.

Rnd 10: Sc in each of next 4 sts, 2 sc in next sc, sc in each of next 3 sc. *(9 sc)*

Rnds 11–15: Sc in each sc around. At end of rnd 15, fasten off, leaving a 10-inch end.

BONE

With white, ch 9, (dc, hdc, sc) in 4th ch from hook, sc in each of next 4 chs, (sc, hdc, dc, ch 2, sl st) in last ch, working in unused lps on opposite side of beg ch, (2 dc, ch 2, sl st) in first ch, sc in each of next 4 chs, (sc, hdc, dc, ch 2, sl st) in next ch, fasten off.

FINISHING

Sew Muzzle to Head, then sew buttons above Muzzle for eyes. Sew Eye Patch around left eye, sew Ears to Head. On Muzzle and with black, embroider nose using satin stitch *(see Fig. 1)* and mouth using straight stitch *(see Fig. 2)*.

Insert ch-5 of Tag between rnds 4 and 5 of Lid Cover, from front to back. Tack ch to back of Tag, tack Head to middle of Lid Cover.

Press Feet flat. With honey, sew last rnd of each foot tog. Using

diagrams as templates, cut paw pads from black felt. Referring to photo for placement, glue 2 small pads and 1 large pad to each foot. Sew Feet to Body.

Press Arms flat. With honey, sew last rnd tog. Sew rnd 1 of Arms to Body.

Sew Tail to back of Body. Sew Bone to front of Body.

**Satin Stitch
Fig. 1**

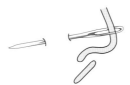

**Straight Stitch
Fig. 2**

Paw Pad
Cut 3 for each foot

Paw Pad
Cut 1 for each foot

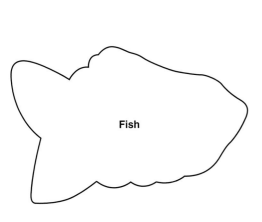

Fish

**Best Friends Treat Holders
Diagrams**

Cat Treat Holder

SKILL LEVEL   ◼◼◻◻
EASY

FINISHED SIZE
Fits 5¼-inch tall coffee can with 12½-inch circumference

MATERIALS
- Medium (worsted) weight yarn:
    7 oz/350 yds/198g light grey
- Bernat Super Value medium (worsted) weight yarn (7 oz/382 yds/197g per skein):
    5 yds each #07391 white, #07438 baby pink, #08879 sky, #07421 black
- Red Heart Super Saver medium (worsted) weight yarn (7 oz/364 yds/198g per skein):
    1 yd #657 dusty teal
- Size H/6/5mm crochet hook or size needed to obtain gauge
- Tapestry needle
- Sewing needle
- Polyester fiberfill
- 14mm black shank style buttons: 2
- Small jingle bell
- Small pieces of pink and orange felt
- Hot glue or tacky craft glue
- Empty coffee can with plastic lid
- Black sewing thread
- Stitch markers

GAUGE
4 sc = 1 inch

PATTERN NOTES
Weave in ends as work progresses.

Join rounds with a slip stitch unless otherwise stated.

Chain-2 at beginning of half double crochet round counts as first half double crochet unless otherwise stated.

Chain-3 at beginning of double crochet round counts as first double crochet unless otherwise stated.

Instructions

HEAD
With light grey, work same as Head for Dog Treat Holder.

CHEEK
Make 2.
Note: Work in continuous rnds, do not join unless specified. Mark beg of rnds.

Rnds 1–3: With white, rep rnds 1–3 of Head for Dog Treat Holder.

Rnds 4 & 5: Sc in each sc around. At end of rnd 5, fasten off.

Stuff Cheeks.

NOSE
With pink, ch 3, sc in 2nd ch from hook, hdc in next ch, fasten off.

EYE
Make 2.
With dusty teal, ch 2, in 2nd ch from hook work [sc, hdc, sc, ch 2, sl st in 2nd ch from hook] twice, join in first sc, fasten off.

EAR
Make 2.
Row 1 (RS): With silver, ch 7, sc in 2nd ch from hook, sc in each of next 5 chs, turn. *(6 sc)*

Row 2: Ch 1, sc in each sc across, turn.

Row 3: Ch 1, **sc dec** *(see Stitch Guide)* in first 2 sc, sc in each of next 2 sc, sc dec in last 2 sc, turn. *(4 sc)*

Row 4: Sc dec in first 2 sc, sc dec in last 2 sc, turn. *(2 sc)*

Row 5: Sc dec in next 2 sts, fasten off. *(1 sc)*

Edging
With silver, make slip knot on hook and join with sc in end of row 1, working up side in ends of rows, sc in each row, (sc, ch 1, sc) in sc of row 5, working down next side in ends of rows, sc in each row, fasten off.

LID COVER
Rnds 1–4: With silver, rep rnds 1–4 of Lid Cover of Dog Treat Holder.

Rnd 5: With sky, rep rnd 5 of Lid Cover of Dog Treat Holder.

BODY
With silver, work same as Body for Dog Treat Holder.

FEET
With white, work same as Feet for Dog Treat Holder.

ARM
Make 2.
Note: Work in continuous rnds, do not join unless specified. Mark beg of rnds.

Rnd 1 (RS): With silver, ch 2, 12 sc in 2nd ch from hook. *(12 sc)*

Rnds 2 & 3: Sc in each sc around.

Rnd 4: *Sc in each of next 3 sc, 2 sc in next sc, rep from * around. *(15 sc)*

Rnd 5: Rep rnd 2.

Rnd 6: *Sc in each of next 4 sc, 2 sc in next sc, rep from * around. *(18 sc)*

Rnd 7: Sc in each sc around, fasten off.

Rnd 8: With white, make slip knot on hook and join with sc in first sc, sc in each of next 4 sc, **sc dec** *(see Stitch Guide)* in next 2 sc, *sc in each of next 4 sc, sc dec in next 2 sc, rep from * around. *(15 sc)*

Rnd 9: *Sc in each of next 3 sc, sc dec in next 2 sc, rep from * around. *(12 sc)*

Rnd 10: [Sc in each of next 2 sc, sc dec in next 2 sc] 3 times, join in first sc, fasten off, leaving a 14-inch end. *(9 sc)*

TAIL
With silver, work same as Tail for Dog Treat Holder.

CONTINUED ON PAGE 112

Granny's Hangers

DESIGNS BY KYLEIGH C. HAWKE

SKILL LEVEL ◼■◻◻
EASY

FINISHED SIZE
To fit over 16¾-inch wide
plastic hanger.

MATERIALS
- Medium (worsted)
  weight yarn:
    40 yds A
    30 yds B
    15 yds C
- Size H/6/5mm crochet
  hook or size needed to
  obtain gauge
- Tapestry needle

GAUGE
Rnds 1 & 2 = 4 inches across

PATTERN NOTES
Weave in ends as work
progresses.

Join rounds with a slip stitch
unless otherwise stated.

Chain-3 at beginning of double
crochet round counts as first
double crochet unless otherwise
stated.

Instructions

COVER
Rnd 1 (RS): With A, ch 8, join
in first ch to form a ring, ch 5
(counts as first tr and ch-1 sp),
[tr in ring, ch 1] 15 times, join
in 4th ch of beg ch-5. *(16 tr,
16 ch-1 sps)*

Rnd 2: Sl st in next ch-1 sp, ch
6 *(counts as first tr and ch-2
sp)*, [tr in next ch-1 sp, ch 2] 15
times, join in 4th ch of beg ch-6,
fasten off. *(16 tr, 16 ch-2 sps)*

Rnd 3: Join B in any ch-2 sp, **ch
3** *(see Pattern Notes)*, (3 dc, ch 2,
4 dc) in same sp, ch 1, sc in next
ch-2 sp, [ch 3, sc in next ch-2 sp]
6 times, ch 1, (4 dc, ch 2, 4 dc)
in next ch-2 sp, ch 1, sc in next

ch-2 sp, [ch 3, sc in next ch-2 sp]
6 times, ch 1, join in 3rd ch of
beg ch-3. *(12 ch-3 sps, 4 ch-1 sps,
2 ch-2 sps)*

Rnd 4: Sl st in each of next 3 dc,
sl st in next ch-2 sp, ch 3, (3 dc,
ch 2, 4 dc) in same sp, ch 1, sk
next ch-1 sp, [4 dc in next ch-3
sp, ch 1] 6 times, sk next ch-1 sp,

CONTINUED ON PAGE 113

Oxygen Tank Covers

DESIGNS BY MARIA MERLINO

SKILL LEVEL ■■□□
EASY

FINISHED SIZES
Instructions given fit 3¼ x 11½-inch tank (B {M6} tank); changes for 4⅖ x 10¾-inch tank (C {M9} tank), 4⅖ x 16½-inch tank (D) and 4⅖ x 25-inch tank (E) are in [ ].

FINISHED COVER SIZES
4 x 12 inches (B {M6} tank) [5 x 11 inches (C {M9} tank), 5 x 18 inches (D tank), 5 x 25 inches (E tank)]

MATERIALS

- Bernat Camouflage medium (worsted) weight yarn (multi: 3½ oz/195 yds/100g per ball): 1 skein each #10420 pink camouflage and #10482 mash
- Size H/6/5mm crochet hook or size needed to obtain gauge
- Tapestry needle
- 1 large hole wooden bead: 2½ inches

GAUGE
Rnds 1–3 = 4 inches across

PATTERN NOTES
Weave in ends as work progresses.

Join rounds with a slip stitch unless otherwise stated.

Chain-3 at beginning of double crochet round counts as first double crochet unless otherwise stated.

Chain-5 at beginning of double treble crochet round counts as first double treble crochet unless otherwise stated.

SPECIAL STITCHES
Beginning petal stitch (beg petal st): Ch 5, keeping last lp of each dtr on hook, 2 dtr in indicated st, sk next 2 sts, 3 dtr in next st, yo and draw through all 6 lps on hook.

Petal stitch (petal st): Keeping last lp of each dtr on hook, 3 dtr in indicated st, sk next 2 sts, 3 dtr in next st, yo and draw through all 6 lps on hook.

Triangle stitch (triangle st): Ch 6, sc in 2nd ch from hook, hdc in next ch, dc in next ch, tr in next ch, dtr in next ch.

Instructions

PETAL STITCH B COVER
Rnd 1 (RS): With pink camouflage, ch 6, join in first ch to form a ring, **ch 3** (see Pattern Notes), 17 dc in ring, join in 3rd ch of beg ch-3. (18 dc)

Rnd 2: Ch 3, dc in same st, 2 dc in each rem dc, join in 3rd ch of beg ch-3. (36 dc)

Rnd 3: Ch 3, dc in each dc, join in 3rd ch of beg ch-3.

Rnds 4–7: Rep rnd 3.

Rnds 8 & 9: Ch 1, sc in same st, sc in each rem st around, join in first sc.

Rnd 10: Beg petal st (see Special Stitches) in same sc, ch 6, *sk next 2 sc, petal st (see Special Stitches) in next 4 sts, ch 6, rep from * around, join in top of beg petal st. (6 petal sts, 6 ch-6 sps)

Rnd 11: Ch 1, sc in same st, 5 sc in next ch-6 sp, *sc in top of next petal st, 5 sc in next ch-6 sp, rep from * around, join in first sc. (36 sc)

Rnd 12: Ch 1, sc in same sc, sc in each rem sc, join in first sc.

Rnds 13–21: [Rep rnds 10–12 consecutively] 3 times.

Rnd 22: Ch 4 (counts as first dc and first ch-1 sp), sk next sc, [dc in next sc, ch 1, sk next sc] 17 times, join in 3rd ch of beg ch-4. (18 dc, 18 ch-1 sps)

Rnd 23: Ch 1, sc in same st, sc in each ch-1 and in each sc around, join in first sc, fasten off. (36 sc)

CORD
With 2 strands of pink camouflage held tog, ch 61, fasten off.

FLOWER
With pink camouflage, ch 4, (2 dc, ch 3, sl st) in 4th ch from hook (petal), [ch 3, 2 dc, ch 3, sl st] 4 times in same ch (4 petals), fasten off. (5 petals)

FINISHING
Weave Cord through ch-1 sps on rnd 22, thread both ends of Cord through center of Flower, pull

Cord, pushing Flower to top of Cover. Knot free ends of Cord with an overhand knot. Trim ends.

PETAL STITCH C COVER
Rnds 1–3: Rep rnds 1–3 of Petal Stitch B Cover.

Rnd 4: Ch 3, dc in same st, dc in each of next 5 dc, *2 dc in next dc, dc in each of next 5 dc, rep from * around, join in 3rd ch of beg ch-3. *(42 dc)*

Rnd 5: Ch 3, dc in each dc, join in 3rd ch of beg ch-3.

Rnds 6 & 7: Ch 1, sc in same st, sc in each dc around, join in first sc.

Rnds 8–21: Rep rnds 10-23 of Petal Stitch B Cover.

Note: There will be 7 petal sts or 42 sc per row.

CORD
Work same as Cord for Petal Stitch B Cover.

FLOWER
Work same as Flower for Petal Stitch B Cover.

FINISHING
Work same as Finishing for Petal Stitch B Cover.

PETAL STITCH D COVER
Rnds 1–5: Rep rnds 1-5 of Petal Stitch C Cover.

Rnds 6–8: Rep rnd 5 of Petal Stitch C Cover.

Rnds 9 & 10: Ch 1, sc in same st, sc in each rem dc around, join in first sc.

Rnd 11: Beg petal st *(see Special Stitches)* in same sc, ch 6, *sk next 2 sc, **petal st** *(see Special Stitches)* in next 4 sts, ch 6, rep from * around, join in top of beg petal st. *(7 petal sts, 7 ch-6 sps)*

Rnd 12: Ch 1, sc in same st, 5 sc in next ch-6 sp, *sc in top of next petal st, 5 sc in next ch-5 sp, rep from * around, join in first sc. *(42 sc)*

Rnd 13: Ch 1, sc in same sc, sc in each rem sc, join in first sc.

Rnds 14–28: [Rep rnds 11–13 consecutively] 5 times.

Rnd 29: Ch 4 (counts as first dc and first ch-1 sp), sk next sc, [dc in next sc, ch 1, sk next sc] 20 times, join in 3rd ch of beg ch-4. (21 dc, 21 ch-1 sps)

Rnd 30: Ch 1, sc in same st, sc in each ch-1 and in each sc around, join in first sc, fasten off. (42 sc)

CORD
Work same as Cord for Petal Stitch B Cover.

FLOWER
Work same as Flower for Petal Stitch B Cover.

FINISHING
Work same as Finishing for Petal Stitch B Cover.

PETAL STITCH E COVER
Rnds 1–13: Rep rnds 1–13 of Petal Stitch C Cover.

Rnds 14–46: [Rep rnds 11–13 of Petal Stitch C Cover consecutively] 11 times.

Rnd 47: Ch 4 (counts as first dc and first ch-1 sp), sk next sc, [dc in next sc, ch 1, sk next sc] 20 times, join in 3rd ch of beg ch-4. (21 dc, 21 ch-1 sps)

Rnd 48: Ch 1, sc in same st, sc in each ch-1 and in each sc around, join in first sc, fasten off. (42 sc)

CORD
Work same as Cord for Petal Stitch B Cover.

FLOWER
Work same as Flower for Petal Stitch B Cover.

FINISHING
Work same as Finishing for Petal Stitch B Cover.

TRIANGLE STITCH B COVER
Rnds 1–8: With mash, rep rnds 1–8 of Petal Stitch B Cover.

Rnd 9: Ch 1, sc in same sc, work **triangle st** (see Special Stitches), sk next 5 sc, *sc in next sc, work triangle st, sk next 5 sc, rep from * around, join in first sc. (6 sc, 6 triangle sts)

Rnd 10: Ch 5 (see Pattern Notes), sc in point of next triangle st, ch 4, *dtr in next sc, sc in point of next triangle st, ch 4, rep from * around, join in 5th ch of beg ch-5. (12 sts, 6 ch-4 sps)

Rnd 11: Ch 1, sc in same st, sc in next sc, 4 sc in next ch-4 sp, *sc in next dtr, sc in next sc, 4 sc in next ch-4 sp, rep from * around, join in first sc. (48 sc)

Rnd 12: Ch 1, sc in same sc, sc in each sc around, join in first sc.

Rnds 13–24: [Rep rnds 9–12 consecutively] 3 times.

Rnd 25: Ch 4 (counts as first dc and first ch-1 sp), sk next sc, [dc in next sc, ch 1, sk next sc] 17 times, join in 3rd ch of beg ch-4. (24 dc, 24 ch-1 sps)

Rnd 26: Ch 1, sc in same st, sc in each ch-1 and in each sc around, join in first sc, fasten off. (48 sc)

CORD
With 2 strands of mash held tog, ch 61, fasten off.

FINISHING
Weave Cord through ch-1 sps on rnd 22, thread both ends of Cord through bead, pull Cord, pushing bead to top of Cover. Knot free ends of Cord with an overhand knot. Trim ends.

TRIANGLE STITCH C COVER
Rnds 1–7: With mash, rep rnds 1–7 of Petal Stitch C Cover.

Rnd 8–11: Rep rnds 9 –12 of Triangle Stitch B Cover. (56 sc at end of last rnd)

Rnds 12–23: [Rep rnds 8–11 consecutively] 3 times.

Rnd 24: Ch 4 (counts as first dc and first ch-1 sp), sk next sc, [dc in next sc, ch 1, sk next sc] 27 times, join in 3rd ch of beg ch-4. (28 dc, 28 ch-1 sps)

Rnd 25: Ch 1, sc in same st, sc in each ch-1 and in each sc around, join in first sc, fasten off. (56 sc)

CORD
Work same as Cord for Triangle Stitch B Cover.

FINISHING
Weave Cord through ch-1 sps on rnd 24, thread both ends of Cord through bead, pull Cord, pushing bead to top of Cover. Knot free ends of Cord with an overhand knot. Trim ends.

TRIANGLE STITCH D COVER
Rnds 1–10: With mash, rep rnds 1–10 of Petal Stitch D Cover.

Rnd 11: Rep rnd 9 of Triangle Stitch B Cover. (7 sc, 7 triangle sts at end of rnd)

Rnd 12: Rep rnd 10 of Triangle Stitch B Cover. (14 sts, 7 ch-4 sps)

Rnd 13: Rep rnd 11 of Triangle Stitch B Cover. (56 sc at end of rnd)

Rnd 14: Rep rnd 12 of Triangle Stitch B Cover.

CONTINUED ON PAGE 113

Heart Pocket Note Holder

DESIGN BY TERRY DAY

SKILL LEVEL ■■□□
EASY

FINISHED SIZE
8¼ inches at widest part x
8 inches long

MATERIALS
• Elmer-Pisgah Peaches
  & Créme medium **4**
  (worsted) weight cotton **MEDIUM**
  yarn (2½ oz/122 yds/
  71g per ball):
    1½ oz #1 white
    1 oz #51 apple green
• Size F/5/3.75mm crochet
  hook or size needed to
  obtain gauge
• Tapestry needle
• Fabric glue
• Magnets (optional)

GAUGE
Rnds 1 & 2 = 2½ inches across

PATTERN NOTES
Weave in ends as work progresses.

Join rounds with a slip stitch
unless otherwise stated.

Chain-3 at beginning of double
crochet round counts as first double
crochet unless otherwise stated.

Instructions

SQUARE
**Make 2 white
and 1 apple green.**
Rnd 1 (RS): Ch 4, join in first
ch to form a ring, **ch 3** (see

Pattern Notes), 2 dc in ring, ch 2,
[3 dc in ring, ch 2] 3 times, join
in 3rd ch of beg ch-3. *(12 dc,
4 ch-2 sps)*

Rnd 2: Sl st in each of next 2
dc, sl st in next ch-2 sp, ch 3, in
same ch-2 sp work (2 dc, ch 2,
3 dc) *(beg corner)*, ch 1, [in next
ch-2 sp work (3 dc, ch 2, 3 dc in
same ch-2 sp *(corner)*, ch 1] 3
times, join in 3rd ch of beg ch-3.
(24 dc, 4 ch-1 sps, 4 ch-2 sps)

Rnd 3: Sl st in each of next 2 dc,
sl st in next ch-2 sp, beg corner in
same ch-2 sp, *ch 1, 3 dc in next

ch-1 sp, ch 1, corner in next ch-2
sp, rep from * twice, ch 1, 3 dc in
next ch-1 sp, ch 1, join in 3rd ch
of beg ch-3. *(36 dc, 8 ch-1 sps,
4 ch-2 sps)*

Rnd 4: Sl st in each of next 2 dc,
sl st in next ch-2 sp, beg corner in
same ch-2 sp, *ch 1, [3 dc in next
ch-1 sp, ch 1] twice, corner in
next ch-2 sp, rep from * twice,
ch 1, [3 dc in next ch-1 sp, ch 1]
2 times, join in 3rd ch of beg ch-3,
fasten off. *(48 dc, 12 ch-1 sps,
4 ch-2 sps)*

CONTINUED ON PAGE 114

Tooth Fairy Pillow

DESIGN BY MARIA MERLINO

SKILL LEVEL ◼◻◻◻ EASY

FINISHED SIZE
6½ x 9 inches

MATERIALS

- Bernat Softee Baby light (light worsted) weight yarn (5 oz/ 455 yds/140g per skein): 1 skein each #02000 white and #02004 mint
- Size H/8/5mm crochet hook or size needed to obtain gauge
- Tapestry needle
- Polyester fiberfill

GAUGE
With 2 strands held tog:
3 sc = 1 inch; 4 sc rows = 1 inch

PATTERN NOTES
Weave in ends as work progresses.

Join rounds with a slip stitch unless otherwise stated.

Pillow is worked with 2 strands held together.

Instructions

FRONT
Row 1 (RS): With mint, ch 19, sc in 2nd ch from hook and in each rem ch, turn. *(18 sc)*

Row 2: Ch 1, sc in each sc, turn.

Row 3: Ch 1, sc in each of first 5 sc, **changing color** *(see Stitch Guide)* to white in last sc, sc in next sc, changing color to mint, sc in each of next 6 sc, changing color to white in last sc, sc in next sc, changing color to mint, sc in each of last 5 sc, turn.

Rows 4–14: Ch 1, sc in each sc across, changing colors according to corresponding rows on chart.

Row 15: Ch 1, sc in each of first 3 sc, changing color to white in last sc, sc in each of next 4 sc, ch 5, sk next 5 sc, sc in each of next 4 sc, changing color to mint in last sc, sc in each of last 2 sc, turn.

Row 16: Ch 1, sc in each of first 2 sc, changing color to white in last sc, sc in each of next 4 sc, sc in each of next 5 chs, sc in each of next 4 sc, changing color to mint in last sc, sc in each of last 3 sc, turn.

Rows 17–21: Ch 1, sc in each sc across, changing colors according to corresponding rows on chart. At end of last row, fasten off.

POUCH
Rnd 1: With WS facing, join white in first skipped sc of row 15, ch 1, sc in same sc, sc in each of next 4 sk sc, turn, working in unused lps on opposite of ch-5 sp made on row 15, sc in each of next 5 chs, turn. *(10 sc)*

Rnd 2: Ch 1, sc in each sc, turn.

Rnds 3–8: Rep rnd 2.

Row 9: Flatten pouch, sl st across 2 or 3 sts to get to edge of piece, ch 1, turn, working through both sides at same time, sc in each of next 5 sc to close, fasten off.

BACK
Row 1: With mint, ch 19, sc in 2nd ch from the hook and in each rem ch, turn. *(18 sc)*

Row 2: Ch 1, sc in each sc across, turn.

Rows 3–21: Rep row 2.

Edging
Holding pieces with WS tog and working through both thicknesses, ch 1, sc in each sc across to last sc, sk last sc *(corner)*, 2 sc in end of next 2 rows, [sk next row, 2 sc in next row] across to last 2 rows, sk next row, 2 sc in next row *(corner)*, sc in each sc across to last sc, sk next sc *(corner)*, [sk next row, 2 sc in next row] across, drop mint, draw up lp with white in first sc, join in first sc. *(78 sc)*

BORDER
Rnd 1: Ch 1, in same st as joining work (sc, ch 3, sc) *(corner)*, sc to last sc of row, in last sc work (sc, ch 3, sc) *(corner)*, working across next side in ends of rows, sc in each row, working across next side, in first st work (sc, ch 3, sc) *(corner)*, sc to last sc of row, in last sc work (sc, ch 3, sc) *(corner)*, working across next side in ends of rows, sc in each row, join in first sc. *(82 sc, 4 ch-3 sps)*

Rnd 2: Ch 1, sc in same sc, ch 3, sk next 2 sc, *sc in next sc or ch-3 sp, ch 3, sk next 2 sc, rep from * around, join in first sc.

Rnd 3: Ch 1, *sc in next sc, in ch-3 sp work (sc, hdc, 2 dc, hdc, sc), rep from * around, join in first sc, fasten off. ∎

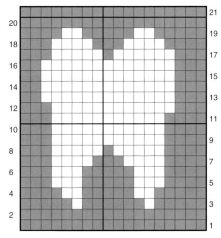

Tooth Fairy Pillow Chart

COLOR KEY
■ #02004 Mint
□ #02000 White

Easy Elegant Jar Covers

DESIGNS BY ELIZABETH ANN WHITE

FINISHED SIZES
Fits a wide-mouth quart jar, small-mouth pint jar and small mouth half-pint jar.

MATERIALS
- Red Heart Super Saver medium (worsted) weight yarn (7 oz/364 yds/ 198g per skein):
    1 skein #316 soft white
- Size H/8/5mm crochet hook or size needed to obtain gauge
- Tapestry needle
- 1 yd 1½-inch wide yellow polka-dotted satin ribbon

GAUGE
Quart Jar
Jar Cover: Rnds 1–3 = 4 inches
Lid Cover: Rnds 1–3 = 3½ inches

Pint Jar
Jar Cover: Rnds 1–3 = 3¾ inches
Lid Cover: Rnds 1–3 = 3 inches

Half-Pint Jar
Jar Cover: Rnds 1 & 2 = 2 inches
Lid Cover: Rnds 1–3 = 2½ inches

PATTERN NOTES
Weave in ends as work progresses.

Join rounds with a slip stitch unless otherwise stated.

Chain-3 at beginning of double crochet round counts as first double crochet unless otherwise stated.

SPECIAL STITCHES
Beginning V-stitch (beg v-st): Ch 4, dc in indicated st.

V-stitch (v-st): (Dc, ch 1, dc) in indicated st.

Instructions

QUART JAR COVER
Rnd 1 (RS): Starting at bottom, ch 4, join in first ch to form a ring, **ch 3** *(see Pattern Notes)*, 11 dc in ring, join in 3rd ch of beg ch-3. *(12 dc)*

Rnd 2: Ch 3, dc in first dc, 2 dc in each rem dc, join in 3rd ch of beg ch-3. *(24 dc)*

Rnd 3: Ch 3, dc in first dc, dc in next dc, *2 dc in next dc, dc in next dc, rep from * around, join in 3rd ch of beg ch-3. *(36 dc)*

Rnd 4: Ch 1, working in **back lps** *(see Stitch Guide)* only, sc in each dc, join in first sc.

Rnd 5: Ch 1, sc in first sc, sk next sc, **V-st** *(see Special Stitches)* in next sc, sk next sc, *sc in next sc, sk next sc, V-st in next sc, sk next sc, rep from * around, join in first sc. *(9 sc, 9 V-sts)*

Rnd 6: Beg V-st *(see Special Stitches)* in first sc, sc in ch-1 sp of next V-st, *V-st in next sc, sc in ch-1 sp of next V-st, rep from * around, join in 3rd ch of beg ch-4.

Rnd 7: Sl st in next ch-1 sp, ch 1, sc in same sp, V-st in next sc, *sc in next ch-1 sp, V-st in next sc, rep from * around, join in first sc.

Rnds 8–17: [Rep rnds 6 and 7 alternately] 5 times.

Rnd 18: Ch 1, sc in first sc, ch 2, sc in ch-1 sp of next V-st, ch 2, *sc in next sc, ch 2, sc in ch-1 sp of next V-st, ch 2, rep from * around, join in first sc, fasten off. *(18 sc, 36 ch-2 sps)*

LID COVER
Rnd 1 (RS): Ch 4, join in first ch to form a ring, **ch 3** *(see Pattern Notes)*, 11 dc in ring, join in 3rd ch of beg ch-3. *(12 dc)*

Rnd 2: Ch 3, dc in first st, 2 dc in each rem dc, join in 3rd ch of beg ch-3. *(24 dc)*

Rnd 3: Ch 3, dc in first st, dc in next st, *2 dc in next dc, dc in next st, rep from * around, join in 3rd ch of beg ch-3. *(36 dc)*

Rnd 4: Ch 4 *(counts as first dc and ch-1 sp)*, sk next st, *dc in next st, ch 1, sk next st, rep from * around, join in 3rd ch of beg ch-4. *(18 dc, 18 ch-1 sps)*

Rnd 5: Ch 3, 3 dc in next ch-1 sp, dc in next dc, *3 dc in next ch-1 sp, dc in next dc, rep from * around, join in 3rd ch of beg ch-3. *(72 dc)*

Rnd 6: Ch 1, sc in same ch as joining, ch 3, sk next dc, *sc in next dc, ch 3, sk next dc, rep from * around, join in first sc, fasten off. *(36 sc, 36 ch-3 sps)*

TIE
Ch 50, fasten off.

FINISHING
Weave Tie through ch-2 sps on rnd 18 of Jar Cover; tie ends in bow. Weave ribbon through ch-1 sps of rnd 4 of Lid Cover, tie ends in bow.

PINT JAR COVER
Rnds 1–7: Rep rnds 1–7 of Quart Jar Cover.

Rnds 8–11: [Rep rnds 6 and 7 of Quart Jar Cover alternately] twice.

Rnd 12: Rep rnd 6 of Quart Jar Cover.

Rnd 13: Sl st in next ch-1 sp, ch 1, sc in same sp, ch 2, sc in next sc, ch 2, *sc in ch-1 sp of next V-st, ch 2, sc in next sc, ch 2, rep from * around, join in first sc, fasten off. *(18 sc, 36 ch-2 sps)*

LID COVER
Rnds 1 & 2: Rep rnds 1 and 2 of Lid Cover for Quart Jar Cover.

Rnd 3: Ch 1, sc in each st, join in first sc.

Rnd 4: Ch 4 *(counts as first dc and ch-1 sp)*, sk next sc, *dc in next sc, ch 1, sk next sc, rep from * around, join in 3rd ch of beg ch-4. *(12 dc, 12 ch-1 sps)*

Rnd 5: Ch 3, 3 dc in next ch-1 sp, *dc in next dc, 3 dc in next ch-1 sp, rep from * around, join in 3rd ch of beg ch-3. *(48 dc)*

Rnd 6: Ch 1, sc in same ch as joining, ch 3, sk next dc, *sc in next dc, ch 3, sk next dc, rep from * around, join in first sc, fasten off. *(24 sc, 24 ch-3 sps)*

CONTINUED ON PAGE 114

Dog Bed

DESIGN BY ELAINE BARTLETT

SKILL LEVEL ■■□□
EASY

FINISHED SIZES
Dog Bed: 40 x 54 inches before assembly
Pillow: 70 x 10 inches before assembly

MATERIALS
- Red Heart Super Saver medium (worsted) weight yarn (7 oz/ 364 yds/198g per skein): 5 skeins #336 warm brown
- Medium (worsted) weight yarn: 15 oz/750 yds/425g browns variegated
- Size I/9/5.5mm crochet hook or size needed to obtain gauge
- Tapestry needle
- 50 oz polyester fiberfill

GAUGE
10 sts = 3½ inches

PATTERN NOTE
Weave in ends as work progresses.

Instructions

BED BASE
Row 1 (RS): With warm brown, ch 123, sc in 2nd ch from hook, *dc in next ch, sc in next ch, rep from * across to last ch, sc in last ch, turn. *(62 sc, 60 dc)*

Row 2: Ch 1, sc in first sc, *dc in next sc, sc in next dc, rep from * across to last sc, sc in last sc, turn.

Rep row 2 until piece measures 25 inches from beg, ending with a RS row. At end of last row, fasten off.

Next Row: With warm brown make slip knot on hook and join with sc in 7th st of last row, *dc in next sc, sc in next dc, rep from * across to last 7 sts, sc in next sc, leaving last 6 sts unworked, turn. *(56 sc, 54 dc)*

Next 5 Rows: Rep row 2. At end of last row, fasten off.

BED TOP
Row 1: With RS facing and with browns variegated, make slip knot on hook and join with sc in first st of last row, *dc in next sc, sc in next dc, rep from * across to last st, sc in last sc, turn. *(56 sc, 54 dc)*

Row 2: Ch 1, sc in first sc, *dc in next sc, sc in next dc, rep from * across to last st, sc in last sc, turn.

Rep row 2 until piece measures 25 inches from beg, ending on a RS row. At end of last row, fasten off.

BACK FLAP
Row 1: Hold piece with beg ch at top and WS facing, sk first 6 sts, with warm brown make slip knot on hook and join with sc in next st, *sc in next dc, dc in next sc, rep from * across to last 7 sts, sc in next st, leaving last 6 sts unworked, turn. *(56 sc, 54 dc)*

Row 2: Ch 1, sc in first sc, *sc in next dc, dc in next sc, rep from * across to last st, sc in last st, turn.

Rows 3–6: Rep row 2. At end of last row, fasten off.

ASSEMBLY
Note: The extra 2 inches of warm brown on all sides will be used to make sides of Bed.

Fold piece with RS tog; with warm brown, sew each adjacent short sides tog. Sew sides of Top to sides of bottom, leaving back open for turning inside out and filling. Turn inside out so RS is now facing. Stuff with fiberfill. With brown, sew back closed. Mark center back of Dog Bed for Pillow placement.

PILLOW
Row 1 (RS): With warm brown and leaving a 12-inch end, ch 213, sc in 2nd ch from hook and in each ch across, turn. *(212 sc)*

Row 2: Ch 1, sc in each sc across, turn.

Rep row 2 until piece measures 10 inches from beg, ending with a WS row. Fasten off, leaving a 12-inch end for sewing.

ASSEMBLY
Referring to assembly diagram (page 115) and with tapestry needle, weave beg end over and under end sts (short side) being

CONTINUED ON PAGE 115

Eyeglasses Cases

DESIGNS BY DELORES SPAGNUOLO

Small Case

SKILL LEVEL

EASY

FINISHED SIZE
2¾ x 6 x 1¼ inches

MATERIALS

- Red Heart Super Saver medium (worsted) weight yarn (7 oz/364 yds/ 198g per skein):
  1½ oz #316 soft white
- Size G/6/4mm crochet hook or size needed to obtain gauge
- Tapestry needle

GAUGE
4 sc = 1 inch; 4 sc rows = 1 inch

PATTERN NOTES
Weave in ends as work progresses.

Join rounds with a slip stitch unless otherwise stated.

SPECIAL STITCH
Puff stitch (puff st): Yo, insert hook in indicated st, yo, pull up ½-inch lp, [yo, insert hook in same st, yo, pull up ½-inch lp] twice, yo, draw through all 7 lps on hook.

Instructions

SIDE
Make 2.
Row 1: Ch 4, sc in 2nd ch from hook, dc in next ch, sc in last ch, turn. *(3 sts)*

Rows 2–21: Ch 1, sc in each st across, turn.

Edging
Ch 1, 3 sc in first sc *(corner)*, sc in next sc, 3 sc in last sc *(corner)*, working across next side in ends of rows, sk first row, sc in each row, working across next side in unused lps on opposite side of foundation ch, 2 sc in first ch, sc in next ch, 2 sc in last ch,

working across next side in ends of rows, sc in each row to last row, sk last row, join in first sc, fasten off. *(52 sc)*

FRONT/BACK
Row 1 (WS): Starting at front, ch 8, sc in 2nd ch from hook, sc in each ch across, turn. *(7 sc)*

Row 2 (RS): Ch 1, sc in each sc across, turn.

Row 3: Ch 1, sc in each of first 3 sc, **puff st** (see Special Stitch) in next sc, sc in each of last 3 sc, turn. (6 sc, 1 puff st)

Row 4: Ch 1, sc in each st across, turn. (7 sc)

Row 5: Ch 1, sc in each of first 2 sc, puff st in next sc, sc in next sc, puff st in next sc, sc in each of last 2 sc, turn. (5 sc, 2 puff sts)

Row 6: Rep row 4.

Row 7: Ch 1, sc in first sc, puff st in next sc, sc in each of next 3 sc, puff st in next sc, sc in last sc, turn.

Row 8: Rep row 4.

Row 9: Ch 1, sc in each of first 2 sc, puff st in next sc, sc in next sc, puff st in next sc, sc in each of last 2 sc, turn.

Row 10: Rep row 4.

Row 11: Ch 1, sc in each of first 3 sts, puff st in next sc, sc in each of last 3 sts, turn. (6 sc, 1 puff st)

Row 12: Rep row 4.

Rows 13–44: [Rep rows 5-12 consecutively] 4 times.

Edging
Ch 1, 3 sc in first sc (corner), sc in next 5 sc, 3 sc in last sc (corner), working across next side in ends of rows, sc in each row, working across next side in unused lps on opposite side of foundation ch, 3 sc in first ch (corner), sc in next 5 chs, 3 sc in last ch (corner), working across next side in ends of rows, sc in each row across, join in first sc, fasten off. (110 sc)

FLAP
Row 1: Ch 8, sc in 2nd ch from hook, dc in each of next 5 chs, sc in last ch, turn. (7 sts)

Rows 2–13: Ch 1, sc in each st across, turn.

Edging
Ch 1, 3 sc in first sc (corner), sc in each of next 5 sc, 3 sc in last sc (corner), working across next side in ends of rows, sk first row, sc in each row across, working across next side in unused lps on opposite side of foundation ch, 2 sc in first ch (corner), sc in each of next 5 chs, 2 sc in last ch (corner), working across next side in ends of rows, sc in each row to last row, sk last row, join in first sc, fasten off. (46 sc)

STRAP
Ch 12, 4 sc in 2nd sc from hook, sc in each of next 9 chs, 4 sc in last ch, working in unused lps on opposite side of foundation ch, sc in each ch across, join in first sc, fasten off.

ASSEMBLY
Working in **back lps** (see Stitch Guide) only, easing to fit, and matching corner sts, sl st WS of 1 long edge on Side to 1 End. Rep with other End. For back, sl st top edge on Flap to 1 edge of Side. Sew ends of Strap to seams 1 inch below edge on Front.

Large Case

SKILL LEVEL ◼◼◻◻
EASY

FINISHED SIZE
2¾ x 7 x 1¾ inches

MATERIALS
- Red Heart Super Saver medium (worsted) weight yarn (7 oz/364 yds/ 198g per skein):
  2 oz #631 light sage
- Size G/6/4mm crochet hook or size needed to obtain gauge
- Tapestry needle

GAUGE
4 sc = 1 inch; 4 sc rows = 1 inch

PATTERN NOTES
Weave in ends as work progresses.

Join rounds with a slip stitch unless otherwise stated.

SPECIAL STITCH
Puff stitch (puff st): Yo, insert hook in indicated st, yo, pull up ½-inch lp, [yo, insert hook in same st, yo, pull up ½-inch lp] twice, yo, draw through all 7 lps on hook.

Instructions

SIDE
Make 2.
Row 1: Ch 6, sc in 2nd ch from hook, dc in each of next 3 chs, sc in last ch, turn. (5 sts)

Rows 2–25: Ch 1, sc in each st across, turn.

Edging
Ch 1, 3 sc in first sc (corner), sc in next sc, 3 sc in last sc (corner), working across next side in ends of rows, sk first row, sc in each

CONTINUED ON PAGE 116

Kitchen Gift Set

DESIGNS BY BEVERLY DAVIS

SKILL LEVEL ■■□□
EASY

FINISHED SIZES
Towel: 12 x 20 inches
Pot Holder: 7 x 7 inches

MATERIALS
- Lily Sugar 'n Cream medium (worsted) weight cotton yarn (Solids: 2½ oz/120 yds/70g per ball; Ombres: 2 oz/95 yds/56g per ball):
    1 ball each #01130 warm brown and #00228 natural ombre
- Size G/6/4mm crochet hook or size needed to obtain gauge
- Tapestry needle
- 1-inch white button

GAUGE
10 dc = 1 inch; 2 dc rows = 1 inch

PATTERN NOTES
Weave in ends as work progresses.

Chain-3 at beginning of double crochet row counts as first double crochet unless otherwise stated.

SPECIAL STITCHES
Cross-stitch (cross-st): Sk indicated st, dc in next st, working over dc just made, dc in sk st.

Textured stitch (textured st): Insert hook in **back lp** *(see Stitch Guide)* of indicated st and then in **front lp** *(see Stitch Guide)* in

st on 2nd row below, yo, draw through both lps, yo and draw through 2 lps on hook.

Instructions

TOWEL
Row 1: With warm brown, ch 41, sc in 2nd ch from hook, sc in each rem ch, turn. *(40 sc)*

Rows 2 & 3: Ch 1, sc in each sc across, **changing color** *(see Stitch Guide)* to natural ombre in last sc of row 3, turn.

Row 4: Ch 3 *(see Pattern Notes)*, *cross-st *(see Special Stitches)* in next 2 sc, rep across to last st, dc

in last st, changing color to warm brown in last dc, turn.

Row 5: Rep row 4.

Row 6: Ch 1, sc in each st across, turn.

Row 7: Ch 1, sc in each sc across, changing color to natural ombre in last sc, turn.

Rows 8–35: [Rep rows 4–7 consecutively] 7 times, change color to warm brown in last sc of row 35.

Row 36: Ch 1, **sc dec** *(see Stitch Guide)* in first 2 sc, *sc dec in next 2 sc, rep from * across, turn. *(20 sc)*

Row 37: Ch 1, sc dec in first 2 sc, [sc dec in next 2 sc] 9 times, turn. *(10 sc)*

Row 38: Ch 1, sc in each st across, turn.

Rows 39–54: Rep row 38.

Edging
Ch 1, sc in each of first 5 sc, ch 5 *(button lp)*, sk next sc, sc in each of next 4 sc, working around outer edge, sc evenly spaced to first sc, join in first sc.

FINISHING
Sew button to row 40.

POT HOLDER
Row 1 (RS): With warm brown, ch 26, sc in 2nd ch from hook, sc in each rem ch, turn. *(25 sc)*

Row 2: Ch 1, working in **back lps** *(see Stitch Guide)* only, sc in each sc, turn.

Row 3: Ch 1, **textured st** *(see Special Stitch)* in first sc, textured st in each rem sc across, turn.

Rows 4–19: Ch 1, textured st in each st across, turn.

Row 20: Ch 1, *insert hook in first st, and then in front lp of st on 2nd row below, yo, draw through lp and st, yo and draw through 2 lps on hook, rep from * across, turn.

Edging
Ch 1, 2 sc in first st, sc in each st to last st, 2 sc in last st, working across next side in ends of rows, sc evenly spaced to next corner, working across next side in unused lps of foundation ch, 2 sc in first ch, sc in each ch to last ch, 2 sc in last ch, working across next side in ends of rows, sc evenly spaced to first sc, join in first sc, fasten off. ■

Pooch Pullovers

DESIGNS BY NANCY PRUSINSKI

Small Pooch Pullover

SKILL LEVEL ■■□□
EASY

FINISHED SIZE
To fit a small (2–5 lbs) dog

MATERIALS
- Red Heart Super Saver medium (worsted) weight yarn (solids: 7 oz/ 364 yds/198g per skein; multis: 5 oz/255 yds/141g per skein):
  1 skein each #321 gold and #950 Mexicana
- Size J/10/6mm crochet hook or size needed to obtain gauge
- Tapestry needle
- Stitch markers
- 1⅛-inch shank style button

GAUGE
3 sc = 1 inch

PATTERN NOTES
Weave in ends as work progresses.

Join rounds with a slip stitch unless otherwise stated.

Chain-3 at beginning of double crochet row counts as first double crochet unless otherwise stated.

Instructions

COLLAR
Row 1 (RS): With gold, ch 8, sc in 2nd ch from hook, sc in each rem ch, turn. *(6 sc)*

Rows 2–19: Ch 1, sc in each sc across, turn.

Row 20: Ch 1, sc in each sc across, turn.

Row 21: Ch 1, carefully matching sts, bring row 1 up to WS of piece, working through both thicknesses, sl st in each st across, **do not turn.**

BODY
Rnd 1 (RS): Ch 1, working across next side in ends of rows, sc in each row, join in first sc. *(21 sc)*

Rnd 2: Ch 1, sc in each sc around, join in first sc.

Rnd 3: Ch 1, sc in each of first 5 sc, 2 sc in next sc, [sc in each of next 4 sc, 2 sc in next sc] 3 times, join in first sc. *(25 sc)*

Rnd 4: Rep rnd 2. Fasten off.

BACK
Row 1 (RS): Sk first 5 sc, join gold in next sc, ch 1, sc in same sc, 2 sc in next sc, sc in each of next 12 sc, 2 sc in next sc, turn, leaving rem sc unworked. *(17 sc)*

Row 2: Ch 1, sc in sc across, turn.

Row 3: Ch 1, sc in next sc, 2 sc in next sc, sc in next 14 sc, 2 sc in next sc, turn. *(19 sc)*

Row 4: Ch 1, sc in each sc across, ch 14 *(base of belt)*, turn. *(19 sc, 14 chs)*

Row 5: Ch 1, sc in each ch of ch-14, sc in each sc across, turn. *(33 sc)*

Rows 6 & 7: Rep row 2.

Row 8: Ch 1, sc in each of next 20 sc, turn, leaving rem sc unworked. *(20 sc)*

Row 9: Rep row 2.

Row 10: Ch 3 *(see Pattern Notes)*, dc in each sc across, turn. *(20 dc)*

Row 11: Ch 3, **dc dec** *(see Special Stitches)* in next 2 dc, dc in each rem dc across, turn. *(19 dc)*

Row 12: Ch 1, sc dec in first 2 dc, sc in each of next 15 sc, sc dec in last 2 sc, turn. *(17 sc)*

Row 13: Ch 1, sc dec in first 2 sc, sc in each of next 13 sc, sc dec in last 2 sc, fasten off. *(15 sc)*

Edging
Rnd 1: With RS facing, join gold in first sc of row 13, ch 1, sc in same sc, sc in each sc across, ch 1, working in ends of rows and in sts across next sides, sc in each row and st to last st of belt, sc in last st of belt, working across edge of belt in ends of rows, sc in first row, ch 2 *(buttonhole)*, sk next 2 rows, sc in last row, ch 1, working across next

sides, sc in each st and in end of each row to first sc, join in first sc.

Rnd 2: Ch 1, loosely sl st in each st, join in first sl st, fasten off.

TURTLENECK

Rnd 1: Hold piece with Collar at top, join Mexicana in seam, ch 1, sc in same sp, working in ends of rows, sc in each row, join in first sc. *(21 sc)*

Rnds 2–6: Ch 1, sc each sc around, join in first sc.

Rnd 7: Ch 1, sl st in each sc, join in first sl st, fasten off.

FINISHING

Place Pullover on dog. Adjust Belt to fit and mark placement of button opposite buttonhole. Remove from dog and sew button to Pullover.

Large Pooch Pullover

SKILL LEVEL ■■□□
EASY

FINISHED SIZE
To fit a large (75-90 lbs) dog

MATERIALS
- Red Heart Super Saver medium (worsted) weight yarn (7 oz/364 yds/ 198g per skein):
  1 skein each #312 black and #332 ranch red
- Medium (worsted) weight yarn:
  7 oz/350 yds/198g dark plum
- Size J/10/6mm crochet hook or size needed to obtain gauge
- Tapestry needle
- Stitch markers
- 1⅛-inch shank style button: 3
- 2 metal conchos

GAUGE
3 sc = 1 inch

PATTERN NOTES
Weave in ends as work progresses.

Join rounds with a slip stitch unless otherwise stated.

Chain-3 at beginning of double crochet round counts as first double crochet unless otherwise stated.

Instructions

COLLAR
Row 1 (WS): With black, ch 16, sc in 2nd ch from hook, sc in each rem ch, turn. *(15 sc)*

Rows 2–40: Ch 1, sc in each sc across, turn.

Row 41: Ch 1, carefully matching sts, bring row 1 up to WS of piece, working through both thicknesses, sl st in each st across, **do not turn.**

BODY
Rnd 1 (RS): Ch 1, working across next side in ends of rows, sc in each row, join in first sc. *(40 sc)*

Rnds 2–4: Ch 1, sc in each sc around, join in first sc. At end of last rnd, fasten off.

CHEST
Rnd 1 (WS): Join dark plum in first sc of rnd 4, ch 1, sc in each of first 9 sc, 2 sc in next sc, [sc in each of next 9 sc, 2 sc in next sc] 4 times, join in first sc. *(44 sc)*

Rnd 2: Ch 1, sc in each sc around, join in first sc.

Rnd 3: Ch 1, sc in each of first 10 sc, 2 sc in next sc, [sc in each of next 10 sc, 2 sc in next sc] 3 times, join in first sc. *(48 sc)*

Rnd 4: Rep rnd 2.

Rnd 5: Ch 1, sc in each of first 11 sc, 2 sc in next sc, [sc

in each of next 11 sc, 2 sc in next sc] 3 times, join in first sc. *(52 sc)*

Rnd 6: Rep rnd 2.

Rnd 7: Ch 1, sc in each of first 12 sc, 2 sc in next sc, [sc in each of next 12 sc, 2 sc in next sc] 3 times, join in first sc. *(56 sc)*

Rnd 8: Rep rnd 2.

Rnd 9: Ch 1, sc in each of first 13 sc, 2 sc in next sc, [sc in each of next 13 sc, 2 sc in next sc] 3 times, join in first sc. *(60 sc)*

Rnd 10: Rep rnd 2.

Rnd 11: Ch 1, sc in each of first 14 sc, 2 sc in next sc, [sc in each of next 14 sc, 2 sc in next sc] 3 times, join in first sc. *(64 sc)*

Rnd 12: Rep rnd 2.

Rnd 13: Ch 1, sc in each of first 15 sc, 2 sc in next sc, [sc in each of next 15 sc, 2 sc in next sc] 3 times, join in first sc. *(68 sc)*

Rnd 14: Rep rnd 2.

Rnd 15: Ch 1, sc in each of first 16 sc, 2 sc in next sc, [sc in each of next 16 sc, 2 sc in next sc] 3 times, join in first sc. *(72 sc)*

Rnd 16: Rep rnd 2.

Rnd 17: Ch 1, sc in each of first 17 sc, 2 sc in next sc, [sc in each of next 17 sc, 2 sc in next sc] 3 times, join in first sc. *(76 sc)*

Rnd 18: Rep rnd 2.

Rnd 19: Ch 1, sc in each of first 18 sc, 2 sc in next sc, [sc in each of next 18 sc, 2 sc in next sc] 3 times, join in first sc. *(80 sc)*

Rnd 20: Rep rnd 2. At end of rnd, fasten off.

BACK & BELT

Row 1 (RS): With RS facing, sk first 16 sc on rnd 2, join ranch red in next sc, ch 1, sc in same sc, sc in each of next 47 sc, turn, leaving rem sc unworked. *(48 sc)*

Row 2: Ch 1, sc in first sc, 2 sc in next sc, sc in each sc to last 2 sc, 2 sc in next sc, sc in last sc, turn. *(50 sc)*

Row 3: Ch 1, sc in each sc across, turn.

Row 4: Rep row 2. *(52 sc at end of row)*

Row 5: Rep row 3.

Row 6: Ch 1, sc in first sc, 2 sc in next sc, sc in each sc to last 2 sc, 2 sc in next sc, sc in last sc, turn. *(54 sc)*

Row 7: Ch 1, sc in each sc across, ch 41 *(base of belt)*, turn. *(54 sc, 41 chs)*

Row 8: Ch 1, sc in each ch of ch-41, sc in each sc across, turn. *(95 sc)*

Rows 9–27: Rep row 3. At end of last row, fasten off.

Row 28: With WS facing, sk first 41 sc, join dark plum in next sc, ch 1, sc in same sc, sc in each sc across, turn. *(54 sc)*

Row 29: Ch 1, sc in each sc across, turn.

Rows 30–48: Ch 3 *(see Pattern Notes)*, dc in each st across, turn.

Row 49: Ch 3, **dc dec** *(see Stitch Guide)* in next 2 dc, dc in each dc across to last 2 dc, dc dec in last 2 dc, turn. *(52 dc)*

Row 50: Ch 1, **sc dec** *(see Stitch Guide)* in first 2 dc, sc in each dc across to last 2 dc, sc dec in last 2 dc, turn. *(50 dc)*

Rows 51–55: Rep row 50. *(40 sc at end of last row)*

Row 56: Ch 1, sc in each sc across, fasten off.

Edging

Rnd 1: With RS facing, join dark plum in first sc of row 56, ch 1, sc in same sc, sc in each sc across, ch 1, working in ends of rows and in sts across next sides, sc in each row and st to last st of belt, sc in last st of belt, working across edge of belt in ends of rows, sc in each of first 4 rows, ch 2 *(buttonhole)*, [sk next 2 rows, sc in each of next 3 rows, ch 2 *(buttonhole)* twice, sk next 2 rows, sc in each of last 4 rows, ch 1, working across next sides, sc in each st and in end of each row to first sc, join in first sc.

Rnd 2: Ch 1, sc in each st around, join in first sc.

Rnd 3: Ch 1, loosely sl st in each sc, join in first sl st, fasten off.

FINISHING

Place Pullover on dog. Adjust Belt to fit and mark placement of buttons opposite buttonholes. Remove from dog and sew buttons to Pullover.

Referring to photo for placement and with tapestry needle and black, sew 1 concho to either side of Pullover. ■

Bookmarks

Butterfly

DESIGN BY BARBARA NEID

SKILL LEVEL
EASY

FINISHED SIZE
2⅝ x 10½ inches, including tassel

MATERIALS
- Size 10 crochet cotton: 5 yds shaded pinks
- Size 3/2.10mm steel crochet hook or size needed to obtain gauge
- Tapestry needle

GAUGE
Gauge not important to this project.

PATTERN NOTES
Weave in ends as work progresses.

Join rounds with a slip stitch unless otherwise stated.

Chain-3 at beginning of double crochet round counts as first double crochet unless otherwise stated.

Instructions

Rnd 1 (RS): Ch 8, join in first ch to form a ring, **ch 3** *(see Pattern Notes)*, 2 dc in ring, ch 3, [3 dc in ring, ch 3] 7 times, join in 3rd ch of beg ch-3. *(24 dc, 8 ch-3 sps)*

Rnd 2: Sl st in each of next 2 dc, sl st in next ch-3 sp, ch 3, (3 dc, ch 3, 4 dc) in same sp, (4 dc, ch 3, 4 dc) in each rem ch-3 sp around, join in 3rd ch of beg ch-3. *(64 dc, 8 ch-3 sps)*

Rnd 3: Sl st in each of next 3 sts, sl st in next ch-3 sp, ch 3, (4 dc, ch 3, 5 dc) in same sp, sk next 3 dc, sl st in sp between next 2 dc, *(5 dc, ch 3, 5 dc) in next ch-3 sp, sk next 3 dc, sl st in sp between next 2 dc, rep from * around, join in 3rd ch of beg ch-3, fasten off.

FINISHING
Fold WS of piece in half matching points to form Butterfly. Wrap 1 end of thread around center of butterfly 4 times, tie in knot, ch 60 *(tail)*, sl st in 2nd ch from hook, sl st in each rem ch, fasten off.

TASSEL
Cut 8 strands each 4 inches long. Holding all strands tog, fold in half, insert hook in last ch of Tail, draw fold through, draw ends through fold, tighten.

Heart

DESIGN BY BARBARA NEID

SKILL LEVEL
EASY

FINISHED SIZE
2 x 11½ inches, including tassel

MATERIALS
- Size 10 crochet cotton: 5 yds dark red
- Size 3/2.10mm steel crochet hook or size needed to obtain gauge
- Tapestry needle

GAUGE
Gauge not important to this project.

PATTERN NOTE
Weave in ends as work progresses.

Instructions

HEART CENTER
Row 1: Ch 11, dc in 5th ch from hook (*beg 4 sk chs count as first dc*), *ch 1, sk next ch, dc in next ch, rep from * across, turn. (*5 dc*)

Row 2: Ch 4 (*counts as first dc and ch-1 sp*), sk next ch-1 sp, dc in next dc, *ch 1, sk next ch-1 sp, dc in next dc, rep from * twice, ch 1, dc in 3rd ch of beg 4 sk chs, turn.

Rows 3 & 4: Ch 4, sk next ch-1 sp, dc in next dc, *ch 1, sk next ch-1 sp, dc in next dc, rep from * twice, ch 1, dc in 3rd ch of beg ch-4, turn. At end of last row, **do not turn**.

HEART TOP
Row 1: Ch 1, working across next side in sps formed by edge sts, 2 sc in each of first 2 sps, ch 2, 2 sc in each of last 2 sps, turn. (*8 sc*)

Row 2: Ch 1, sc in first sc, sk next 3 sc, 12 dc in next ch-2 sp, sk next 4 sc, sc in next dc on row 4, 2 sc in each of next 2 ch-2 sps on row 4, ch 2, 2 sc in last 2 ch-1 sps on row 4, turn.

Row 3: Ch 1, sc in first sc, sk next 3 sc, 12 dc in next ch-2 sp, sk next 4 sc, sl st in next sc on row 2, **do not turn**, ch 60 (*tail*), sl st in 2nd ch from hook, sl st in each rem ch across, sl st in same sc on row 2.

Edging
Ch 1, working around outer edge, sc in each st, 2 sc in each ch sp or sp formed by edge dc and 4 sc in tip, join with a sl st in first sc, fasten off.

TASSEL
With dark red, work same as Tassel for Butterfly.

Flower

DESIGN BY BARBARA NEID

SKILL LEVEL
EASY

FINISHED SIZE
2½ x 11½ inches, including tassel

MATERIALS
- Size 10 crochet cotton: 5 yds golden yellow and green
- Size 3/2.10mm steel crochet hook or size needed to obtain gauge
- Tapestry needle

GAUGE
Gauge not important to this project.

PATTERN NOTES
Weave in ends as work progresses.

Join rounds with a slip stitch unless otherwise stated.

Chain-3 at beginning of double crochet row/round counts as first double crochet unless otherwise stated.

Instructions

Rnd 1: Starting at center with golden yellow, ch 6, join in first ch to form a ring, ch 1, 12 sc in ring, join in **front lp** (*see Stitch Guide*) of first sc. (*12 sc*)

Rnd 2: Ch 3 (*see Pattern Notes*), sl st in same lp as joining sl st, working in front lps only, (sl st, ch 3, sl st) in each rem sc, join in **back lp** (*see Stitch Guide*) of joining sl st of rnd 1.

Rnd 3: Working in back lps of sc of rnd 1, *sl st in next st, ch 9, sl st in 2nd ch from hook, sl st in each rem ch (*petal*), sl st in next sc on rnd 1, rep from * around, join in joining sl st. (*6 petals*)

Rnd 4: Working in chs and in sl sts of petals, *sc in each of next 2 sts, hdc in each of next 2 sts, dc in next st, hdc in next st, sc in next st, sl st in next st, ch 1, working on opposite side of petal, sl st in next st, sc in next st, hdc in next st, dc in next st, hdc in each of next 2 sts, sl st in next 2 sts on rnd 2, rep from * around, join in first sc, fasten off.

LEAF
Row 1: Join green in any st on back of Flower, ch 12, sl st in 2nd ch from hook, sl st in each ch across, turn.

Row 2: Sl st in first st, ch 1, sc in next st, hdc in each of next 3 sts, dc in each of next 3 sts, dc in each of next 2 sts, hdc in each of next 2 sts, sc in next st, 2 sc in last st, working on opposite side of foundation ch, sc in each of

CONTINUED ON PAGE 117

Plastic Bag Holder

DESIGN BY TARA SURPRENANT

SKILL LEVEL
EASY

FINISHED SIZE
16 inches long

MATERIALS
- Medium (worsted) weight yarn:
  6 oz/300 yds/170g black
  5 yds each oatmeal, orange, lime green
- Size I/9/5.5mm crochet hook or size needed to obtain gauge
- Tapestry needle
- 1½-inch diameter ponytail holders: 2

GAUGE
10 dc = 1 inch; 2 dc rows = 1 inch

PATTERN NOTES
Weave in ends as work progresses.

Join rounds with a slip stitch unless otherwise stated.

Instructions

BAG HOLDER
Rnd 1 (RS): With black, ch 35, join in first ch to form a ring, ch 1, sc in each ch, join in first sc. *(35 sc)*

Rnd 2: Ch 1, working over 1 ponytail holder, sc in each sc around, join in first sc.

Rnd 3: Ch 2, dc in first sc and in each rem sc around, join in first dc.

Rnd 4: Ch 2, dc in first dc and in each rem dc around, join in first dc.

Rnds 5–30: Rep rnd 4.

Rnd 31: Ch 1, working over 2nd ponytail holder, sc in each dc around, join in first sc.

Rnd 32: Ch 1, sc in first dc, ch 10 *(hanging lp)*, sc in each rem sc around, join in first sc, fasten off.

FLOWER
Make 2.
Rnd 1 (RS): With orange, ch 3, join in first ch to form a ring, ch 4 *(counts as first dc and ch-2 sp)*, [dc in ring, ch 2] 5 times, join in 2nd ch of beg ch-4. *(6 dc, 6 ch-2 sps)*

Rnd 2: Ch 1, in each ch-2 sp work (sc, 3 dc, sc) *(petal)*, join in first sc. *(6 petals)*

Rnd 3: Holding petals made on rnd 2 to front, sl st in back of beg ch-4 of rnd 1, *ch 5, sl st in next dc on rnd 1, rep from * around, join in first sl st, fasten off. *(6 sl sts, 6 ch-5 sps)*

Rnd 4: Join oatmeal in first ch-5 sp, in next ch-5 sp work (dc, 5 tr, dc) *(large petal)*, *sl st in next ch-5 sp, in next ch-5 sp work (dc, 5 tr, dc) *(large petal)*, rep from * 4 times, join in joining sl st, fasten off, leaving an 8-inch end for sewing.

LEAF
Make 4.
With lime green, ch 10, working in **back lps** *(see Stitch Guide)* only, sc in 2nd ch from hook, sc in next ch, ch 1, dc in each of next 2 chs, tr in each of next 3 chs, dc in next ch, 2 dc in last ch, working in unused lps on opposite side of foundation ch, 2 dc in first ch, dc in next ch, tr in each of next 3 chs, dc in each of next 2 chs, sc in each of last 2 chs, join in first sc, fasten off, leaving an 8-inch end for sewing.

FINISHING
Referring to photo for placement, sew Flowers and Leaves to Bag Holder. ■

Golf Club Covers CONTINUED FROM PAGE 83

Rnd 5: Sc in each of first 4 sc, 2 sc in next sc, *sc in each of next 4 sc, 2 sc in next sc, rep from * around. *(36 sc)*

Rnd 6: Sc in each sc around.

Rnd 7: Sc in each of first 5 sc, 2 sc in next sc, *sc in each of next 5 sc, 2 sc in next sc, rep from * around. *(42 sc)*

Rnds 8–12: Rep rnd 6.

Rnd 13: Sc in each of first 5 sc, **sc dec** *(see Stitch Guide)* in next 2 sc, *sc in each of next 5 sc, sc dec in next 2 sc, rep from * around. *(36 sc)*

Rnds 14–17: Rep rnd 6.

Rnd 18: Sc in each of first 4 sc, sc dec in next 2 sc, *sc in each of next 4 sc, sc dec in next 2 sc, rep from * around. *(30 sc)*

Rnds 19–21: Rep rnd 6. At end of last rnd, join in first sc, fasten off.

Rnd 22: Join soft white in first sc, **ch 3** *(see Pattern Notes)*, dc in each of next 2 sc, **dc dec** *(see Stitch Guide)* in next 2 sc, *dc in each of next 3 sc, dc dec in next 2 sc, rep from * around, join in 3rd ch of beg ch-3. *(24 dc)*

Rnd 23: Ch 3, dc in each dc, join in 3rd ch of beg ch-3, fasten off.

Rnd 24: Join warm brown in same ch as joining, ch 3, dc in each dc around, join in 3rd ch of beg ch-3.

Rnds 25–27: Ch 3, dc in each dc, join in 3rd ch of beg ch-3.

Rnd 28: Ch 1, sc in each dc around, join in first sc, fasten off.

#3 COVER
Work same as #1 Cover, using Windsor blue in place of warm brown.

#5 COVER
Work same as #1 Cover, using carrot in place of warm brown.

GOLF BALL
Make 9.
Note: Work in continuous rnds, do not join unless specified. Mark beg of rnds.

Rnd 1 (RS): With F hook and soft white, ch 2, 6 sc in 2nd ch from hook. *(6 sc)*

Rnd 2: 2 sc in each sc around, join in first sc, fasten off.

ASSEMBLY
Referring to photo for placement and with tapestry needle and soft white, sew 1 Golf Ball to #1 Cover, 3 Golf Balls to #3 Cover and 5 Golf Balls to #5 Cover. ■

Best Friends Treat Holders CONTINUED FROM PAGE 88

FINISHING
Sew Cheeks to Head, sew Nose between Cheeks.

For whiskers, cut 6 (6-inch) strands of black sewing thread. Referring to photo for placement, insert hook through st on 1 Cheek, fold 1 length of thread in half and pull fold part way through. Pull ends of thread down through lp and pull tight. Trim ends. Rep twice more on same Cheek. Rep on other Cheek.

Sew Eyes to Head. Sew 1 button on top of each Eye using straight stitches. With tapestry needle and black, outline each Eye.

With black, embroider mouth using straight st.

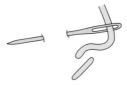

Straight Stitch

Sew Ears to Head.

With sky, sew jingle bell to front middle of rnd 5 of Lid Cover. Sew Head to Lid Cover.

Using drawings, page 87, as templates, cut paw pads from pink felt and fish from orange felt. Referring to photo for placement, glue

2 small pads and 1 large pad to each foot. Sew Feet to Body. Mark eyes, mouth and fins with black felt-tip marker. Glue fish to front of Body.

Stuff Arms lightly. Press flat. With light grey, sew end of each Arm tog and sew to Body.

Sew Tail to back of Body. ■

Granny's Hangers CONTINUED FROM PAGE 89

(4 dc, ch 2, 4 dc) in next ch-2 sp, ch 1, sk next ch-1 sp, [4 dc in next ch-3 sp, ch 1] 6 times, sk next ch-1 sp, join in 3rd ch of beg ch-3, fasten off. *(14 ch-1 sps, 2 ch-2 sps)*

Rnd 5: Join C in any ch-2 sp, ch 3, (3 dc, ch 2, 4 dc) in same sp, 4 dc in each of next 7 ch-1 sps, (4 dc, ch 2, 4 dc) in next ch-2 sp, 4 dc in each of last 7 ch-1 sps, join in 3rd ch of beg ch-3. *(9 {4-dc} groups between each ch-2 sp)*

Rnd 6: Sl st in each of next 3 sts, sl st in next ch-2 sp, ch 3, (3 dc, ch 2, 4 dc) in same sp, 4 dc in sp between each 4-dc group across to next ch-2 sp, (4 dc, ch 2, 4 dc) in ch-2 sp, 4 dc in sp between each 4-dc group across, join in 3rd ch of beg ch-3. *(10 {4-dc} groups between ch-2 sps)*

Rnd 7: Sl st in each of next 3 sts, sl st in next ch-2 sp, ch 3, (3 dc,

ch 2, 4 dc) in same sp, ch 1, [sk next 3 dc, 4 dc in sp between next 2 dc, ch 1] 9 times, (4 dc, ch 2, 4 dc) in next ch-2 sp, ch 1, [sk next 3 dc, 4 dc sp between next 2 dc, ch 1] 9 times, join in 3rd ch of beg ch-3, fasten off. *(10 ch-1 sps between ch-2 sps)*

Rnd 8: Join A in first ch-2 sp, ch 3, 3 dc in same sp, ch 1, [4 dc in next ch-1 sp, ch 1] 10 times, 4 dc in next ch-2 sp, ch 1, [4 dc in next ch-1 sp, ch 1] 10 times, join in 3rd ch of beg ch-3. *(22 ch-1 sps)*

Rnd 9: Sl st in each of next 3 dc, sl st in next ch-1 sp, ch 3, 3 dc in same sp, ch 1, *4 dc in next ch-1 sp, ch 1, rep from* around, join in 3rd ch of beg ch-3, fasten off.

ASSEMBLY

Fold piece in half with ch-2 sps at fold. Insert hanger. Matching sts, with A and tapestry needle and working through both thicknesses, sew first 20 dc and 4 ch-1 sps along top edge tog, sk next 4 sts around curved part of hanger, sew last 20 dc and 4 ch-1 sps tog.

FRINGE

Cut 12 strands of A each 12 inches long. Hold strands tog and fold in half, insert hook in ring formed on rnd 1, draw fold through, draw ends through fold, tighten. Trim ends. ■

Oxygen Tank Covers CONTINUED FROM PAGE 92

Rnds 15–34: [Rep rnds 11–14 consecutively] 5 times.

Rnd 35: Ch 4 *(counts as first dc and first ch-1 sp)*, sk next sc, [dc in next sc, ch 1, sk next sc] 27 times, join in 3rd ch of beg ch-4. *(28 dc, 28 ch-1 sps)*

Rnd 36: Ch 1, sc in same st, sc in each ch-1 and in each sc around, join in first sc, fasten off. *(56 sc)*

CORD

Work same as Cord for Triangle Stitch B Cover.

FINISHING

Weave Cord through ch-1 sps on rnd 35, thread both ends of Cord through bead, pull Cord, pushing bead to top of Cover. Knot free

ends of Cord with an overhand knot. Trim ends.

TRIANGLE STITCH E COVER

Rnds 1–10: With mash, rep rnds 1–10 of Petal Stitch E Cover.

Rnd 11: Rep rnd 9 of Triangle Stitch B Cover. *(7 sc, 7 triangle sts at end of rnd)*

Rnd 12: Rep rnd 10 of Triangle Stitch B Cover. *(14 sts, 7 ch-4 sps)*

Rnd 13: Rep rnd 11 of Triangle Stitch B Cover. *(56 sc at end of rnd)*

Rnd 14: Rep rnd 12 of Triangle Stitch B Cover.

Rnds 15–58: [Rep rnds 11–14 consecutively] 11 times.

Rnd 59: Ch 4 *(counts as first dc and first ch-1 sp)*, sk next sc, [dc in next sc, ch 1, sk next sc] 27 times, join in 3rd ch of beg ch-4. *(28 dc, 28 ch-1 sps)*

Rnd 60: Ch 1, sc in same st, s c in each ch-1 and in each sc around, join in first sc, fasten off. *(56 sc)*

CORD
Work same as Cord for Triangle Stitch B Cover.

FINISHING
Weave Cord through ch-1 sps on rnd 59, thread both ends of Cord through bead, pull Cord, pushing

bead to top of Cover. Knot free ends of Cord with an overhand knot. Trim ends. ∎

Heart Pocket Note Holder CONTINUED FROM PAGE 93

CIRCLE
Make 2.
Rnd 1 (RS): With white, ch 4, join in first ch to form ring, **ch 3** *(see Pattern Notes)*, 12 dc in ring, join in 3rd ch of beg ch-3. *(13 dc)*

Rnds 2 & 3: Ch 3, dc in same st as joining, 2 dc in each dc around, join in 3rd ch of beg ch-3. At end of last rnd, fasten off. *(52 dc at end of last rnd)*

ASSEMBLY
Fold each Circle in half with RS facing. Place 2 white Squares tog; working through both thicknesses, sew fold of 1 Circle to edge of Squares stretching Circle slightly to fit if necessary. Rep for other Circle on adjoining side of Squares.

EDGING
Place WS of apple green Square over RS of 1 white square, carefully matching sts. Working

through all 3 thicknesses, join white in ch-2 sp at bottom corner Squares, ch 2, 5 hdc in same ch-2 sp, *sk next dc, sc in next dc, sk next dc, 6 hdc in next ch-1 sp, rep from * twice, sk next 3 dc, sc in next corner ch-2 sp, working through both thicknesses of Circles only, sk first dc,* 6 hdc in next dc, sk next dc, sc in next dc, sk next dc, rep from * around, adjusting sts if necessary to have 7 (6-hdc) groups on each Circle and sc in st between Circles, working through thicknesses of all 3 Squares, sc in next corner ch-2 sp, sk next 3 dc, *6 hdc in next ch-1 sp, sk next dc, sc in next dc, sk next dc, rep from * twice, join in 2nd ch of beg ch-2, fasten off.

HANGER
Join apple green in sc between 2 Circles, ch 18, join in same sc to form a ring, ch 1, sc evenly in ring covering ch sts completely and

keeping sts smooth and flat, being careful not to bunch them up, join in first sc, fasten off.

FINISHING
Fold down top half of apple green Square to form flap for pocket. Tack down outer corners of flap pocket where it folds to keep it from falling forward when the notepad and pen are placed inside.

For added strength, add a dot of glue to the base of Hanger on WS where Hanger touches Heart.

If using magnets, glue to WS of Heart. ∎

Easy Elegant Jar Covers CONTINUED FROM PAGE 97

TIE
Ch 50, fasten off.

FINISHING
Weave Tie through ch-2 sps on rnd 13 of Jar Cover, tie ends in bow.

HALF-PINT JAR COVER
Rnds 1 & 2: Rep rnds 1 & 2 of Quart Jar Cover.

Rnd 3: Working in **back lps** *(see Stitch Guide)* only, ch 1, sc in

each dc around, join in first sc. *(24 sc)*

Rnd 4: Ch 1, sc in first sc, sk next sc, **V-st** *(see Special Stitches)* in next sc, sk next sc, *sc in next sc, sk next sc, V-st in next sc, sk next sc, rep from * around, join in first sc. *(6 sc, 6 V-sts)*

Rnd 5: Beg V-st *(see Special Stitches)* in first sc, sc in ch-1 sp of next V-st, *V-st in next sc, sc in ch-1 sp of next V-st, rep from *

around, join in 3rd ch of beg ch-4.

Rnd 6: Sl st in next ch-1 sp, ch 1, sc in same sp, V-st in next sc, *sc in ch-1 sp of next V-st, V-st in next sc, rep from * around, join in first sc.

Rnds 7 & 8: Rep rnds 5 and 6.

Rnd 9: Rep rnd 5, fasten off.

LID COVER

Rnds 1 & 2: Rep rnds 1 and 2 of Lid Cover for Quart Jar Cover.

Rnd 3: Ch 4 *(counts as first dc and ch-1 sp)*, sk next dc, *dc in next dc, ch 1, sk next dc, rep from * around, join in 3rd ch of beg ch-4. *(12 dc, 12 ch-1 sps)*

Rnd 4: Sl st in next ch-1 sp, ch 1, sc in same sp, ch 3, *sc in next ch-1 sp, ch 3, rep from * around, join in first sc. *(12 sc, 12 ch-3 sps)*

Rnd 5: Sl st in next ch-1 sp, ch 1, (sc, ch 1, sc, ch 1, sc) in same sp, ch 1, work [sc, ch 1] 3 times in each rem ch-1 sp around, join in first sc, fasten off. *(36 sc, 36 ch-1 sps)*

FINISHING

Cut 16-inch strand of yarn, weave through sts of rnd 9 of Half-Pint Jar Cover, tie ends in bow. ∎

Dog Bed CONTINUED FROM PAGE 98

careful not to split sts with needle. Pull yarn end tightly to close end of Pillow. When closed as tightly as possible, secure end of yarn in end of Pillow. Rep on other end of Pillow. Turn Pillow ends inside out so clean side is facing. Mark center of long side. With warm brown, sew long side of Pillow closed, stuffing with

fiberfill as you sew, making sure Pillow isn't so full that it won't bend.

Match marked sts on both Bed and Pillow. With warm brown, sew Pillow in place. Pillow should fit across back and about half way down both sides of Dog Bed. ∎

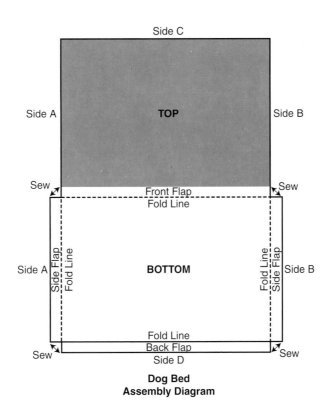

**Dog Bed
Assembly Diagram**

Eyeglasses Cases CONTINUED FROM PAGE 101

row, working across next side in unused lps on opposite side of foundation ch, 2 sc in first ch, sc in next ch, 2 sc in last ch, working across next side in ends of rows, sc in each row to last row, sk last row, join in first sc, fasten off. *(64 sc)*

FRONT/BACK
Row 1 (WS): Starting at front, ch 8, sc in 2nd ch from hook, sc in each ch across, turn. *(7 sc)*

Row 2 (RS): Ch 1, sc in each sc across, turn.

Row 3: Ch 1, sc in each of first 3 sc, **puff st** *(see Special Stitch)* in next sc, sc in each of last 3 sc, turn. *(6 sc, 1 puff st)*

Row 4: Ch 1, sc in each st across, turn. *(7 sc)*

Row 5: Ch 1, sc in first sc, puff st in next sc, sc in next sc, puff st in next sc, sc in each of last 2 sc, turn. *(5 sc, 2 puff sts)*

Row 6: Ch 1, sc in each sc across, turn.

Row 7: Ch 1, sc in first sc, puff st in next sc, sc in each of next 3 sc, puff st in next sc, sc in last sc, turn.

Row 8: Ch 1, sc in each sc across, turn.

Row 9: Ch 1, sc in each of first 2 sc, puff st in next sc, sc in next

sc, puff st in next sc, sc in each of last 2 sc, turn.

Row 10: Rep row 2.

Row 11: Ch 1, sc in each of first 3 sts, puff st in next sc, sc in each of last 3 sts, turn. *(6 sc, 1 puff st)*

Row 12: Rep row 2.

Rows 13–28: [Rep rows 5-12 consecutively] twice.

Row 29: Ch 1, sc in each of first 2 sc, puff st in next sc, sc in next sc, puff st in next sc, sc in each of last 2 sc, turn.

Row 30: Rep row 2.

Row 31: Ch 1, sc in each of first 3 sts, puff st in next sc, sc in each of last 3 sts, turn.

Row 32: Rep row 2.

Rows 33–56: [Rep rows 5-12 consecutively] 3 times.

Edging
Ch 1, 3 sc in first sc *(corner)*, sc in each of next 5 sc, 3 sc in last sc *(corner)*, working across next side in ends of rows, sc in each row, working across next side in unused lps on opposite side of foundation ch, 3 sc in first ch *(corner)*, sc in next 5 chs, 3 sc in last ch *(corner)*, working across next side in ends of rows, sc in each row across, join in first sc, fasten off. *(134 sc)*

FLAP
Work same as Flap for Small Case.

STRAP
Make 3.
Ch 12, 4 sc in 2nd sc from hook, sc in each of next 9 chs, 4 sc in last ch, working in unused lps on opposite side of foundation ch, sc in each ch across, join in first sc, fasten off.

ASSEMBLY
Working in **back lps** *(see Stitch Guide)* only, easing to fit and matching corner sts, sl st WS of 1 long edge on Side to 1 End. Rep with other End. For back, sl st top edge on Flap to 1 edge of Side. Sew 1 Strap to seams 1 inch below edge on Front. Sewing rem Straps to back of Case *(see Assembly Diagram)*. ∎

Straps

7"

2¾"

**Large Case
Eyeglasses Cases
Assembly Diagram**

Bookmarks CONTINUED FROM PAGE 109

first 2 sts, hdc in each of next 2 sts, dc in each of next 2 sts, hdc in each of next 2 sts, dc in each of next 2 sts, hdc in each of next 3 sts, sc in next st, sl st in last st, ch 60 *(tail)*, sl st in 2nd ch from hook, sl st in each ch across, fasten off.

TASSEL
With green, work same as Tassel for Butterfly.

Apple

DESIGN BY LUELLA HINRICHSEN

SKILL LEVEL   **EASY**

FINISHED SIZE
2 inches x 10 inches, including worm

MATERIALS
• Size 10 crochet cotton:
  5 yds red
  1 yd each green, camel, goldenrod, white
• Size 5/1.90mm steel crochet hook or size needed to obtain gauge
• Tapestry needle

GAUGE
Gauge not important to this project.

PATTERN NOTES
Weave in ends as work progresses.

Join rounds with a slip stitch unless otherwise stated.

Instructions

Row 1: With red, ch 3, 2 sc in 2nd ch from hook, 2 sc in last ch, turn. *(4 sc)*

Row 2: Ch 1, sc in each st across, turn.

Row 3: Ch 1, 2 sc in each sc across, turn. *(8 sc)*

Row 4: Rep row 2.

Row 5: Ch 1, 2 sc in first sc, sc in each st across to last sc, 2 sc in last sc, turn. *(10 sc)*

Row 6: Rep row 2.

Row 7: Rep row 5. *(12 sc at end of row)*

Rows 8–10: Rep row 2.

Row 11: Rep row 5. *(14 sc at end of row)*

Row 12: Rep row 2.

Row 13: Ch 1, **sc dec** *(see Stitch Guide)* in first 2 sc, sc in each sc across to last 2 sc, sc dec in last 2 sc, turn. *(12 sc)*

Row 14: Ch 1, sc dec in first 2 sc, (sc, hdc, sc) in next sc, sc in next sc, sl st in next 4 sc, sc in next sc, (sc, hdc, sc) in next sc, sc dec in last 2 sts, turn. *(14 sts)*

Edging
Ch 1, working around outer edge, sc in each st and in end of each row, join in first sc, fasten off.

STEM
Join camel in 7th sc of Edging, ch 5, sl st in 2nd ch from hook, sl st in each rem ch across, sl st in next sc of Edging, fasten off.

LEAF
Join green in last sl st on Stem, ch 10, sc in 2nd ch from hook, hdc in next ch, dc in next ch, tr in next ch, dc in next ch, hdc in each of next 2 chs, sc in next ch, sl st in last ch, working in unused lps on opposite of foundation ch, sc in next ch, hdc in each of next 2 chs, dc in next ch, tr in next ch, dc in next ch, hdc in next ch, sc in last ch, join in first sc, fasten off.

WORM
With goldenrod, ch 16, sl st in 2nd ch from hook, sc in each of next 3 chs, 3 sc in next ch, sc in next 4 chs, sk next ch, sc in each of next 2 chs, 3 sc in next ch, sc in each of last ch, fasten off.

FINISHING
Join white around **post** *(see Stitch Guide)* of same sc as first sl st on Stem made, ch to measure 6 inches, join in first sc on Worm, fasten off. ■

4

Afghan Beauty

The beauty of these afghans is that they are all quick and easy to make. Not only do these afghans have decorative appeal, but they are also functional. Any one of these Afghan Beauties can add a special look to any room, or become a comforting companion as you snuggle up and relax with a cup of coffee and your favorite book.

Post Stitch Patchwork

DESIGN BY MARTY MILLER

SKILL LEVEL

EASY

FINISHED SIZE
43 x 51 inches

MATERIALS
- Red Heart Super Saver medium (worsted) weight yarn (7 oz/364 yds/ 198g per skein):
    3 skeins #360 cafe
    1 skein each #631 light sage and #320 cornmeal
- Red Heart Classic medium (worsted) weight yarn (3½ oz/ 190 yds/99g per skein):
    4 skeins each #3 off-white and #882 country blue
- Size I/9/5.5mm crochet hook or size needed to obtain gauge
- Tapestry needle

GAUGE
Square = 8 inches

PATTERN NOTES
Weave in ends as work progresses.

Join rounds with a slip stitch unless otherwise stated.

Chain-2 at beginning of double crochet row counts as first double crochet unless otherwise stated.

Two methods for beginning these squares are given—the first method uses the traditional chain and first row of double crochet. The second method uses a foundation double crochet, which creates the chain and first row at the same time. Use either method.

SPECIAL STITCH
Foundation double crochet (foundation dc): Ch 4, yo, insert hook in 4th ch from hook, yo, draw up a lp, ch 1, [yo, draw through 2 lps] twice *(first foundation dc)*, yo, insert hook under 2 lps of ch made in first foundation dc, yo, draw up a lp, ch 1, [yo, draw through 2 lps] twice. *(2 foundation dc)*

Continue in this manner for number of foundation dc needed.

Instructions

SQUARE A
Make 1 of each color.
Method 1
Row 1 (WS): Ch 28, dc in 4th ch from hook *(beg 3 sk chs count as a dc)*, dc in each rem ch across, turn. *(26 dc)*

Method 2
Row 1 (RS): Work 26 **foundation dc** *(see Special Stitch)*, turn. *(26 foundation dc)*

Both Methods
Row 2 (RS): Ch 2 *(see Pattern Notes)*, sk first st, **bpdc** *(see Stitch Guide)* around next st, **fpdc** *(see Stitch Guide)* around next st, [bpdc around each of next 2 sts, fpdc around next st] 7 times, bpdc around next st, hdc in sp before last st, turn. *(26 sts)*

Row 3: Ch 2, sk first st, fpdc around next st, bpdc around next st, [fpdc around each of next 2 sts, bpdc around next st] 7 times, fpdc around next st, hdc in sp before last st, turn.

Row 4: Ch 2, sk first st, bpdc around each of next 24 sts, hdc in sp before last st, turn.

Row 5: Ch 2, sk first st, fpdc around next st, bpdc around next st, [fpdc around each of next 2 sts, bpdc around next st] 7 times, fpdc around next st, hdc in sp before last st, turn.

Row 6: Ch 2, sk first st, bpdc around next st, fpdc around next st, [bpdc around each of next 2 sts, fpdc around next st] 7 times, bpdc around next st, hdc in sp before last st, turn.

Row 7: Ch 2, sk first st, fpdc around each of next 24 sts, hdc in sp before last st, turn.

Rows 8–13: Rep rows 2-7.

Rows 14–18: Rep rows 2-6. At end of last row, fasten off.

SQUARE B
Make 2 cornmeal and 1 each off-white, light sage and country blue.

Method 1
Row 1 (WS): Ch 28, dc in 4th ch from hook *(beg 3 sk chs count as a dc)*, dc in each rem ch across, turn. *(26 dc)*

Method 2
Row 1 (WS): Work 26 **foundation dc** *(see Special Stitches)*, turn. *(26 foundation dc)*

Both Methods
Row 2 (RS): Ch 2, sk first st, *fpdc around each of next 2 sts, bpdc around each of next 2 sts, rep from * across to last st, hdc in sp before last st, turn. At end of last row, fasten off. *(26 sts)*

Rows 3–18: Rep row 2. At end of last row, fasten off.

SQUARE C
Make 2 each off-white and cafe and 1 country blue.
Method 1
Row 1 (WS): Ch 28, dc in 4th ch from hook *(beg 3 sk chs count as a dc)*, dc in each rem ch across, turn. *(26 dc)*

Method 2
Row 1 (WS): Work 26 **foundation dc** *(see Special Stitches)*, turn. *(26 foundation dc)*

Both Methods
Row 2 (RS): Ch 2 *(see Pattern Notes)*, sk first st, *fpdc around next st, bpdc around next st, rep from * across to last st, hdc in sp before last st, turn. *(26 sts)*

Row 3: Ch 2, sk first st, *bpdc around next st, fpdc around next st, rep from * across to last st, hdc in sp before last st, turn.

Rows 4–17: [Rep rows 2 and 3 alternately] 7 times.

Row 18: Rep row 2. At end of row, fasten off.

SQUARE D
Make 2 each cornmeal and light sage and 1 country blue.
Method 1
Row 1 (WS): Ch 28, dc in 4th ch from hook *(beg 3 sk chs count as a dc)*, dc in each rem ch across, turn. *(26 dc)*

Method 2
Row 1 (WS): Work 26 foundation dc *(see Special Stitches)*, turn. *(26 foundation dc)*

Both Methods
Row 2 (RS): Ch 2 *(see Pattern Notes)*, sk first st, *fpdc around next st, bpdc around next st, rep from * across to last st, hdc in sp before last st, turn. *(26 sts)*

Rows 3–18: Rep row 2. At end of last row, fasten off.

SQUARE E
Make 2 cafe and 1 each off-white, country blue and light sage.
Method 1
Row 1 (WS): Ch 28, dc in 4th ch from hook *(beg 3 sk chs count as a dc)*, dc in each rem ch across, turn. *(26 dc)*

Method 2
Row 1 (WS): Work 26 **foundation dc** *(see Special Stitches)*, turn. *(26 foundation dc)*

Both Methods
Row 2 (RS): Ch 2 *(see Pattern Notes)*, sk first st, bpdc around next st, fpdc around next st, bpdc around each of next 8 sts, fpdc around next st, bpdc around each of next 2 sts, fpdc around next st, bpdc around each of next 8 sts, fpdc around next st, bpdc around next st, hdc in sp before last st, turn. *(26 sts)*

Row 3: Ch 2, sk first st, fpdc around each of next 2 sts, bpdc around next st, fpdc around each of next 6 sts, bpdc around next st, fpdc around each of next 4 sts, bpdc around next st, fpdc around each of next 6 sts, bpdc around next st, fpdc around each of next 2 sts, hdc in sp before last st, turn.

Row 4: Ch 2, sk first st, bpdc around each of next 3 sts, fpdc around next st, bpdc around each of next 4 sts, fpdc around next st, bpdc around each of next 6 sts, fpdc around next st, bpdc around each of next 4 sts, fpdc around next st, bpdc around each of next 3 sts, hdc in sp before last st, turn.

Row 5: Ch 2, sk first st, fpdc around each of next 4 sts, bpdc around next st, fpdc around each of next 2 sts, bpdc around next st, fpdc around each of next 8 sts, bpdc around next st, fpdc around each of next 2 sts, bpdc around next st, fpdc around each of next 4 sts, hdc in sp before last st, turn.

Row 6: Ch 2, sk first st, bpdc around each of next 4 sts, fpdc around next st, bpdc around each of next 2 sts, fpdc around next st, bpdc around each of next 8 sts, fpdc around next st, bpdc around each of next 2 sts, fpdc around next st, bpdc around each of next 4 sts, hdc in sp before last st, turn.

Row 7: Ch 2, sk first st, fpdc around each of next 3 sts, bpdc around next st, fpdc around each of next 4 sts, bpdc around next st, fpdc around each of next 6 sts, bpdc around next st, fpdc around each of next 4 sts, bpdc around next st, fpdc around each of next 3 sts, hdc in sp before last st, turn.

Row 8: Ch 2, sk first st, bpdc around each of next 2 sts, fpdc around next st, bpdc around each of next 6 sts, fpdc around next st, bpdc around each of next 4 sts, fpdc around next st, bpdc around each of next 6 sts, fpdc around next st, bpdc around each of next 2 sts, hdc in sp before last st, turn.

Row 9: Ch 2, sk first st, fpdc around next st, bpdc around next st, fpdc around each of next 8 sts, bpdc around next st, fpdc around each of next 2 sts, bpdc around next st, fpdc around each of next 8 sts, bpdc around next st, fpdc around next st, hdc in sp before last st, turn.

Rows 10–17: Rep rows 2–9.

Row 18: Rep row 2. At end of row, fasten off.

SQUARE F
Make 1 of each color.
Method 1
Row 1 (WS): Ch 28, dc in 4th ch from hook *(beg 3 sk chs count as a dc)*, dc in each rem ch across, turn. *(26 dc)*

Method 2
Row 1 (WS): Work 26 **foundation dc** *(see Special Stitches)*, turn. *(26 foundation dc)*

Both Methods
Row 2 (RS): Ch 2 *(see Pattern Notes)*, sk first st, bpdc around each of next 3 sts, [fpdc around each of next 4 sts, bpdc around each of next 4 sts] twice, fpdc around each of next 4 sts, bpdc around next st, hdc in sp before last st, turn. *(26 sts)*

Row 3: Ch 2, sk first st, *bpdc around each of next 2 sts, fpdc around next st, bpdc around each of next 2 sts, fpdc around each of next 3 sts, rep from * twice, hdc in sp before last st, turn.

Row 4: Ch 2, sk first st, fpdc around next st, [bpdc around each of next 2 sts, fpdc around each of next 2 sts] 5 times, bpdc around each of next 2 sts, fpdc around next st, hdc in sp before last st, turn.

Row 5: Ch 2, sk first st, *fpdc around each of next 3 sts, bpdc around each of next 2 sts, fpdc around next st, bpdc around each of next 2 sts, rep from * twice, hdc in sp before last st, turn.

Row 6: Ch 2, sk first st, bpdc around next st, [fpdc around each of next 4 sts, bpdc around each of next 4 sts] twice, fpdc around each of next 4 sts, bpdc around each of next 3 sts, hdc in sp

before last st, turn.

Row 7: Ch 2, sk first st, fpdc around each of next 3 sts, bpdc around each of next 3 sts, [fpdc around each of next 5 sts, bpdc around each of next 3 sts] twice, fpdc around each of next 2 sts, hdc in sp before last st, turn.

Row 8: Ch 2, sk first st, bpdc around each of next 3 sts, fpdc around each of next 2 sts, [bpdc around each of next 6 sts, fpdc around each of next 2 sts] twice, bpdc around each of next 3 sts, hdc in sp before last st, turn.

Row 9: Ch 2, sk first st, fpdc around each of next 2 sts, [bpdc around each of next 3 sts, fpdc around each of next 5 sts] twice, bpdc around each of next 3 sts, fpdc around each of next 3 sts, hdc in sp before last st, turn.

Rows 10–17: Rep rows 2–9.

Row 18: Rep row 2. At end of row, fasten off.

FINISHING
Referring to Assembly Diagram, arrange squares with RS facing and last row of each Square at top. To join Squares, hold 2 Squares with RS tog and carefully match sts. With tapestry needle and matching yarn of 1 Square, sew Squares tog across 1 side. Rep with rem Squares.

BORDER
Rnd 1 (RS): With RS facing join cafe in end of row 1 in bottom right-hand corner, ch 1, working across side in ends of rows, sc in each row, working across next side, 3 sc in first st *(corner)*, sc in each st to last st, 3 sc in last st *(corner)*, working across next side in ends of rows, sc in each row, working across

next side in unused lps of beg ch, 3 sc in first lp *(corner)*, sc in each lp to last lp, 3 sc in last lp *(corner)*, join in first sc.

Rnd 2: Ch 3 *(counts as first dc)*, dc in each sc to 2nd sc of next corner, 3 dc in 2nd sc *(dc corner)*, rep from * 3 times, join in 3rd ch of beg ch-3.

Rnd 3: Ch 2, sk first st, *fpdc around next st, bpdc around next st, rep from * around, working each corner as follows: A: (fpdc, hdc, fpdc) or B: (bpdc, hdc, bpdc) around 2nd dc of each corner, depending on st immediately preceding corner. If the previous st was a bpdc, then work A; if it was fpdc, then work B, join in 2nd ch of beg ch-2.

Rnd 4: Ch 2, sk first st, *fpdc around next st, bpdc around next st, rep from * around, working either an A or a B corner around hdc of each corner, join in 2nd ch of beg ch-2.

Rnd 5: Rep rnd 4. At end of rnd, fasten off. ■

Square A Cornmeal	Square B Off-White	Square C Country Blue	Square D Light Sage	Square E Cafe
Square F Off-White	Square A Country Blue	Square B Light Sage	Square C Cafe	Square D Cornmeal
Square E Country Blue	Square F Light Sage	Square A Cafe	Square B Cornmeal	Square C Off-White
Square D Light Sage	Square E Cafe	Square F Cornmeal	Square A Off-White	Square B Country Blue
Square C Cafe	Square D Cornmeal	Square E Off-White	Square F Country Blue	Square A Light Sage
Square B Cornmeal	Square C Off-White	Square D Country Blue	Square E Light Sage	Square F Cafe

Post Stitch Afghan
Assembly Diagram

Sonata in Shells

DESIGN BY DARLA SIMS

SKILL LEVEL

EASY

FINISHED SIZE
45 x 62 inches

MATERIALS
- Patons Décor medium  (worsted) weight yarn (3½ oz/210 yds/100g per ball):
  - 5 balls #01614 winter white
  - 3 balls each #16523 new green, #16522 pale new green and #16524 rich new green
- Sizes G/6/4mm and H/8/5mm crochet hooks or size needed to obtain gauge
- Tapestry needle

GAUGE
With H hook: [Shell, sk 4 chs] 3 times = 4 inches

PATTERN NOTES
Weave in ends as work progresses.

Chain-3 at beginning of double crochet row or round counts as first double crochet unless other-wise stated.

Color sequence: 2 rows winter white, 2 rows new green, 2 rows winter white, 2 rows pale new green, 2 rows winter white, 2 rows rich new green.

SPECIAL STITCHES
Shell: (2 dc, ch 1, 2 dc) in indi-cated st.

Large shell: (3 dc, ch 1, 3 dc) in indicated st.

Long double crochet (long dc): Yo, insert hook in indicated sp, yo, draw lp up to height of working row, [yo, draw through 2 lps on hook] twice.

Instructions

CENTER
Row 1 (WS): With H hook and new green, ch 164, **shell** *(see Special Stitches)* in 6th ch from hook *(beg 5 chs count as dc, 2 sk chs)*, *sk next 4 chs, shell in next ch, rep from * 30 times, sk next 2 chs, dc in last ch, turn. *(32 shells, 2 dc)*

Row 2 (RS): Ch 3 *(see Pattern Notes)*, *shell in ch-1 sp of next shell, rep from * across to beg 5 sk chs, dc in next ch of beg 5 sk chs, **change color** *(see Stitch Guide)* to winter white in last dc, turn.

Row 3: Ch 5 *(counts as first dc, ch-2 sp)*, sc in ch-1 sp of next shell, ch 2, working in next sp between same shell and next shell, **long dc** *(see Special Stitches)* in sp between first 2 shells on 2nd row below, ch 2, sc in ch-1 sp of next shell, ch 2, *working in next sp between same shell and next shell, long dc in sp between next 2 shells on 2nd row below, ch 2, sc in ch-1 sp of next shell, rep from * across to beg ch-3, ch 2, dc in 3rd ch of beg ch-3, turn. *(32 sc, 31 long dc, 2 dc)*

Row 4: Ch 1, sc in first dc, *ch 4, sc in next long dc, rep from * across to beg ch-5, ch 4, sc in 3rd ch of beg ch-5, change to pale new green in last sc, turn. *(33 sc)*

Row 5: Ch 3, 2 dc in first sc, *sk next ch-4 sp, shell in next sc, rep from * across to last ch-4 sp, sk last ch-4 sp, dc in last sc, turn. *(31 shells)*

Row 6: Ch 3, 2 dc in first dc, *shell in ch-1 sp of next shell, rep from * across to beg ch-3, dc in 3rd ch of beg ch-3, change to winter white in last dc.

Row 7: Ch 1, sc in first dc, ch 2, sk next dc, working in sp between next dc and next shell, long dc in corresponding sp on 2nd row below, *ch 2, on working row, sc in ch-1 sp of next shell, *ch 2, working in sp between same shell and next shell, long dc in corresponding sp on 2nd row below, rep from * across to last shell, ch 2, sc in ch-1 sp of next shell, ch 2, working in sp between same shell and next 3-dc group, long dc in corresponding sp on 2nd row below, ch 2, sc in 3rd ch of beg ch-3, turn.

Row 8: Ch 1, sc in first sc, ch 2, *sc in long dc, ch 4, rep from * across to last long dc, sc in last long dc, ch 2, sc in last sc, change to rich new green in last sc, turn.

Row 9: Ch 3, *shell in next sc, rep from * across to last sc, dc in last sc, turn.

Row 10: Ch 3, *shell in ch-1 sp of next shell, rep from * across to beg ch-3, dc in 3rd ch of beg ch-3, change to winter white in last dc.

Rows 11–122: [Rep rows 3–10 consecutively] 14 times following **color sequence** *(see Pattern Notes)*.

Row 123: Rep row 3. At end of row, fasten off.

BORDER

Rnd 1 (RS): With G hook and winter white, make slip knot on hook and join with sc in any corner, sc evenly spaced around outer edge, working 3 sc in each corner, ending with 2 sc in same st as first sc, join in first sc. Change to H hook.

Rnd 2: Ch 3 *(see Pattern Notes)*, 2 dc in same sc, sk next sc, sc in next sc, sk next sc, *large shell *(see Special Stitches)* in next sc, sk next 2 sc, rep from * to beg ch-3, 3 dc in same sc as beg ch-3 made, ch 1, join in 3rd ch of beg ch-3.

Rnd 3: Sl st in ch-1 sp just made, ch 3, sl st in next sc, ch 3, *sl st in ch-1 sp of next large shell, ch 5, (sl st, ch 7, sl st, ch 5, sl st) in same sp, ch 3, sl st in next sc, ch 3, rep from * around to same ch-1 sp as beg sl st made, (sl st, ch 5, sl st, ch 7, sl st, ch 5, sl st) in same sp, join in beg sl st, fasten off. ■

Catherine Wheel

DESIGN BY KATHLEEN STUART

SKILL LEVEL
■■□□
EASY

FINISHED SIZE
46 x 66 inches

MATERIALS
- TLC Essentials medium (worsted) weight yarn (6 oz/312 yds/170g per skein):
    5 skeins #2313 Aran
    1 skein each #2254 persimmon, #2675 dark thyme, #2915 cranberry
- Size J/10/6mm crochet hook or size needed to obtain gauge
- Tapestry needle

GAUGE
1 cl = 1 inch

PATTERN NOTES
Weave in ends as work progresses.

Color sequence: 4 rows Aran, 2 rows persimmon, 4 rows Aran, 2 rows dark thyme, 4 rows Aran, 2 rows cranberry.

When changing colors, fasten off contrasting colors. Carry Aran along edge side.

SPECIAL STITCHES
Beginning cluster (beg cl): Yo, insert hook in indicated st, yo and draw lp through, yo, draw through 2 lps on hook, *yo, insert hook in next st, yo and draw lp through, yo, draw through 2 lps on hook, rep from * twice, yo and draw through all 5 lps on hook.

Cluster (cl): Yo, insert hook in indicated st, yo and draw lp through, yo, draw through 2 lps on hook, *yo, insert hook in next st, yo and draw lp through, yo, draw through 2 lps on hook, rep from * 5 times, yo and draw through all 8 lps on hook.

Ending cluster (ending cl): Work same as beg cl.

Instructions

CENTER
Row 1 (RS): With Aran, ch 182, sc in 2nd ch from hook and in each ch across, turn. *(181 sc)*

Row 2: Ch 1, sc in each of first 2 sc, *sk next 3 sc, 7 dc in next sc, sk next 3 sc, sc in each of next 3 sc, rep from * 16 times, sk next 3 sc, 7 dc in next sc, sk next 3 sc, sc in each of last 2 sc, turn. *(18 7-dc groups, 55 sc)*

Row 3: Ch 2, **beg cl** *(see Special Stitches)* in first 4 sts, *ch 3, sc in each of next 3 dc, ch 3, **cl** *(see Special Stitches)* in next 7 sts, rep from * across to last 6 sts, ch 3, sc in each of next 3 dc, ch 3, **ending cl** *(see Special Stitches)* in last 4 sts, turn. *(17 cls, 1 beg cl, 1 ending cl)*

Row 4: Ch 1, sc in first st and in next ch, *sk next 2 chs and next sc, 7 dc in next sc, sk next sc and next 2 chs, sc in next ch, sc in next cl, sc in next ch, rep from * 16 times, sk next 2 chs and next sc, 7 dc in next sc, sk next sc and next 2 chs, sc in next ch, sc in next cl, **change color** *(see Stitch Guide)* to next color in **color sequence** *(see Pattern Notes)* in last sc, turn.

Rows 5–110: Rep rows 3 and 4 alternately, changing colors as indicated in color sequence.

Row 111: Rep row 3.

Row 112: Ch 1, sc in each st across, turn.

BORDER
Ch 1, 3 sc in first sc *(corner)*, sc evenly spaced around outer edge, working 3 sc in each rem corner, join in first sc, fasten off. ■

Harlequin

DESIGN BY JOYCE NORDSTROM

SKILL LEVEL

■■□□
EASY

FINISHED SIZE
47 x 57 inches

MATERIALS
- TLC Essentials medium (worsted) weight yarn (6 oz/312 yds/ 170g per skein): **4** MEDIUM
  3 skeins each #2332 linen and #2821 paradise blue
- Size I/9/5.5 mm crochet hook or size needed to obtain gauge
- Tapestry needle

GAUGE
(Sl st, ch 3, V-st) = 1 inch

PATTERN NOTES
Weave in ends as work progresses.

Join rounds with a slip stitch unless otherwise stated.

Color sequence: 1 row linen, 7 rows paradise blue, 2 rows linen, 6 rows paradise blue, 3 rows linen, 5 rows paradise blue, 4 rows linen, 4 rows paradise blue, 5 rows linen, 3 rows paradise blue, 6 rows linen, 2 rows paradise blue, 7 rows linen, 1 row paradise blue.

Work backward through colors, substituting linen for paradise blue and paradise blue for linen.

SPECIAL STITCH
V-stitch (V-st): (Dc, ch 1, dc) in indicated st.

Instructions

CENTER
Row 1 (WS): With linen, ch 6, **V-st** *(see Special Stitch)* in 4th ch from hook, sk next ch, dc in last ch, **change color** *(see Stitch Guide)* to paradise blue in last dc, turn.

Row 2 (RS): Ch 6, V-st in 4th ch from hook *(beg group)*, (sl st, ch 3, V-st) in ch-1 sp of next V-st *(group)*, turn. *(2 groups)*

Row 3: Ch 6, V-st in 4th ch from hook—*beg group made*, (sl st, ch 3, V-st) in ch-1 sp of next V-st *(group)*, (sl st, ch 3, V-st) in next ch-3 sp *(group)*, turn. *(3 groups)*

Rows 4–52: Rep row 3, having 1 more group in each row and changing colors following **Color Sequence** *(see Pattern Notes)*. *(52 groups at end of last row)*

Row 53: Ch 6, V-st in 4th ch from hook *(beg group)*, *(sl st, ch 3, V-st) in ch-1 sp of next V-st *(group)*, (sl st, ch 3, V-st) in next ch-3 sp *(group)*, rep from * across to last V-st, (sl st, ch 3, V-st) in ch-1 sp of last V-st, sl st in next ch-3 sp, turn. *(52 groups)*

Note: Mark for dec side.

Row 54: Ch 1, sl st in next dc, sl st in next ch, sl st in next dc, ch 3, V-st in next ch-3 sp, group, work in pattern across row, turn.

Row 55: Rep Row 53.

Rows 56–61: Continue in st pattern as set up in rows 2–13, dec at each dec side and inc at other side.

Continue in st pattern as set up, working dec at each side until 1 group remains.

Last row: Ch 1, sl st in each st across, fasten off.

BORDER
Rnd 1: Join linen in any corner, ch 4 *(counts as first hdc, ch-1 sp)*, *hdc in side of next dc, ch 1, hdc inside of V-st, ch 1, hdc in other side of V-st, ch 1, rep from * to next corner, (hdc, ch 1) 4 times in corner, **hdc in side of next dc, ch 1, hdc alongside of V-st, ch 1, hdc along other side of V-st, ch 1, rep from ** to next corner, [hdc, ch 1] 4 times in corner, ***hdc in side of next dc, ch 1, hdc alongside of V-st, ch 1, hdc along other side of V-st, ch 1, rep from *** to next corner, [hdc, ch 1] 4 times in corner, ****hdc in side of next dc, ch 1, hdc along-side of V-st, ch 1, hdc along other side of V-st, ch 1, rep from **** to next corner, [hdc, ch 1] 4 times in same sp as beg ch-4 made, join in 3rd ch of beg ch-4. *(332 hdc, 332 ch-1 sps)*

Rnd 2: Sl st in next ch-1 sp, ch 4 *(counts as first hdc, ch-1 sp)*, *hdc in next ch-1 sp, sk next hdc, ch 1, rep from * around, working (hdc, ch 2, hdc) in center ch-1 sp of ea corner, join in 3rd ch of beg ch-4, fasten off.

Rnd 3: Join paradise blue in any corner ch-2 sp, ch 4 *(counts as first hdc, ch-1 sp)*, *hdc in next ch-1 sp, sk next hdc, ch 1, rep from * around, working [hdc, ch 1] 4 times in each ch-2 corner sp, [hdc, ch 1] 3 times in same sp as beg ch-4, join in 3rd ch of beg ch-4.

Rnd 4: Rep rnd 2.

Rnd 5: Sl st in next ch-1 sp, *ch 2, sl st in next ch-1 sp, rep from * around, join in first sl st, fasten off. ■

Sand & Sea

DESIGN BY ELAINE BARTLETT

SKILL LEVEL ■■□□
EASY

FINISHED SIZE
45 x 50 inches

MATERIALS
• Lion Brand Wool-Ease **6**
  Thick & Quick super   **SUPER BULKY**
  bulky (super chunky) weight
  yarn (6 oz/106 yds/170g
  per ball):
    4 balls each #110 navy
      and #122 taupe
    3 balls #099 fisherman
• Size N/15/10mm crochet
  hook or size needed to
  obtain gauge
• Tapestry needle

GAUGE
7 dc = 4 inches

PATTERN NOTES
Weave in ends as work progresses.

Join rounds with a slip stitch
unless otherwise stated.

Chain-2 at beginning of double
crochet row counts as first double
crochet unless otherwise stated.

Instructions

CENTER
Row 1 (WS): With navy, ch 77,
dc in 4th ch from hook *(beg 3 sk
chs count as a dc)*, dc in each ch
across, turn. *(75 dc)*

Row 2 (RS): Ch 2 *(see Pattern
Notes)*, dc in each of next 2 dc,
*ch 1, sk next dc, dc in each of
next 3 dc, rep from * across, turn.
(57 dc, 18 ch-1 sps)

Row 3: Ch 2, dc in each dc and
in each ch-1 sp across, **change
color** *(see Stitch Guide)* to fisher-
man in last dc, turn. *(75 dc)*

Row 4: Ch 1, sc in first dc, sc
in each rem dc across, change
to taupe in last sc, turn.

Row 5: Ch 2, dc in each sc
across, turn.

Rows 6 & 7: Rep rows 2 and 3.

Row 8: Rep row 4, change to
navy in last sc.

Row 9: Ch 2, dc in each sc
across, turn.

Rows 10 & 11: Rep rows 2 and 3.

Rows 12–59: [Rep rows 4–11
consecutively] 6 times.

Edging
Rnd 1 (RS): Ch 1, sc in first dc,
sc in each dc across to last dc,
3 sc in last dc *(corner)*, working
across next side in ends of rows,
sc in first dc row, 2 sc in end
of each dc row across (sk all sc
rows), working across next side
in unused lps of beg ch, 3 sc in
first unused lp *(corner)*, sc in
each unused lp across to last
unused lp, 3 sc in last unused lp
(corner), working across next
side in ends of rows, sc in first dc
row, 2 sc in end of each dc row
across (sk all sc rows), 2 sc in
same dc as beg sc made, join in
first sc. *(336 sc)*

Rnd 2: Ch 1, *[sc in next sc, sk
next sc, 4 dc in next sc, sk next
sc] 18 times, sc in next sc, sk next
sc, 6 dc in next sc, sk next sc, [sc
in next sc, sk next sc, 4 dc in next
sc, sk next sc] 22 times, sc in next
sc, sk next sc, 6 dc in next sc, sk
next sc, rep from * around, join in
first sc, fasten off. ■

Shades of Autumn

DESIGN BY RHONDA DODDS

SKILL LEVEL ◼☐☐☐
BEGINNER

FINISHED SIZE
42 x 52 inches

MATERIALS
• Lion Brand Wool-Ease Chunky bulky (chunky) weight yarn (5 oz/153 yds/140g per ball): 8 balls #127 walnut
• Lion Brand Jiffy bulky (chunky) weight yarn (3 oz/135 yds/85g per ball): 4 balls #134 avocado 2 balls #133 paprika
• Size P/15/10mm crochet hook or size needed to obtain gauge
• Tapestry needle

GAUGE
With 2 strands of yarn held tog, square = 9½ inches

PATTERN NOTES
Weave in ends as work progresses.

Entire afghan is worked with 2 strands of yarn held together.

Join rounds with a slip stitch unless otherwise stated.

Chain-3 at beginning of double crochet round counts as first double crochet unless otherwise stated.

SPECIAL STITCH
Cross-stitch (cross-st): Sk indicated st, dc in next st, working in dc just made, dc in sk st.

Instructions

SQUARE
Make 20.
Rnd 1 (RS): With paprika, ch 5, join in first ch to form a ring, **ch 3** *(see Pattern Notes)*, 3 dc in ring, ch 2, [4 dc in ring, ch 2] 3 times, join in 3rd ch of beg ch-3, fasten off. *(16 dc, 4 ch-2 sps)*

Rnd 2: Join avocado in any ch-2 sp, ch 3, (dc, ch 2, 2 dc) in same sp *(beg corner)*, [dc in each of next 4 dc, (2 dc, ch 2, 2 dc) in next ch-2 sp *(corner)*] twice, dc in next 4 sc, join in 3rd ch of beg ch-3, fasten off. *(32 dc, 4 ch-2 sps)*

Rnd 3: Join walnut in any corner ch-2 sp, ch 1, 3 sc in same sp *(sc corner)*, [sc in each of next 8 dc, 3 sc in next corner ch-2 sp *(sc corner)*] twice, sc in each of next 8 dc, join in first sc. *(50 sc)*

Rnd 4: Sl st in next sc, ch 3, (dc, ch 2, 2 dc) in same sc *(beg corner)*, *[**cross-st** (see *Special Stitch*) in next 2 sc] 5 times, (2 dc, ch 2, 2 dc) in next sc *(corner)*, rep from * twice, [cross-st in next 2 sc] 5 times, join in 3rd ch of beg ch 3, fasten off. *(20 cross-sts, 4 ch-2 sps)*

ASSEMBLY
With tapestry needle and walnut and working in **back lps** *(see Stitch Guide)* only, sew Squares tog with RS facing, carefully matching sts. Sew Squares tog in 5 rows of 4 Squares each.

BORDER
Rnd 1 (RS): With RS facing, join paprika in any corner ch-2 sp, ch 1, 3 sc in same sp *(corner)*, *sc evenly spaced to next corner ch-2 sp, 3 sc in corner sp *(corner)*, rep from * twice, sc evenly spaced to first sc, join in first sc, fasten off.

Rnd 2: Join avocado in 2nd sc of any corner, ch 1, 3 sc in same sc *(corner)*, *sc in each sc to 2nd sc of next corner, 3 sc in 2nd sc *(corner)*, rep from * twice, sc in each sc to first sc, join in first sc, fasten off.

Rnd 3: Join walnut in any sc, ch 3, cross-st in next 2 sc, *sk next sc, dc in next sc, cross-st in next 2 sc, rep from * around to beg ch-3, join in 3rd ch of beg ch-3, fasten off. ■

Raspberry Twist

DESIGN BY CINDY ADAMS

SKILL LEVEL

EASY

FINISHED SIZE
40 x 37 inches, excluding
Fringe

MATERIALS
- Bernat Softee Chunky
  Twists bulky (chunky)
  weight yarn (2¾ oz/128 yds/
  80g per ball):
    7 balls #86730 tango
    twists
- Size J/10/6mm crochet
  hook or size needed to
  obtain gauge
- Tapestry needle

GAUGE
11 dc = 4 inches

PATTERN NOTES
Weave in ends as work
progresses.

Chain-2 at beginning of double
crochet row counts as first double
crochet unless otherwise stated.

Instructions

Foundation row: Ch 112, dc
in 3rd ch from hook *(beg 2 sk
chs count as a dc)*, dc in each ch
across, turn. *(111 dc)*

Row 1: Ch 1, sc in each of first 2
dc, *ch 2, sk next 2 dc, sc in each of

next 2 dc, rep from * across to last
dc and beg 2 sk chs, sc in last dc,
sc in 2nd ch of beg 2 sk chs, turn.

Row 2: Ch 2 *(see Pattern Notes)*,
sk first sc, dc in next sc, *2 dc in
next ch-2 sp, dc in each of next
2 sc, rep from * across, turn.

Rep rows 1 and 2 consecutively
until piece measures 40 inches,
ending with row 1. At end of last
row, fasten off.

Hold piece with RS facing and
foundation row at top, join yarn
in unused lp of first ch, ch 1,

working in unused lps of beg ch,
sc in each of first 2 unused lps,
*ch 2, sk next 2 unused lps, sc in
each of next 2 unused, rep from
* across to last unused lp and beg
2 sk chs, sc in last unused, sc in
next ch, fasten off.

FRINGE
Cut 108 strands of yarn 12 inches
long. For each knot of fringe, fold
2 strands in half. From RS side,
draw folded end through first
ch-2 sp on 1 short end. Draw ends
through fold and tighten knot.
Place knots in rem ch-2 sps on
both short ends. Trim ends even. ■

One Row

DESIGN BY CINDY ADAMS

SKILL LEVEL

EASY

FINISHED SIZE
48 x 60 inches

MATERIALS
- Patons Shetland Chunky bulky (chunky) weight yarn (3½ oz/ 148 yds/100g per ball):
    11 balls #3212 imperial variegated
    1 ball #03520 russet
- Size J/10/6mm crochet hook or size needed to obtain gauge
- Tapestry needle

GAUGE
(Sc, ch 3, 3 dc) = 2 inches

PATTERN NOTE
Weave in ends as work progresses.

Instructions

CENTER
Row 1: With imperial, ch 166, sc in 2nd ch from hook, sk next 2 chs, 3 dc in next ch, *ch 3, sk next 3 chs, sc in next ch, sk next 2 chs, 3 dc in next ch, rep from * across, turn. *(24 sc, 72 dc, 24 ch-3 sps)*

Row 2: Ch 1, sc in first dc, 3 dc in next sc, *ch 3, sc in next ch-3 sp, 3 dc in next sc, rep from * across, turn.

Rep row 2 until piece measures 59 inches.

Last row: Ch 1, sc in first dc, 3 dc in next sc, *ch 3, sc in next ch-3 sp, 3 dc in next sc, rep from * across, **change color** *(see Stitch Guide)* to russet in last sc, turn.

Edging
Ch 1, sc in first dc, 3 dc in next sc, *ch 3, sc in next ch-3 sp, 3 dc in next sc, rep from * across, working across next side in ends of rows, **sc in next sc row, 3 dc in next dc row, ch 3, rep from ** to last sc row, sc in last sc row, sk next dc, row, 3 dc in last sc row, ch 3, working across next side, sc in sp formed by next 3 sk chs of row 1, ***dc in unused lp of ch at base of next 3-dc group on row 1, ch 3, sc in sp formed by next 3 sk chs of row 1, rep from *** to last 3 sk chs of row 1, 3 dc in sp formed by last 3 sk chs, ch 3, working across next side in ends of rows, ****sc in row 1, 3 dc in next dc row, ch 3, rep from **** to last sc row, sc in last sc row, 3 dc in side of first sc, fasten off. ■

Hopscotch

DESIGN BY NAZANIN FARD

SKILL LEVEL

BEGINNER

FINISHED SIZE
52 x 48 inches

MATERIALS
- Bernat Black Lites bulky (chunky) weight yarn (3½ oz/60 yds/100g per ball):
  14 balls #82728 cherry chill
- Patons Rumor bulky (chunky) weight yarn (2¾ oz/84 yds/80g per ball):
  10 balls #69530 duberry heather
- Size K/10½/6.5mm crochet hook or size needed to obtain gauge
- Tapestry needle

GAUGE
10 dc = 4 inches

PATTERN NOTES
Weave in ends as work progresses.

Chain-3 at beginning of double crochet row counts as first double crochet unless otherwise stated.

Join rounds with slip stitch unless otherwise stated.

Instructions

CENTER
Row 1 (RS): With duberry heather, ch 131, dc in 4th ch from hook *(beg 3 sk chs count as a dc)*, dc in each ch across, turn. *(129 dc)*

Row 2: Ch 1, sc in each dc across, **change color** *(see Stitch Guide)* to cherry chill in last sc, turn.

Row 3: Ch 3 *(see Pattern Notes)*, dc in next sc, ***fptr** *(see Stitch Guide)* around post of next dc on 2nd below, dc in each of next 3 sc on working row, rep from * 30 times, fptr around post of next dc on 2nd row below, dc in each of last 2 sc, turn. *(97 dc, 32 fptr)*

Row 4: Ch 1, sc in each st across, change to duberry heather in last sc, turn.

Row 5: Ch 3, *dc in each of next 3 sc, fptr around next dc on 2nd row below, rep from * to last 4 sc, dc in each of last 4 sc, turn. *(98 dc, 31 fptr)*

Rows 6–84: [Rep rows 2–5 consecutively] 20 times. At end of last row, **do not turn.**

BORDER
Rnd 1: Working across next side in ends of rows, 2 sc in each dc row, sc in each sc row, working across next side in unused lps of beg ch, sc in each lp, working across next side in ends of rows, 2 sc in each dc row, sc in each sc row, working across row 84, sc in each sc, join in first sc.

Rnd 2: Ch 1, working left to right, work **reverse sc** *(see Fig. 1)* in each sc around, join in first reverse sc, fasten off. ∎

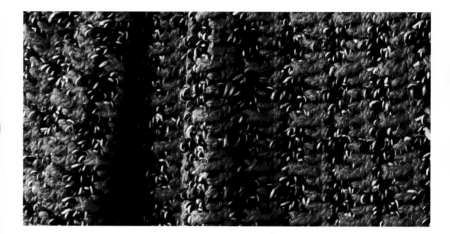

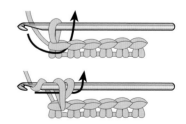

**Reverse Single Crochet
Fig. 1**

Heather Dawn

DESIGN BY CINDY ADAMS

SKILL LEVEL
EASY

FINISHED SIZE
48 x 50 inches

MATERIALS
• Lion Brand Wool-Ease
  medium (worsted)
  weight yarn (3 oz/197 yds/
  85g per ball):
    5 balls each #152 oxford
    grey and #140
    rose heather
• Size I/9/5.5mm crochet
  hook or size needed to
  obtain gauge
• Tapestry needle

GAUGE
14 sts = 4 inches

PATTERN NOTE
Weave in ends as work progresses.

Instructions

CENTER
Row 1 (WS): With oxford grey,
ch 164, sc in 4th ch from hook,
*ch 1, sk next ch, sc in next ch,
rep from * across, turn. *(81 sc, 80
ch-1 sps)*

Row 2 (RS): Ch 2, *sc in next
ch-1 sp, ch 1, rep from * across
to sp formed by beg 3 sk chs,

sc in sp formed by beg 3 sk chs,
change color *(see Stitch Guide)*
to rose heather in last sc, turn.
Fasten off oxford grey.

Row 3: Ch 2, *sc in next ch-1
sp, ch 1, rep from * across to
beg ch-2, sc in sp formed by
beg ch-2, turn.

Rep row 2, alternating colors
every 2 rows until piece measures
50 inches, ending with 2 rows of
oxford grey. At end of last row,
fasten off.

SIDE BORDER
Row 1: Hold piece with WS
facing and last row worked to left,
join oxford grey in end of row 1,
ch 2, sk next row, *working in
ends of rows, sc in next row, ch
1, sk next row, rep from * to last
row, sc in last row, turn.

Row 2: Ch 2, *sc in next ch-1
sp, ch 1, rep from * across to beg
ch-2, sc in sp formed by beg ch-2,
fasten off.

Rep on opposite side. ∎

Lace Fan

DESIGN BY NANCY NEHRING

FINISHED SIZE
45 x 55 inches

MATERIALS

- Patons Lacette fine (sport) weight yarn (1¾ oz/235 yds/50g per ball):
  8 balls #30415 hint of rose
- Size K/10½/6.5 mm crochet hook or size needed to obtain gauge
- Tapestry needle

GAUGE
(Fan, 3 sk dc, sc, ch 1, fan) = 5 inches

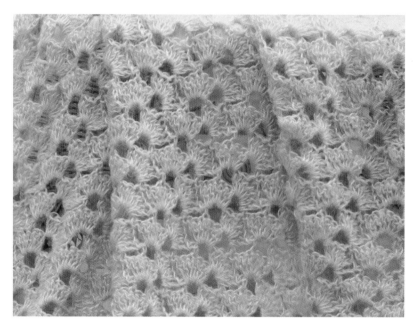

SPECIAL STITCH
Fan: 7 dc in indicated st.

PATTERN NOTES
Weave in ends as work progresses.

Chain-3 at beginning of double crochet row counts as first double crochet unless otherwise stated.

Instructions

Row 1 (RS): Ch 126, 3 dc in 4th ch from hook *(beg 3 sk chs count as a dc)*, sk next 2 chs, *sc in next ch, ch 1, sk next 2 chs, 3 dc in next ch, 4 dc in next ch, sk next 2 chs, rep from * 16 times, sc in last ch, turn. *(123 dc, 18 sc, 17 ch-1 sps)*

Row 2: Ch 3 *(see Pattern Notes)*, 3 dc in first sc, *sk next 3 dc, sc in next dc, ch 1, **fan** *(see Special Stitch)* in next ch-1 sp, rep from * 16 times, sc in sp formed by beg 3 sk chs, turn. *(17 fans, 4 dc, 17 sc, 17 ch-1 sps)*

Row 3: Ch 3, 3 dc in first sc, *sk next 3 dc, sc in next dc, ch 1, fan in next ch-1 sp, rep from * 16 times, sc in sp formed by beg ch-3, turn.

Rows 4–82: Rep row 3. At end of last row, fasten off. ∎

Crosshatch Stitch

DESIGN BY NANCY NEHRING

SKILL LEVEL

EASY

FINISHED SIZE
34 x 42 inches

MATERIALS
- Patons Lacette fine (sport) weight yarn (1¾ oz/235 yds/50g per ball): 4 balls #30128 beautiful blue
- Size K/10½/6.5 mm crochet hook or size needed to obtain gauge
- Tapestry needle

GAUGE
1 crosshatch st = 2 inches

Note: Crosshatch st is extremely flexible making it difficult to measure gauge. Matching gauge is not critical; if gauge is tighter, additional yarn may be needed.

PATTERN NOTES
Weave in ends as work progresses.

Chain-3 at beginning of double crochet row counts as first double crochet unless otherwise stated.

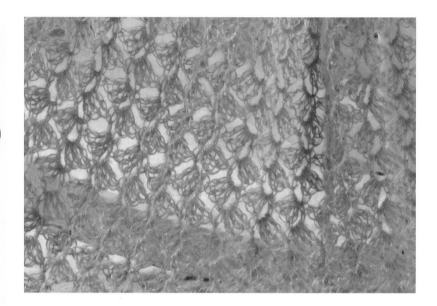

SPECIAL STITCH
Crosshatch stitch (crosshatch st): (Sc, ch 2, 3 dc) in indicated sp.

Instructions

Row 1 (RS): Ch 152, 2 dc in 4th ch from hook *(beg 3 sk chs count as a dc)*, *sk next 3 chs, sc in next ch, ch 2, dc in each of next 3 chs, rep from * 20 times, sc in last ch, turn. *(66 dc, 21 sc, 21 ch-1 sps)*

Row 2: Ch 3 *(see Pattern Notes)*, 2 dc in first sc, sk next 3 dc, **crosshatch st** *(see Special Stitch)* in next ch-2 sp, *sk next sc and next 3 dc, crosshatch st in next ch-2 sp, rep from * 19 times, sc in sp formed by beg 3 sk chs, turn. *(21 crosshatch sts, 3 dc, 1 sc)*

Row 3: 2 dc in first sc, sk next 3 dc, crosshatch st in ch-2 sp of next crosshatch st, *sk next sc and next 3 dc, crosshatch st in ch-2 sp of next crosshatch st, rep from * 19 times, sc in sp formed by beg ch-3, turn.

Rows 4–62: Rep row 3. At end of last row, fasten off. ■

5

Fashionable Accessories

Accessories make an outfit. Any one of these projects would make a great gift for a friend. Or, splurge and treat yourself to a Fashionable Accessory that is sure to take your outfits from basic to beautiful.

Easy Tie Wrap

DESIGN BY DARLA SIMS

FINISHED SIZE
17 x 71 inches

MATERIALS
- Patons Décor medium (worsted) weight yarn (3½ oz/210 yds/100g per ball):
  4 balls #1626 aubergine
- Sizes G/6/4mm and H/8/5mm crochet hooks or size needed to obtain gauge
- Tapestry needle

GAUGE
With H hook: 4 dc = 1 inch

PATTERN NOTES
Weave in ends as work progresses.

Join rounds with a slip stitch unless otherwise stated.

Chain-3 at beginning of double crochet row counts as first double crochet unless otherwise stated.

SPECIAL STITCH
Shell: (Dc, ch 3, 3 dc around **post**—*see Stitch Guide*—of dc just made) in indicated st.

Instructions

FIRST HALF
Row 1: With H hook, ch 4, 2 dc in 4th ch from hook *(beg 3 sk chs count as a dc)*, turn. *(3 dc)*

Row 2: Ch 3 *(see Pattern Notes)*, dc in first dc, dc in next dc, 2 dc in 3rd ch of beg 3 sk chs, turn. *(5 dc)*

Row 3: Ch 3, dc in first dc, dc in each of next 3 dc, 2 dc in 3rd ch of beg ch-3, turn. *(7 dc)*

Row 4: Ch 3, dc in each dc and in 3rd ch of beg ch-3, turn.

Row 5: Ch 3, dc in first dc, dc in each of next 5 dc, 2 dc in 3rd ch of beg ch-3, turn. *(9 dc)*

Rows 6 & 7: Rep row 4.

Row 8: *Ch 2, dc in next dc, dc in each of next 5 dc, **dc dec** *(see Stitch Guide)* in next dc and in 3rd ch of beg ch-3, turn. *(7 dc)*

Row 9: Ch 2, dc in each of next 4 dc, dc dec in next dc and in 3rd ch of beg ch-3, turn. *(5 dc)*

Row 10: Ch 2, dc in next dc, dc dec in next dc and in 3rd ch of beg ch-3, turn. *(3 dc)*

Rows 11–13: Rep row 4.

Row 14: Ch 3, 2 dc in first dc, 3 dc in each dc and in 3rd ch of beg ch-3, turn. *(9 dc)*

Row 15: Rep row 4.

Row 16: Ch 3, 2 dc in first dc, 3 dc in each dc and in 3rd ch of beg ch-3, turn. *(27 dc)*

Row 17: Ch 3, 2 dc in each dc to last dc, dc in last dc and in 3rd ch of beg ch-3, turn. *(51 dc)*

Row 18: Ch 3, dc in each of next 2 dc, *sk next 2 dc, **shell** *(see Special Stitch)* in next dc, sk next 2 dc, dc in each of next 3 dc, rep from * 4 times, shell in next dc, sk next 2 dc, dc in each of next 2 dc and in 3rd ch of beg ch-3, turn. *(6 shells)*

Rows 19–53: Ch 3, dc in each of next 2 dc, *shell in next ch-3 sp, dc in each of next 3 dc, rep from * to last ch-3 sp, shell in last ch-3 sp, dc in each of next 2 dc and in 3rd ch of beg ch-3, turn. At end of last row, fasten off.

2ND HALF
Rows 1–52: Rep rows 1–52 of First Half. At end of last row, fasten off, leaving 24-inch end for sewing.

ASSEMBLY
Hold pieces facing with last row worked held tog at top, with tapestry needle and 24-inch end, sew pieces through **back lps** *(see Stitch Guide)* only across last row.

EDGING
Rnd 1 (RS): With G hook, join in unused lp of beg ch at tip of 1 piece, ch 1, 3 sc in same sp, sc evenly spaced around outer edge, working 3 sc in unused lp of beg ch a tip of 2nd piece, join in first sc.

Rnd 2: Ch 1, sc in same sc as joining, ch 5, sc in next sc, ch 5, rep from * around, join in first sc, fasten off. ■

Red Cord Accessories

DESIGNS BY MARY MELICK

SKILL LEVEL ■■□□ EASY

FINISHED SIZE
One size fits all

MATERIALS

- Red Heart Luster-Sheen fine (sport) weight yarn (4 oz/335 yds/ 113g per skein):
  150 yds #0915 cherry red
- Size E/4/3mm crochet hook
- Size 6/1.80mm steel crochet hook
- Tapestry needle
- Necklace clasp
- Barrel clasp with jump rings
- Craft glue

GAUGE
Gauge is not important to the project.

PATTERN NOTE
Weave in ends as work progresses.

Instructions

NECKLACE
Note: Cut 3 strands each 25 yds long.

With E hook and 3 strands held tog, ch 2, sc in 2nd ch from hook, without removing hook, turn piece to left so back of sc just made is facing you, insert hook in 3 single strands at top

CONTINUED ON PAGE 170

Beaded Cockleshell Choker Set

DESIGN BY LAURA GEBHARDT

SKILL LEVEL
EASY

FINISHED SIZE

Choker: Approx 13 inches long, unclasped

Earrings: 1¼ inches wide x 1¼ inches long, excluding wire

MATERIALS

- DMC Traditions size 10 crochet cotton:
  60 yds #5369 light green
- Size 7/1.65mm steel crochet hook or size needed to obtain gauge
- Tapestry needle
- 156 blues and greens E-beads
- 1 gold necklace clasp
- 2 gold ear wires

GAUGE

Gauge is not important to these projects.

PATTERN NOTE

Weave in ends as work progresses.

SPECIAL STITCHES

Bottom beaded double crochet (bottom beaded dc):
Yo, insert hook in indicated st, slide bead up to hook, yo, draw through, [yo, draw through 2 lps on hook] twice.

Top beaded double crochet (top beaded dc): Yo, insert

hook in indicated st, yo, draw through st and 1 lp on hook, slide bead up to hook, [yo, draw through 2 lps on hook] twice.

Instructions

CHOKER

Note: Before beg, string 130 beads on crochet cotton.

Row 1 (RS): Leaving an 8-inch end, ch 11, dc in 7th ch from hook, ch 3, sk next 3 chs, dc in last ch, turn. *(2 dc, 1 ch-3 sp)*

Row 2: Ch 7, sk first dc, dc in next ch-3 sp, ch 3, sk next dc, dc in sp formed by beg 6 sk chs, turn.

CONTINUED ON PAGE 170

Magic Mitts & Ski Hat

DESIGNS BY JENNIFER BORNE

SKILL LEVEL

SKILL LEVEL

■■■□ INTERMEDIATE

SIZES

Mitts: Instructions given fit child's age 10 size and Adult small, medium and large

Hat: Instructions given fit child's age 10 size and Adult

MATERIALS

- Patons Kroy Socks (super fine) fingering weight yarn (1¾ oz/ 203 yds/50g per ball):
    4 balls #54602 country jacquard
- Size C/2/2.75mm crochet hook or size needed to obtain gauge for age 10 size and Adult size small Mitts
- Size D/3/3.25mm crochet hook or size needed to obtain gauge for Adult size medium Mitts
- Size E/4/3.5mm crochet hook or size needed to obtain gauge for Adult size large Mitts
- Size F/5/8mm crochet hook or size needed to obtain gauge for Hat
- Tapestry needle
- Stitch markers

GAUGE

With C hook: 12 sts = 2 inches

With D hook: 13 sts = 2 inches

With E hook: 14 sts = 2 inches

PATTERN NOTES

Weave in ends as work progresses.

Join rounds with a slip stitch unless otherwise stated.

Chain-2 at beginning of half double crochet round counts as first half double crochet unless otherwise stated.

Instructions

MITT
Make 2.
Ribbing
Row 1: With appropriate size hook, ch 51, sc in 2nd ch from hook, sc in each ch across, turn. *(50 sc)*

Row 2: Ch 1, working in **back lps** *(see Stitch Guide)* only, sc in each sc across, turn.

Rows 3–19: Rep row 2.

Thumb Opening
Row 20: Ch 1, working in back lps only, sc in each of first 28 sc, ch 14 *(thumb opening)*, sk next 14 sc, sc in each of last 8 sc, turn. *(36 sc, 14 chs)*

Row 21: Ch 1, working in back lps only, sc in each sc and in each ch across, turn. *(50 sc)*

Rows 22–45: Rep row 2. At end of last row, fasten off, leaving a 12-inch end for sewing.

ASSEMBLY
With tapestry needle and long end, sew last row 45 to beg ch.

Finger Openings
Rnd 1: Hold piece with RS facing, join in end of row 20, ch 1, sc in same row, working in ends of rows of piece, sc in each row around, join in first sc. *(45 sc)*

Rnd 2: Ch 1, sc in same sc as joining and in each of next 9 sc *(mark last sc made)*, sc in each of next 5 sc *(mark last sc made)*, sc in each of next 5 sc *(mark last sc made)*, sc in each of next 10 sc, (ch 2, join in last marked sc, ch 1, turn, sc in each of next 2 chs, continuing on working rnd, sc in each of next sc, ch 2, join in next marked sc, ch 1, turn, sc in each of next 2 chs, continuing on working rnd, sc in each of next 5 sc, ch 2, join in first marked sc, ch 1, turn, sc in each of next 2 chs, continuing on working rnd, sc in each of last 5 sc), join in first sc.

Index Finger
Note: Fingers are worked in rnds. If any finger is too snug, undo rows and work again adding an extra sc around.

Rnd 1: Ch 1, sc in same sc, sc in each of next 8 sc, working between finger openings, sc in each of next 2 connecting sc, sc in each of next 5 sc, join in first sc. *(16 sc)*

Rnds 2–5: Ch 1, sc in same sc as joining and in each sc around, join in first sc, fasten off.

Middle Finger
Rnd 1: Join in any sc of next

finger opening, ch 1, sc in same sc and in each of next 4 sc, sc in each of next 2 chs, sc in each of next 5 sc, sc in unused lp of each of next 2 sc at base of index finger, join in first sc. *(14 sc)*

Rnds 2–5: Ch 1, sc in same sc as joining and in each sc around, join in first sc, fasten off.

Ring Finger

Rnd 1: Join in any sc of next finger opening, ch 1, sc in same sc and in each of next 4 sc, sc in each of next 2 chs, sc in each of next 5 sc, sc in unused lp of each of next 2 sc at base of index finger, join in first sc. *(14 sc)*

Rnds 2–4: Ch 1, sc in same sc as joining and in each sc around, join in first sc, fasten off.

Little Finger

Rnd 1: Join in any sc of next finger opening, ch 1, sc in same sc and in each of next 3 sc, sc in each of next 2 chs, sc in each of next 4 sc, sc in unused lp of each of next 2 sc at base of index finger, join in first sc. *(12 sc)*

Rnds 2 & 3: Ch 1, sc in same sc as joining and in each sc around, join in first sc, fasten off.

Thumb

Rnd 1: Hold piece with Thumb Opening facing up and fingers to left, join in first unused sc of Thumb Opening, ch 1, sc in same sc, sc in each of next 13 sc, working in unused lps of chs on opposite side of thumb opening, sc in each of next 12 lps, **sc dec** *(see Stitch Guide)* in next 2 lps, join in first sc. *(27 sc)*

Rnd 2: Ch 1, sc in same sc as joining and in each sc around to last 2 sc, sc dec in last 2 sc, join in first sc. *(26 sc)*

Thumb Bottom Shaping

Row 1: Ch 1, now working in rows, sc in same sc as joining and in each of next 2 sc, sl st in next sc, turn, leaving rem sc unworked.

Row 2: Ch 1, sc in each of first 2 sc, sc dec in last sc and in last of rnd 2, sc in each of next 3 sc on rnd 2, sl st in next sc, turn, leaving rem sts unworked.

Row 3: Ch 1, sc in each of first 2 sc, sc dec in last sc and in next sc on working rnd, sc in each of next 2 sc, sc in next sc after the first sl st joining on rnd below, sl st in next sc, turn

Row 4: Ch 1, sc in each of next 2 sc, sc dec, sc in each of next 2 sc, sc in next sc in rnd below, sl st in next sc, turn

Row 5: Ch 1, sc in each of next 2 sc, sc dec, sc in each of next 2 sc, sc in next sc in rnd below, sc in each of last 13 sc, join in first sc.

Rnds 3–6: Ch 1, now working in rnds, sc in same sc as joining and in each sc around, join in first sc. *(19 sc)*

Rnd 7: Ch 1, sc in same sc as joining, sc dec in next 2 sc, sc in each of next 16 sc, join in first sc. *(18 sc)*

Rnd 8: **Ch 2** *(see Pattern Notes)*, hdc in next sc, dc in each of next 2 sc, hdc in each of next 3 sc, sc in each of next 8 sc, hdc in last sc, join in 2nd ch of beg ch-2.

Rnd 9: Ch 1, sc in same ch as joining and in each st around, join in first sc, fasten off.

SKI HAT

Note: Hat is worked in **back lps** *(see Stitch Guide) only.*

Row 1: Leaving a 12-inch end for sewing, ch 51, sc in 2nd ch from hook, sc in each rem ch across, turn. *(50 sc)*

Row 2: Ch 1, sc in each sc across, turn.

Row 3: Ch 1, sc in each sc to last 2 sc, turn, leaving last 2 sc unworked. *(48 sc)*

Row 4: Rep row 2.

Rows 5–20: [Rep rows 3 and 4 alternately] 8 times. *(32 sc at end of last row)*

Row 21: Ch 1, sc in each sc across, sc in next sc on next row below (leaving last st of that row unworked), turn. *(33 sc)*

Row 22: Rep row 2.

Row 23: Ch 1, sc in each sc across, sc in last st of row below, sc in next st of next row down (leaving last st of that row unworked), turn. *(35 sc)*

Row 24: Rep row 2.

Rows 25–38: [Rep rows 23 and 24 alternately] 7 times. *(49 sc at end of last row)*

Row 39: Ch 1, sc in each sc across, sc in next st on next row below, turn. *(50 sc)*

Row 40: Rep row 2.

Rows 41–116: [Rep rows 3–40 consecutively] twice.

Rows 117–154: Rep rows 3–38 consecutively. At end of last row, fasten off.

FINISHING

Sew last row to first row. ■

Coat Hanger Hideaway

DESIGN BY BARBARA ROY

SKILL LEVEL

INTERMEDIATE

FINISHED SIZE

15 inches wide x 7½ inches deep

MATERIALS

- Medium (worsted) weight yarn
  3½ oz/175 yds/99g country rose
- Size G/6/4mm crochet hook or size needed to obtain gauge
- Tapestry needle
- 30 inches ¼-inch wide white ribbon
- 16¼-inch wide plastic coat hanger

GAUGE

4 dc = 1 inch; 4 sc rows = 1 inch

PATTERN NOTE

Weave in ends as work progresses.

Instructions

POCKET

Row 1 (RS): Ch 52, sc in 2nd sc from hook, sc in each rem ch across, turn. *(51 sc)*

Row 2: Ch 1, sc in each sc across, turn.

Rows 3–25: Rep row 2.

Row 26: Ch 1, working in **back lps** *(see Stitch Guide)* only, sc in each sc across, turn.

Rows 27–46: Rep row 2. At end of last row, **do not turn**.

Row 47: Fold piece at row 26, working across next side through both thicknesses at same time, sl st in each row, working across next side, sl st in each unused lp on row 25, working across next side through both thicknesses, sl st in each row to row 1. **Do not turn**.

Row 48: Ch 1, working in unused lps on opposite side of foundation ch, sc in each ch across, turn. *(51 sc)*

Row 49: Rep row 2.

Row 50: Ch 1, holding hanger in front and working over hanger, sc in each of next 51 sc, working across next side, sl st in each row to row 47, fasten off.

FINISHING

Cut ribbon in 10-inch lengths. Referring to photo for placement, weave 1 length of ribbon through both thicknesses around center st at top of pocket, tie ends in bow. Attach 1 length at each end of hanger around end st tie ends in bow. ■

Winter Royal Set

DESIGNS BY WHITNEY CHRISTMAS

FINISHED SIZES
Hat: fits 22-inch circumference head
Mittens: 5 inches across palm
Scarf: 5½ x 58 inches

MATERIALS
- Patons Classic Merino Wool medium (worsted) weight yarn (3½ oz/ 223 yds/100g per ball):
    5 balls #00212 royal purple
    3 balls #00204 old gold
- Sizes I/9/5.5mm, J/10/6mm, and K/10½/6.5mm crochet hook or size needed to obtain gauge
- Tapestry needle
- Stitch marker

GAUGE
With K hook: Rnds 1 and 2 = 1¾ inches

PATTERN NOTE
Weave in ends as work progresses.

Instructions

HAT
Rnd 1: With K hook and 2 strands of purple, ch 4, join in first ch to form a ring, ch 1, 8 sc in ring, join in first sc. *(8 sc)*

Rnd 2: Ch 2, 2 hdc in each sc around, join in first hdc. *(16 hdc)*

Rnd 3: Ch 1, 2 sc in same hdc as joining, sc in next sc, [2 sc in next hdc, sc in next hdc] 7 times, join in first sc. *(24 sc)*

Rnd 4: Ch 2, 2 hdc in same sc as joining, hdc in each of next 2 sc, [2 hdc in next st, hdc in each of next 2 sts] 11 times, join in first hdc. *(32 hdc)*

Rnd 5: Ch 1, 2 sc in same hdc as joining, sc in each of next 3 hdc, [2 sc in next hdc, sc in each of next 3 hdc] 7 times, join in first sc. *(40 sc)*

Rnd 6: Ch 2, 2 hdc in same sc as joining, hdc in each of next 4 sc, [2 hdc in next sc, hdc in each of next 4 sc] 7 times, join in first hdc. *(48 hdc)*

Rnd 7: Ch 1, 2 sc in same hdc as joining, sc in each of next 5 hdc, [2 sc in next st, sc in each of next 5 sts] 7 times, join in first sc. *(56 sc)*

Rnd 8: Ch 2, 2 hdc in same sc as joining, hdc in each of next 6 sc, [2 hdc in next sc, hdc in each of next 6 sc] 7 times, join in first hdc. *(64 hdc)*

Rnd 9: Ch 1, sc in each hdc around, join in first sc.

Rnd 10: Ch 2, hdc in each sc around, join in first hdc.

Rnds 11–18: [Rep rnds 9 and 10 alternately] 4 times.

Rnd 19: Rep rnd 9, **change color** *(see Stitch Guide)* to old gold in last sc.

Rnd 20: Rep rnd 10, change to purple in last hdc.

Rnds 21 & 22: Rep rnds 9 and 10, change to old gold in last hdc of rnd 10.

Rnd 23: Ch 1, working left to right, work **reverse sc** *(see Fig. 1)* in each sc, join in first reverse sc, fasten off.

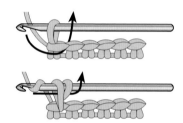

Reverse Single Crochet
Fig. 1

MITTENS
Make 2.
Cuff
Row 1: With I hook and 2 strands of purple held tog, ch 12, sc in 2nd ch from hook, sc in each rem ch across, turn. *(11 sc)*

Row 2: Ch 1, working in **back lps** *(see Stitch Guide)* only, sc in each sc across, turn.

Rows 3–27: Rep row 2. At end of last row, **do not turn**.

Row 28: With J hook and working across next side in ends of rows, ch 1, sc in each row across, turn. *(28 sc)*

CONTINUED ON PAGE 171

Confetti Waves

DESIGNS BY WHITNEY CHRISTMAS

SKILL LEVEL

FINISHED SIZES
Instructions given fit child's size 4 yrs; changes for child's size 6 yrs are in [ ].

MATERIALS
- Red Heart Super Saver medium (worsted) weight yarn (solids: 7 oz/364 yds/198g per skein; prints: 5 oz/244 yds/141g per skein):
    1 skein each #381 light blue and #310 Monet print
- Sizes H/8/5mm and J/10/6mm crochet hooks or size needed to obtain gauge
- Tapestry needle

GAUGE
With J hook: 3 sts = 1 inch

PATTERN NOTES
Weave in ends as work progresses.

Join rounds with a slip stitch unless otherwise stated.

Chain-4 at beginning of treble crochet row counts as first double crochet unless otherwise stated.

Instructions

SCARF
Row 1: With J hook and Monet print, ch 182, sc in 2nd ch from hook, *hdc in next ch, dc in next ch, tr in next ch, dc in next ch, tr in next ch, dc in next ch, hdc in next ch, sc in next ch, rep from * across, **change color** (see Stitch Guide) to light blue in last sc, turn. (181 sts)

Row 2: Ch 4 (see Pattern Notes), dc in next st, hdc in next st, *sc in next st, hdc in next st, dc in next st, tr in next st, dc in next st, hdc in next st, rep from * across to last 4 sts, sc in next st, hdc in next st, dc in next st, tr in last st, change to Monet print in last tr, turn.

Row 3: Ch 1, sc in first st, *hdc in next st, dc in next st, tr in next st,

dc in next st, hdc in next st, sc in next st, rep from * across, turn.

Rows 4–7: [Rep rows 2 and 3 alternately] twice. At end of last row, fasten off.

Border

With J hook, join light blue in any corner, ch 1, working left to right, work 2 **reverse sc** (see Fig. 1) in same sp, work reverse sc evenly spaced around outer edge and work 2 reverse sc in each rem corner, join in first reverse sc, fasten off.

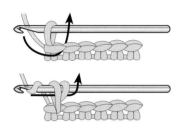

**Reverse Single Crochet
Fig. 1**

CORNER HAT
Row 1: With H hook and light blue, ch 5 [7], sc in 2nd ch from hook, sc in each rem ch across, turn. (4 [6] sc)

Rows 2–36 [2–42]: Ch 1, working in **back lps** (see Stitch Guide) only, sc in each sc across, turn. At end of row 36 [42], change to J hook and Monet print, **do not turn.**

Body
Row 37: Ch 1, working across next side in ends of rows, sc in each row, turn. (36 [42] sc)

Row 38: Ch 1, sc in first sc, hdc in next sc, dc in next sc, tr in next sc, dc in next sc, hdc in next sc, *sc in next sc, hdc in next sc, dc in next sc, tr in next sc, dc in next sc, hdc in next sc, change to light blue in last hdc, rep from * across, turn.

Row 39: Ch 4 (see Pattern Notes), dc in next st, hdc in next st, *sc in next st, hdc in next st, dc in next st, tr in next st, dc in next st, hdc in next st, rep from * across to last 4 sts, sc in next st, hdc in next st, dc in next st, tr in last st, change to Monet print in last tr, turn.

Row 40: Ch 1, sc in first st, *hdc in next st, dc in next st, tr in next st, dc in next st, hdc in next st, sc in next st, rep from * 4 [6] times, hdc in next st, dc in next st, tr in next st, dc in next st, hdc in next st, turn.

FOR SIZE 4 YRS ONLY
Rows 41–44: [Rep rows 39 and 40 alternately] twice. At end of last row, fasten off.

FOR SIZE 6 YRS ONLY
Rows 41–48: [Rep rows 39 and 40 alternately] 4 times. At end of last row, fasten off..

FINISHING
FOR BOTH SIZES
Sew across top and side of Hat.

MITTEN
Make 2.
Row 1: With H hook and light blue, ch 6, sc in 2nd ch from hook, sc in each rem sc across, turn.

Rows 2–18: Ch 1, working in **back lps** (see Stitch Guide) only, sc in each sc across, turn. At end of row 18, change to J hook and Monet print, **do not turn.**

Row 19: Ch 1, working across next side in ends of rows, sc in each row, turn. (18 sc)

Rows 20–25: Ch 2, hdc in each st across, turn.

Row 26: Ch 2, **hdc dec** (see Stitch Guide) in first 2 hdc, hdc in next 5 hdc, [hdc in each of

next 2 hdc] twice, hdc in each of next 5 hdc, hdc dec in last 2 hdc, turn. (14 hdc)

Row 27: Ch 2, hdc dec in first 2 hdc, hdc in each of next 3 hdc, [hdc dec] twice, hdc in each of next 3 hdc, hdc dec in next 2 hdc, turn. (10 hdc)

Row 28: Ch 2, hdc dec in first 2 hdc, hdc in next hdc, [hdc dec in next 2 hdc] twice, hdc in next hdc, hdc dec in next 2 hdc, fasten off. (6 hdc)

THUMB
Note: Thumb is worked in continuous rnds. Do not join; mark beg of rnds.

Rnd 1: With J hook, join light blue in end of row 1 of Body, ch 1, sc in same sp and in end of each of next 4 [5] rows across side, turn piece so opposite end of row 5 [6] is at top, sc in end of row 5 [6], sc in end of each of next 4 [5] rows. (10 [12] sc)

Rnd 2: Sc in each of next 9 [11] sc, **sc dec** (see Stitch Guide) in next sc and in first sc of rnd. (8 [10] sc)

Rnd 3: Sc in each of next 7 [9] sc, sc dec in next sc and in first sc of rnd. (7 [9] sc)

Rnd 4: Sc in each sc around.

FOR SIZE 4 YRS ONLY
Rnd 5: [Sc dec in next 2 sc] 3 times, sc dec in next sc and in first sc of rnd, fasten off, pulling end firmly to inside. (3 sc)

FOR SIZE 6 YRS ONLY
Rnd 5: Sc in each sc around.

Rnd 6: [Sc dec in next 2 sc] 4 times, sc dec in next sc and in first sc of rnd, fasten off, pulling end firmly to inside. (5 sc) ∎

Felted Fall Essentials

DESIGN BY NAZANIN FARD

FINISHED SIZES
Hat: 22½ inches in circumference, excluding brim
Purse: 11 x 14 x 2½ inches

MATERIALS
- Lion Brand Lion Wool medium (worsted) weight yarn (3 oz/ 150 yds/85g per ball):
  6 balls #133 pumpkin
  3 yds each #147 purple and #123 sage
- Sizes P/15mm and J/10/6mm crochet hooks or size needed to obtain gauge
- Tapestry needle
- Sewing needle
- 2 gold 1-inch D-rings for purse
- 1-inch piece hook & eye closure such as Velcro in matching color
- Matching thread
- Stitch marker

GAUGE
With P hook: 5 sc = 2 inches

PATTERN NOTES
Weave in ends as work progresses.

Chain-3 at beginning of double crochet row counts as first double crochet unless otherwise stated.

Instructions

HAT
Rnd 1: Beg at center of crown, with pumpkin, make slip knot on hook, ch 1, 8 sc in slip knot, pull short end tight to close center hole. *(8 sc)*

Rnd 2: Ch 1, 2 sc in each sc around, join in first sc. *(16 sc)*

Rnd 3: Ch 1, sc in each sc around, join in first sc.

Rnd 4: Rep rnd 2. *(32 sc at end of rnd)*

Rnd 5: Rep rnd 3.

Rnd 6: Rep rnd 2. *(64 sc at end of rnd)*

Rnds 7–11: Rep rnd 3.

Rnd 12: Ch 1, *sc in next sc, 2 sc in next sc, rep from * around, join in first sc. *(96 sc)*

Rnd 13–33: Rep rnd 3.

Rnd 34: Ch 1, *sc in next sc, 2 sc in next sc, rep from * around, join in first sc. *(144 sc)*

CONTINUED ON PAGE 172

Jewelry Organizer

DESIGN BY PAMELA BARKER

FINISHED SIZE
9¾ x 16¾ inches unfolded
and 9¾ x 6½ folded

MATERIALS
• Medium (worsted)
  weight yarn:
    3½ oz/175 yds/99g
      dark plum
    1 oz/50 yds/28g burgundy
    1 yd gold
• Sizes E/4/3.5mm and
  F/5/3.75mm crochet
  hooks or size needed
  to obtain gauge
• Tapestry needle
• Sewing needle
• 2 pieces 1-inch wide x
  1½-inches-long hook & eye
  closure such as Velcro in
  matching color
• ⅝-inch shank button
• Hot glue gun and glue
• Black nylon thread
• Pins

GAUGE
With F hook: 9 sc = 2¼
inches, 9 sc rows = 2¼ inches

PATTERN NOTES
Weave in ends as work
progresses.

Join rounds with a slip stitch
unless otherwise stated.

Instructions

BACK
Note: Back is worked in continuous rnds. Do not join unless specified; mark beg of rnds.

Rnd 1 (RS): With F hook and dark plum, ch 22, 3 sc in 2nd ch from hook, sc in each of next 19 chs, 3 sc in last ch, working in unused lps on opposite side of beg ch, sc in each of next 19 chs. *(44 sc)*

Rnd 2: [2 sc in each of next 3 sc, sc in each of next 19 sc] twice. *(50 sc)*

Rnd 3: [2 sc in each of next 6 sc, sc in each of next 19 sc] twice. *(62 sc)*

Rnd 4: Sc in each of next 3 sc, 2 sc in each of next 6 sc, sc in next 25 sc, 2 sc in each of next 6 sc, sc in each of last 22 sc. *(74 sc)*

Rnd 5: Sc in each sc around.

Rnd 6: Sc in each of next 3 sc, [2 sc in next sc, sc in next sc] 5 times, 2 sc in next sc, sc in each of next 26 sc, [2 sc in next sc, sc in next sc] 5 times, 2 sc in next sc, sc in each of last 23 sc. *(86 sc)*

Rnd 7: Rep rnd 5.

Rnd 8: Sc in each of next 5 sc, [2 sc in next sc, sc in each of next 2 sc] 4 times, 2 sc in next sc, sc in each of next 30 sc, [2 sc in next sc, sc in each of next 2 sc] 4 times, 2 sc in next sc, sc in each of last 25 sc. *(96 sc)*

Rnd 9: Rep rnd 5.

Rnd 10: Sc in each of next 4 sc, [2 sc in next sc, sc in each of next 2 sc] 6 times, 2 sc in next sc, sc in each of next 29 sc, [2 sc in next sc, sc in each of next 2 sc] 6 times, 2 sc in next sc, sc in each of last 25 sc. *(110 sc)*

Rnd 11: Rep rnd 5.

Rnd 12: Sc in each of next 4 sc, [2 sc in next sc, sc in each of next 2 sc] 8 times, 2 sc in next sc, sc in each of next 30 sc, [2 sc in next sc, sc in each of next 2 sc] 8 times, 2 sc in next sc, sc in each of last 26 sc. *(128 sc)*

Rnd 13: Rep rnd 5.

Rnd 14: Sc in each of next 5 sc, [2 sc in next sc, sc in each of next 2 sc] 10 times, 2 sc in next sc, sc in each of next 33 sc, [2 sc in next sc, sc in each of next 2 sc] 10 times, 2 sc in next sc, sc in each of last 28 sc. *(150 sc)*

Rnd 15: Rep rnd 5.

Rnd 16: Sc in each of next 6 sc, hdc in each of next 6 sc, dc in each of next 5 sc, hdc in each of next 6 sc, sc in each of next 5 sc, hdc in each of next 6 sc, dc in each of next 5 sc, hdc in each of next 6 sc, sc in each of next 36 sc, hdc in each of next 6 sc, dc in each of next 5 sc, hdc in each of next 6 sc, sc in each of next 5 sc, hdc in each of next 6 sc, dc in each of next 5 sc, hdc in each of next 6 sc, sc in each of last 30 sc, turn.

Rnd 17: Sc in each of next 10 sc, [2 sc in next sc, sc in each of next 2 sc] 10 times, sc in each of next 45 sc, [2 sc in next sc, sc in each of next 2 sc] 10 times, sc in each of last 35 sc, join in first sc, fasten off. *(170 sc)*

INSIDE BOTTOM POCKET

Row 1 (RS): With F hook and dark plum, ch 34, sc in 2nd ch from hook, sc in each rem ch across, turn. *(33 sc)*

Rows 2–10: Ch 1, sc in each sc across, turn.

Row 11: Ch 1, sk first sc, **sc dec** *(see Stitch Guide)* in next 2 sc, sc in each sc across to last 3 sc, sk next sc, sc dec in last 2 sc, turn. *(29 sc)*

Row 12: Rep row 2.

Row 13: Ch 1, sk first sc, sc dec in next 2 sc, sc in each sc across to last 3 sc, sk next sc, sc dec in last 2 sc, turn. *(25 sc)*

Row 14: Rep row 2.

Rows 15–17: Ch 1, sk first sc, sc dec in next 2 sc, sc in each sc across to last 3 sc, sk next sc, sc dec in last 2 sc. At end of last row, fasten off. *(13 sc at end of last row)*

Trim

Hold piece with beg ch at top, with F hook make slip knot on hook with burgundy and join with sc in first unused lp of beg ch of Inside Bottom Pocket, working in rem unused lps of beg ch, sc in each lp across, fasten off.

CENTER POCKET

Row 1: With F hook and dark plum, ch 38, sc in 2nd ch from hook, sc in each rem ch across, turn. *(37 sc)*

Rows 2–17: Ch 1, sc in each sc across, turn. At end of last row, fasten off.

Trim

Hold piece with beg ch at top, with F hook make slip knot on hook with burgundy and join with sc in first unused lp of beg ch, working in rem unused lps of beg ch of Center Pocket, sc in each lp across, fasten off.

Pocket Flap

Row 1: Starting at bottom with F hook and dark plum, ch 30, sc in 2nd ch from hook, sc in each rem ch across, turn. *(29 sc)*

Rows 2–29: Ch 1, sc in each sc across, turn.

Rows 30–33: Ch 1, sk first sc, sc dec in next 2 sc, sc in each sc across to last 3 sc, sk next sc, sc dec in last 2 sc, turn. At end of last row, fasten off. *(13 sc at end of last row)*

Trim

Hold piece with beg ch at top, with F hook make slip knot on hook with burgundy and join with sc in first unused lp of beg ch of Pocket Flap, working in rem unused lps of beg ch, sc in each lp across, fasten off.

CONTINUED ON PAGE 173

Strawberries & Kiwi

DESIGNS BY WHITNEY CHRISTMAS

SKILL LEVEL ■■□□ EASY

FINISHED SIZES
Hat: Fits 21-inch circumference head
Scarf: 3 x 72 inches
Hand Warmers: 1 size fits most

MATERIALS

- Lion Brand Homespun bulky (chunky) weight yarn (6 oz/185 yds/170g per skein):
    1 skein each #392 cotton candy and #389 spring green
- Sizes J/10/6mm, K/10½/6.5mm and M/13/9mm crochet hooks or size needed to obtain gauge
- Tapestry needle

GAUGE
With M hook: [Dc, ch 1] twice = 1 inch

PATTERN NOTES
Weave in ends as work progresses.

Join rounds with a slip stitch unless otherwise stated.

Chain-3 at beginning of double crochet row or round counts as first double crochet unless otherwise stated.

Instructions

SCARF
Row 1: With M hook and spring green, ch 4, dc in 4th ch from hook, turn. *(1 dc)*

Row 2: Ch 4 *(counts as first dc, ch-1 sp)*, (dc, ch 1, dc) in sp formed by beg 3 sk chs, turn. *(3 dc, 2 ch-1 sps)*

Row 3: Ch 4, dc in next ch-1 sp, ch 1, dc in sp formed by beg ch-4, ch 1, dc in 3rd ch of beg ch-4, turn. *(4 dc, 3 ch-1 sps)*

Row 4: Ch 4, [dc in next ch-1 sp, ch 1] twice, dc in sp formed by beg ch-3, ch 1, dc in 3rd ch of beg ch-4, turn. *(5 dc, 4 ch-1 sps)*

Row 5: Ch 1, sc in each dc, in each ch-1 sp, in sp formed by beg ch-4 and in 3rd ch of beg ch-4, turn. *(9 sc)*

Row 6: Ch 3 *(see Pattern Notes)*, dc in each sc across, turn. *(9 dc)*

Row 7: Ch 3, dc in each dc and in 3rd ch of beg ch-3, turn.

Rep row 7 until piece measures 65 inches from beg.

End point
Row 1: Ch 4, sk next dc, [dc in next dc, ch 1, sk next dc] 3 times, dc in 3rd ch of beg ch-3, turn. *(5 dc, 4 ch-1 sps)*

Row 2: Ch 4, sk next ch-1 sp, dc in next ch-1 sp, ch 1, dc in sp formed by beg ch-4, ch 1, dc in 3rd ch of beg ch-4, turn. *(4 dc, 3 ch-1 sps)*

Row 3: Ch 4, sk next dc, dc in next ch-1 sp, ch 1, dc in 3rd ch of beg ch-4, turn.

Row 4: Ch 4, dc in 3rd ch of beg ch-4, fasten off.

HAT
Rnd 1: With M hook and cotton candy, ch 4, join in first ch to form a ring, ch 2, 10 dc in ring, join in first dc. *(10 dc)*

Rnd 2: Ch 2, 2 dc in each dc around, join in first dc. *(20 dc)*

Rnd 3: Ch 2, 2 dc in first dc, dc in next dc, [2 dc in next dc, dc in next dc] 9 times. *(30 dc)*

Rnd 4: Ch 2, 2 dc in first dc, dc in each of next 2 dc, [2 dc in next dc, dc in each of next 2 dc] 9 times. *(40 dc)*

Rnds 5–8: Ch 2, dc in each dc around, join in first dc, fasten off.

Rnd 9: With J hook, join spring green in same dc as joining, ch 1, sc in same dc, sc in each dc around, join in first sc

Rnd 10: Ch 1, sc in each sc around, join in first sc, fasten off.

HAND WARMER
Make 2.
Cuff
Row 1: With J hook and cotton candy, ch 6, sc in 2nd ch from hook, sc in each rem ch across, turn. *(5 sc)*

CONTINUED ON PAGE 173

Slippers for the Family

DESIGNS BY MARIA MERLINO

SIZES

Instructions given fit Women's shoe size small; changes for shoe sizes medium and large are in [ ].

Instructions given fit Men's shoe size small; changes for shoe sizes medium and large are in [ ].

Instructions given fit Child's foot length 6½ inches *(small)*; changes for 7 inches *(medium)* and 7½ inches *(large)* are in [ ].

MATERIALS

- Medium (worsted) weight yarn: 7 oz/350 yds/198g each blue, brown, variegated, and dark brown
- Size J/10/6mm crochet hook or size needed to obtain gauge for Women's and Child's sizes
- Size K/10½/6.5mm crochet hook or size needed to obtain gauge for Men's sizes
- Tapestry needle
- Stitch marker

GAUGE

With J hook: Ch 16 [19, 22], pushing ch st over thumb rest of hook = 5½ [6¼, 7¼] inches

With K hook: Ch 16 [19, 22], pushing ch st over thumb rest of hook = 7¼ [8¼, 9¼] inches

PATTERN NOTES

Weave in ends as work progresses.

Join rounds with a slip stitch unless otherwise stated.

Ch-3 at beginning of double crochet round counts as first double crochet unless otherwise stated.

Instructions

WOMEN'S SLIPPER

Make 2.

Sole

Note: Sole is worked in continuous rnds. Do not join unless specified; mark beg of rnds.

Rnd 1 (RS): With J hook and 2 strands of blue held tog, ch 19 [22, 25], 3 sc in 2nd ch from hook, sc in each of next 16 [19, 22] chs, 3 sc in last ch, working in unused lps on opposite side of beg ch, sc in each of next 16 [19, 22] lps. *(38 [44, 50] sc)*

Rnd 2: *2 sc in next sc, 3 sc in next sc, 2 sc in next sc, sc in each of next 16 [19, 22] sc, rep from * once. *(46 [52, 58] sc)*

Rnd 3: Sc in each of next 2 sc, 2 sc in next sc, 3 sc in next sc, 2 sc in next sc *(toe section)*, sc in each of next 21 [24, 27] sc, 3 sc in next sc *(heel section)*, sc in each of next 19 [22,25] sc. *(52 [58, 64] sc)*

Rnd 4: Sc in each of next 4 sc, 2 sc in next sc, 3 sc in next sc, 2 sc in next sc, sc in each of last 45 [51, 57] sc. *(56 [62, 68] sc)*

Side

Rnds 5–7: Sc in each sc around.

Rnd 8: Sc in each of next 3 sc, [**sc dec** *(see Stitch Guide)* in next 2 sc] twice, sc in next sc, [sc dec in next 2 sc] twice, sc in each of last 44 [50, 56] sc. *(52 [58, 64] sc)*

Rnd 9: Sc in next sc, [sc dec in next 2 sc] twice, sc in next sc, [sc dec in next 2 sc] 4 times, sc in each of next 34 [40, 46] sc, [sc dec in next 2 sc] twice, fasten off. *(44 [50, 56] sc)*

Fold piece lengthwise, and mark center sc at toe edge.

Vamp

Row 1: Hold with RS facing and toe pointing up, with J hook and 2 strands held tog, join variegated in 3rd sc to left of marked sc, sl st in next sc, sc in next sc, sc in marked sc, remove marker, sc in next sc *(mark this sc)*, sl st in each of next 2 sc, turn, leaving rem sc unworked. *(6 sts)*

Row 2: Ch 1, sk first 2 sl sts, sc in next sc, remove marker, sc in next sc, sc in next sc *(mark this sc)*, sk each of next 2 sl sts, sl st in each of next 2 sc of rnd 9 of piece, turn, leaving rem sc unworked. *(5 sts)*

Row 3: Ch 1, sk first 2 sl sts, 2 sc in marked sc, remove marker, sc in next sc, 2 sc in next sc, *(mark last sc made)*, sk each of next 2 sl sts, sl st in each of next 2 sc on rnd 9. *(7 sts)*

Rnd 4: Now working in rnds, ch 1, sk next 2 sl sts, 2 sc in marked sc, remove marker, sc in each of next 3 sc, 2 sc in next sc, *(mark last sc made)*, sk next 2 sl sts, working in rem 36 [39, 42] sc on rnd 9, sc in marked sc, remove marker, sc in each rem 6 sc of Vamp join in first sc, turn. *(43 [46, 49] sc)*

Rnd 5: Ch 1, sc in each sc around, join in first sc, turn.

Rnd 6: Ch 1, sc in each sc around, join in first sc, fasten off.

FLOWER

Note: *Flower is worked in continuous rnds. Do not join unless specified; mark beg of rnds.*

Rnd 1 (RS): With J hook and 1 strand of variegated, ch 2, 5 sc in 2nd ch from hook. *(5 sc)*

Rnd 2: 3 sc in each sc around. *(15 sc)*

Rnd 3: 3 sc in each sc around, join in first sc, fasten off, leaving an 8-inch end for sewing. *(45 sc)*

FINISHING

Referring to photo for placement, sew Flower to center of row 2 of Vamp.

CHILD'S SLIPPER
Make 2.
Sole
Rnd 1: With J hook and 2 strands of dark brown held tog, ch 16 [19, 22], 3 sc in 2nd ch from hook, sc in each of next 13 [16, 19] chs, 3 sc in last ch, working in unused lps on opposite side of beg ch, sc in each of next 13 [16, 19] lps. *(32 [38, 44] sc)*

Rnd 2: *2 sc in next sc, 3 sc in next sc, 2 sc in next sc, sc in each

of next 13 [16, 19] sc, rep from * once. *(40 [46, 52] sc)*

Rnd 3: Sc in each of next 2 sc, 2 sc in next sc, 3 sc in next sc, 2 sc in next sc *(toe section)*, sc in each of next 18 [21, 24] sc, 3 sc in next sc *(heel section)*, sc in each of next 16 [19, 21] sc. *(46 [52, 48] sc)*

Rnd 4: Sc in each of next 4 sc, 2 sc in next sc, 3 sc in next sc, 2 sc in next sc, sc in each of last 39 [45, 51] sc. *(50 [56, 62] sc)*

Side

Rnd 5: Sc in each sc around.

Rnd 6: Hdc in each sc around.

Rnd 7: Sc in each of next 3 hdc, [sc dec in next 2 hdc] twice, sc in next sc, [sc dec in next 2 hdc] twice, sc in each of last 38 [44, 50] sc. *(46 [52, 58] sc)*

Rnd 8: Sc in next sc, [sc dec in next 2 sc] twice, sc in next sc, [sc dec in next 2 sc] 4 times, sc in each of next 28 [34, 40] sc, [sc dec in next 2 sc] twice, fasten off. *(38 [44, 50] sc)*

Fold piece lengthwise and mark center sc at toe edge.

Vamp

Rows 1–3: Rep rows 1–3 of Women's Vamp.

Rnd 4: Now working in rnds, ch 1, sk first 2 sl sts, 2 sc in marked sc, remove marker, sc in each of next 3 sc, 2 sc in next sc, *(mark last sc made)*, sk next 2 sl sts, working in rem 30 [33, 36] sc of rnd 9, sk sl sts, sc in marked sc, remove marker, sc in each rem 6 sc of instep, join in first sc, turn. *(37 [40, 43] sc)*

Rnd 5: Ch 1, sc in each sc around, join in first sc, turn.

Rnd 6: Ch 1, sc in each sc around, join in first sc, fasten off.

FLOWER

Work same as Flower for Women's Slipper.

FINISHING

Work same as Finishing for Women's Slipper.

MEN'S SLIPPER
Make 2.
Sole
Note: Sole is worked in continuous rnds. Do not join unless specified; mark beg of rnds.

Rnd 1: With K hook and 2 strands of dark brown held tog, ch 19 [22, 25], 3 sc in 2nd ch from hook, sc in each of next 16 [19, 22] chs, 3 sc in last ch, working in unused lps on opposite side of beg ch, sc in each of next 16 [19, 22] lps. *(38 [44, 50] sc)*

Rnd 2: *2 hdc in next sc, 3 hdc in next sc, 2 hdc in next sc, hdc in each of next 16 [19, 21] sc, rep from * once. *(46 [52, 58] hdc)*

Rnd 3: Hdc in each of next 2 hdc, 2 hdc in next hdc, 3 hdc in next hdc, 2 hdc in next hdc *(toe section)*, hdc in each of next 21 [24, 27] hdc, 3 hdc in next hdc *(heel section)*, hdc in each of next 19 [22, 25] hdc. *(52 [58, 64] hdc)*

Rnd 4: Hdc in each of next 4 hdc, 2 hdc in next hdc, 3 hdc in next hdc, 2 hdc in next hdc, hdc in each of next 12 hdc, sc in each of next 25 [31, 37] hdc, hdc each of next 8 hdc. *(56 [62, 68] hdc)*

Side

Rnds 5–7: Sc in each st around.

Rnd 8: Sc in each of next 3 sc, [sc dec *(see Stitch Guide)* in next 2 sc] twice, sc in next sc, [sc dec in next 2 sc] twice, sc in each of last 44 [50, 56] sc. *(52 [58, 64] sc)*

Rnd 9: Sc in next sc, [sc dec in next 2 sc] twice, sc in next sc, [sc dec in next 2 sc] 4 times, sc in each of next 34 [40, 46] sc, [sc dec in next 2 sc] twice, fasten off. *(44 [50, 56] sc)*

Fold piece lengthwise, and mark center sc at toe edge.

Vamp

Row 1: Hold outside of piece facing and toe pointing up, with J hook and 2 strands held tog, join brown in 3rd sc to left of marked sc, sl st in next sc, sc in next sc, sc in marked sc, remove marker, sc in next sc *(mark this sc)*, sl st in each of next 2 sc, turn, leaving rem sc unworked. *(6 sts)*

Row 2: Ch 1, sk first 2 sl sts, sc in next sc, remove marker, sc in next sc, sc in next sc *(mark this sc)*, sk each of next 2 sl sts, sl st in each of next 2 sc of rnd 9 of piece, turn, leaving rem sc unworked. *(5 sts)*

Row 3: Ch 1, sk first 2 sl sts, 2 sc in marked sc, remove marker, sc in next sc, 2 sc in next sc, *(mark last sc made)*, sk each of next 2 sl sts, sl st in each of next 2 sc on rnd 9. *(7 sts)*

Rnd 4: Now working in rnds, ch 1, sk next 2 sl sts, 2 sc in marked sc, remove marker, sc in each of next 3 sc, 2 sc in next sc, *(mark last sc made)*, sk next 2 sl sts, working in rem 36 [39, 42] sc on rnd 9, sc in marked sc, remove marker, sc in each rem 6 sc of instep, join in first sc, turn. *(43 [46, 49] sc)*

Rnd 5: Ch 1, sc in each sc around, join in first sc, turn.

Rnd 6: Ch 1, sc in each sc around, join in first sc, fasten off. ■

Snakes Alive

DESIGN BY ELAINE BARTLETT

SKILL LEVEL
EASY

FINISHED SIZE
5½ inches at widest part x
53 inches long

MATERIALS
• Red Heart Super Saver
  Economy Size medium
  (worsted) weight yarn (5 oz/
  244 yds/141g per skein):
    1 skein #975 amazon
    12-inch length of
      #332 ranch red
• Size H/8/5mm crochet hook
  or size needed to obtain gauge
• Tapestry needle
• Small amount polyester fiberfill
• 2 yellow ⅜-inch buttons
  with holes
• Small amount black
  embroidery floss
• Stitch marker

GAUGE
4 sc = 1 inch

PATTERN NOTES
Weave in ends as work progresses.

Chain-2 at beginning of double
crochet row counts as first double
crochet unless otherwise stated.

Instructions

HEAD
Make 2.
Row 1 (RS): Ch 2, sc in 2nd ch
from hook, turn. *(1 sc)*

Row 2: Ch 1, 3 sc in first sc, turn.
(3 sc)

Row 3: Ch 1, 2 sc in first sc,
sc in next sc, 2 sc in last sc,
turn. *(5 sc)*

Row 4: Ch 1, sc in each sc
across, turn.

Row 5: Ch 1, 2 sc in first sc, sc
in each sc across to last sc, 2 sc
in last sc. *(7 sc)*

Rows 6–17: [Rep rows 4 and 5
alternately] 6 times. *(19 sc at end
of last row)*

Rows 18–22: Rep row 4.

Row 23: Ch 1, sk first sc, sc in
each sc to last sc, turn, leaving
last sc unworked. *(17 sc)*

Rows 24 & 25: [Rep rows 2 and
3 alternately] twice. *(13 sc)*

Rows 26 and 27: Rep row 4. At
end of last row, fasten off.

Eyes
For eyes, with black embroidery
floss, sew buttons to row 18 on
RS of 1 piece.

ASSEMBLY
Hold Head pieces with RS tog,
sew along both sides and across
row 1, leaving row 27 open.

Tongue
Thread red in tapestry needle.
Insert needle from RS into middle
of where row 1 of both Head

pieces are joined to WS of Head, leaving a few inches of yarn on RS, sew yarn to WS *(inside of Head)*, then pass needle back through middle of row 1s to RS. Cut yarn ends to desired length for tongue.

Turn Head inside out. Stuff with polyester fiberfill.

BODY

Row 1: Hold Head with RS facing and row 27 at top, working through both thicknesses, with

amazon make slip knot on hook and join with sc in first sc, sc in each sc across, turn. *(13 sc)*

Rows 2–5: Ch 1, sc in each sc across. *(13 sc)*

Rows 6–8: Ch 2 *(see Pattern Notes)*, dc in each sc across.

Rows 9–13: Rep row 2.

Rows 14–125: [Rep rows 6–13 consecutively] 14 times.

Tail

Row 1: Ch 1, **sc dec** *(see Stitch Guide)* in first 2 sc, sc in each sc across to last 2 sc, sc dec in last 2 sc, turn. *(11 sc)*

Rows 2 & 3: Ch 1, sc in each sc across, turn.

Rows 4–15: [Rep rows 1–3 consecutively] 4 times. *(3 sc at end of last row)*

Row 16: Rep row 2. At end of row, fasten off. ∎

Red Cord Accessories CONTINUED FROM PAGE 150

left *(see Fig. 1)*, yo, draw through strands, yo, draw through 2 lps on hook, without removing hook, turn piece to left so back of sc just made is facing you, sc loosely in 2 groups of 3 strands at top left *(see Fig. 2)*, rep until piece measures 42 inches. To fasten off, cut yarn 6 inches from piece, turn, sl st in 2 strands at top left, fasten off.

FINISHING
Tie ends tog in knot. Fold in half with ends as 1 fold. Tie

overhand knot in center between folds. Attach ends of necklace clasp through fold and through knotted end.

BRACELET

Fig. 1   **Fig. 2**

Note: Cut 3 strands each 5 yds long.

Work same as Necklace until piece measures same as wrist measurement. Fasten off as for Necklace.

FINISHING
Attach ends of barrel clasp to ends of piece. ∎

Beaded Cockelshell Choker Set CONTINUED FROM PAGE 151

Row 3: Ch 5, sk first dc, dc in next ch-3 sp, ch 3, sk next dc, **top beaded dc** *(see Special Stitches)* in sp formed by beg ch-7, [**bottom beaded dc** *(see Special Stitches)*, top beaded dc] 6 times in same sp, turn. *(14 dc, 1 ch-3 sp)*

Row 4: Ch 3, sk first 2 dc, sc in next dc, [ch 3, sk next dc, sc in next dc] 5 times, ch 3, dc in next ch-3 sp, ch 3, dc in sp formed by beg ch-5, turn. *(6 sc, 2 dc, 7 ch-3 sps)*

Row 5: Ch 5, sk first dc, dc in next ch-3 sp, ch 3, sk next dc, dc in next ch-3 sp, turn, leaving rem sts and ch-3 sps unworked. *(2 dc, 1 ch-3 sp)*

Rows 6–37: [Rep rows 2–5 consecutively] 8 times.

Rows 38–40: Rep rows 2–4. At end of last row, fasten off, leaving 8-inch end.

FINISHING
Using ends, join ends of piece to ends of necklace clasp.

EARRING
Make 2.
Note: Before beg, string 13 beads on crochet cotton.

Rnd 1 (RS): Leaving an 8-inch end, ch 2, 6 sc in 2nd ch from hook, join in first sc, turn. *(6 sc)*

Row 2: Now working in rows, ch 4, dc in first sc, turn, leaving rem sc unworked.

Row 3: Ch 5, sl st in sp formed by beg ch-4, turn.

Row 4: Ch 2, slide bead up, ch 1, [**bottom beaded dc** (see Special Stitches), **top beaded dc** (see

Special Stitches)] 6 times in sp formed by beg ch-5, turn. *(12 dc)*

Row 5: Ch 1, sc in first dc, [ch 3, sk next dc, sc in next dc] 5 times,

ch 3, sk next dc, sc in sp formed by beg ch-2, fasten off.

FINISHING
Using 8-inch beg end, join rnd 1 of each piece to ear wires. ∎

Winter Royal Set CONTINUED FROM PAGE 156

Row 29: Ch 2, hdc in first sc, hdc in each sc across, turn.

Row 30: Ch 1, sc in each hdc across, turn.

Rows 31–38: [Rep rows 29 and 30 alternately] 4 times, **change color** (see Stitch Guide) to old gold in last sc of last row.

Rows 39 & 40: Rep rows 29 and 30, change to purple in last sc of last row.

Row 41: Ch 2, **hdc dec** (see Stitch Guide) in next 2 sc, hdc in each of next 9 sc, [hdc dec in next 2 sc] twice, hdc in each of next 9 sc, hdc dec in last 2 sc, turn, leaving rem hdc unworked. *(22 hdc)*

Row 42: Ch 1, sc in each hdc across, turn.

Row 43: Ch 2, hdc dec in first 2 sc, hdc in each of next 7 sc, [hdc dec in next 2 sc] twice, hdc in each of next 7 sc, hdc dec in last 2 sc, turn. *(18 hdc)*

Row 44: Ch 1, sc in each hdc across, fasten off.

Thumb
Note: Thumb is worked in continuous rows. Do not join; mark beg of rnds.

Rnd 1: With J hook, join 2 strands of purple in end of row 29, ch 1, sc in same sp, sc in end of each of next 6 rows across side, turn piece so opposite end of row 35 is at top, sc in end of

row 35, sc in end of each of next 6 rows. *(14 sc)*

Rnd 2: Sc in first sc, hdc in each of each of next 11 sc, **hdc dec** (see Stitch Guide) in next 2 sc. *(13 sts)*

Rnd 3: Sc in each st around.

Rnd 4: Sc in first sc, hdc in each of next 10 sc, hdc dec in next 2 sc. *(12 sts)*

Rnd 5: *Sc dec (see Stitch Guide) in next 2 sc, sc in next sc, rep from * around. *(8 sc)*

Rnd 6: [Sc dec in next 2 sc] 4 times, fasten off, pulling end firmly to inside.

ASSEMBLY
Sew side seam of each Mitten with 1 strand of purple.

SCARF
Center
Row 1 (RS): With I hook and 1 strand of old gold, ch 201, sk first ch from hook, *sc in each of next 5 chs, dc in each of next 5 chs, rep from * across, turn. *(100 sc, 100 dc)*

Row 2: Ch 1, sc in each of first 5 dc, dc in each of next 5 sc, *sc in each of next 5 dc, dc in each of next 5 sc, rep from * across, turn.

Rows 3–7: Rep row 2, **change color** (see Stitch Guide) to purple in last dc of last row.

Rows 8 & 9: Rep row 2, change to old gold in last dc of last row.

Rows 10 & 11: Rep row 2, change to purple in last dc of last row.

Rows 12 & 13: Rep row 2, change to old gold in last dc of last row.

Row 14: Rep row 2. At end of row, fasten off.

Border
Join 1 strand of purple in any corner, ch 1, working left to right, work **reverse sc** (see Fig. 1) evenly spaced around outer edge and working 2 reverse sc in each corner, join in first reverse sc, fasten off. ∎

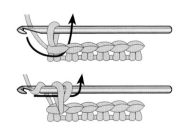

**Reverse Single Crochet
Fig. 1**

Felted Fall Essentials CONTINUED FROM PAGE 160

Rnds 35–44: Rep rnd 3. At end of last rnd, fasten off.

ROSE

Row 1: With purple, (ch 4, tr in 4th ch from hook) 13 times, turn. *(13 ch-4 sps, 13 tr)*

Row 2: (Sc, ch 1, 5 dc, ch 1, sc) in each of first 5 ch-4 sps, (sc, ch 1, dc, 3 tr, dc, ch 1, sc) in each of next 8 ch-4 sps, fasten off.

LEAF

Row 1: With sage, ch 4, 3 dc in 4th ch from hook *(beg 3 sk chs count as a dc)*, turn. *(4 dc)*

Row 2: Ch 3 *(see Pattern Notes)*, 2 dc in each of next 2 sts, dc in 3rd ch of beg 3 sk chs, turn. *(6 dc)*

Row 3: Ch 2, [**dc dec** *(see Stitch Guide)* in next 2 dc] twice, dc in 3rd ch of beg ch-3, turn. *(3 dc)*

Row 4: Ch 2, dc dec in next 2 dc, ch 2, sl st in 2nd ch from hook, working across edge, ch 2, sl st in base of end st on row 4, ch 2, sl st in base of end st on row 3, ch 2, sl st in base of end st on row 2, ch 2, sl st in first ch made, fasten off.

FINISHING

Felt Hat, Flower and Leaf according to Felting Instructions. Let dry. Wrap ribbon around brim.

Roll Rose to form flower, tack Leaf to back of Rose, and tack Rose and Leaf in place to ribbon.

PURSE
Front/Back
Make 2.
Row 1: With pumpkin, ch 46, sc in 2nd ch from hook, sc in each rem ch across, turn. *(45 sc)*

Rows 2–60: Ch 1, sc in each sc across, turn. At end of last row, fasten off.

Gusset

Row 1: Ch 10, sc in 2nd ch from hook, sc in each ch across, turn. *(9 sc)*

Rows 2–195: Ch 1, sc in each sc across, turn. At end of last row, fasten off.

Handle

Row 1: Ch 5, sc in 2nd ch from hook, sc in each rem ch across, turn. *(4 sc)*

Rows 2–4: Ch 1, sc in each sc across, turn.

Rnd 5: Now working in rnds, ch 1, sc in each sc across, join in first sc.

Note: Work rnds 6–60 in continuous rnds. Do not join, mark beg of rnds.

Rnd 6: Sc in each sc.

Rnds 7–60: Rep rnd 6.

Row 61: Ch 1, now working in rows, sc in each sc across, turn.

Row 62–65: Ch 1, sc in each sc across, turn. At end of last row, fasten off.

FINISHING

Join Front piece to Gusset as follows: Leaving 15 rows of Gusset for joining to Handle, join in first edge st of Front and Gusset, working through both thicknesses, *sl st in edge st of Front and Gusset, rep from * last 15 rows on Gusset, fasten off.

Repeat with Back and Gusset.

Felt Purse and Handle according to Felting Instructions. Let dry. Cut about 10-inch strand pumpkin

and use just 2 strands for sewing Gusset to D-rings. Insert end of Gusset in D-ring and sew top edge to bottom edge. Rep on other side. Sew 1 end of Handle to D-ring. Rep for the other end. With sewing needle and thread, sew pieces of hook and eye closure to inside edge of Purse opposite each other.

FELTING INSTRUCTIONS

Place Hat, Rose and Leaf in 1 pillowcase and Purse pieces in another. Secure top of each pillowcase with rubber band. Fill washing machine with hot water, and add some mild detergent. Add both pillowcases and a pair of old jeans or towels and let machine run for a few minutes. Remove Hat. Squeeze water out and try Hat on. If Hat fits well, it is time for rinsing. Otherwise rep procedure several times, until Hat, Rose and Leaf are desired size. Remove Purse when desired size is reached.

For drying Purse, stuff with plastic bags to hold shape and let dry.

For drying Hat, find a bowl about the same size as desired. Wrap bowl in clean unmarked plastic bag. Place crown of Hat on bowl and straighten as desired. Let dry. ■

Jewerly Organizer CONTINUED FROM PAGE 163

ASSEMBLY

Hold WS of Pocket Flap and Pocket tog, working through both thicknesses and easing to fit, with F hook make slip knot on hook with burgundy and join with sc in first st in right-hand corner, sc in each st across, fasten off.

FINISHING

Center and sew smooth side of 1 hook and eye closure to top edge on WS of Pocket Flap. Sew other side of hook and eye closure to RS of Pocket matching closure on Pocket Flap. Close Pocket Flap.

Matching bottom edges of Inside Bottom Pocket to WS on Back, pin in place. Glue bottom edge of Pocket ½ inch from top edge of Inside Bottom Pocket, pin in place. With RS of Back facing and pieces still pinned in place, working through all thicknesses, around outer edge, with F hook make slip knot on hook with burgundy and join with sc in any st on outer edge, sc evenly spaced around, join in first sc, fasten off. Remove pins.

Center and sew smooth side of rem hook and eye closure to top edge on WS of Back. Sew other side of closure to RS of Back, matching closure on inside of Back.

FLOWER

Rnd 1 (RS): With E hook and gold, ch 6, join in first ch to form a ring, ch 1, 10 sc in ring, join in first sc. *(10 sc)*

Rnd 2: (Ch 4, 3 tr, ch 4, sl st) in same sc as joining *(beg petal)*, sl st in next sc, *(sl st, ch 4, 3 tr, ch 4, sl st) in next sc *(petal)*, sl st in next sc, rep from * around, join in joining sl st, fasten off. *(5 petals)*

FINISHING

With gold, sew Flower to RS of Back ½ inch from bottom edge of trim. ■

Strawberry & Kiwi CONTINUED FROM PAGE 164

Rows 2–21: Ch 1, working in **back lps** *(see Stitch Guide)* only, sc in each sc across, turn.

Row 22: Ch 1, working in back lps only, sc in each sc across, **do not turn**.

Palm

Row 23: With K hook and working across next side in ends of rows, ch 1, sc in each each row across, turn. *(22 sc)*

Rows 24–30: Ch 2, dc in each st across, turn. At end of last row, fasten off.

Row 30: With J hook, join spring green in first dc, ch 1, sc in each dc across, turn.

Row 31: Ch 1, sc in each sc across, fasten off.

FLOWER

Make 5.
Rnd 1 (RS): With K hook and spring green, ch 3, join in first ch to form a ring, ch 1, 9 sc in ring, fasten off. *(9 sc)*

Rnd 2: With K hook and pink, join in any sc, *ch 2, 3 dc in same sc *(petal)*, sl st in each of next 2 sc, rep from * 3 times, ch 2, 3 dc in same sc as last sl *(petal)*, sl st in next sc and in joining sl st, fasten off. *(5 petals)*

FINISHING

Fold Warmer in half and sew ends of rows tog, leaving a 1-inch opening for thumb approximately 2 inches below spring green top edge.

With spring green, sew around edges of petals of each Flower. Sew 1 Flower to each point of Scarf, to outside wrist of each Hand Warmer and at bottom edge of Hat. ■

General Instructions

Please review the following information before working the projects in this book. Important details about the abbreviations and symbols used are included in the information below.

HOOKS

Crochet hooks are sized for different weights of yarn and thread. For most thread crochet, you will use a steel crochet hook. Steel crochet-hook sizes range from size 00 to 14. The higher the number of the hook, the smaller your stitches will be. For example, a size 1 steel crochet hook will give you much larger stitches than a size 9 steel crochet hook. Keep in mind that the hook sizes given with the pattern instructions were obtained by working with the size thread or yarn and hook given in the materials list. If you work with a smaller hook, depending on your gauge, your project size will be smaller; if you work with a larger hook, your project's finished size will be larger.

GAUGE

Gauge is determined by the tightness or looseness of your stitches, and affects the finished size of your project. If you are concerned about the finished size of the project matching the size given, take time to crochet a small section of the pattern and then check your gauge. For example, if the gauge called for is 10 dc = 1 inch, and your gauge is 12 dc

to the inch, you should switch to a larger hook. On the other hand, if your gauge is only 8 dc to the inch, you should switch to a smaller hook.

If the gauge given in the pattern is for an entire motif, work one motif and then check your gauge.

UNDERSTANDING SYMBOLS

As you work through a pattern, you'll quickly notice several symbols in the instructions. The following symbols are used to clarify the pattern for you: brackets [], curlicue braces {}, parentheses () and asterisks *.

Brackets [] are used to set off a group of instructions worked a specific number of times. For example, "[ch 3, sc in next ch-3 sp] 7 times" means to work the instructions inside the [] seven times.

Occasionally, a set of instructions inside a set of brackets needs to be repeated, too. In this case, the text within the brackets to be repeated will be set off with curlicue braces {}. For example, "[dc in each of next 3 sts, ch 1, {shell in next ch-1 sp} 3 times, ch 1] 4 times." In this case, in

each of the four times you work the instructions included in the brackets, you will work the section included in the curlicue braces three times.

Parentheses () are used to set off a group of stitches to be worked all in one stitch, space or loop. For example, the parentheses () in this set of instructions, "Sk 3 sc, (3 dc, ch 1, 3 dc) in next st" indicate that after skipping 3 sc, you will work 3 dc, ch 1 and 3 more dc all in the next stitch.

Single asterisks * are also used when a group of instructions is repeated. For example, "*Sc in each of the next 5 sc, 2 sc in next sc, rep from * around, join with a sl st in beg sc" simply means you will work the instructions from the first * around the entire round.

Double asterisks ** are used to indicate when a partial set of repeat instructions are to be worked. For example, "*Ch 3, (sc, ch 3, sc) in next ch-2 sp, ch 3**, shell in next dc, rep from * 3 times, ending last rep at **" means that on the third repeat of the single asterisk instructions, you will stop at the double asterisks.

174

STITCH GUIDE

Abbreviations

beg	begin/beginning
bpdc	back post double crochet
bpsc	back post single crochet
bptr	back post treble crochet
CC	contrasting color
ch	chain stitch
ch-	refers to chain or space previously made (i.e., ch-1 space)
ch sp	chain space
cl	cluster
cm	centimeter(s)
dc	double crochet
dec	decrease/decreases/decreasing
dtr	double treble crochet
fpdc	front post double crochet
fpsc	front post single crochet
fptr	front post treble crochet
g	gram(s)
hdc	half double crochet
inc	increase/increases/increasing
lp(s)	loop(s)
MC	main color
mm	millimeter(s)
oz	ounce(s)
pc	popcorn
rem	remain/remaining
rep	repeat(s)
rnd(s)	round(s)
RS	right side
sc	single crochet
sk	skip(ped)
sl st	slip stitch
sp(s)	space(s)
st(s)	stitch(es)
tog	together
tr	treble crochet
trtr	triple treble crochet
WS	wrong side
yd(s)	yard(s)
yo	yarn over

Chain—ch: Yo, pull through lp on hook.

Slip stitch—sl st: Insert hook in st, pull through both lps on hook.

Single crochet—sc: Insert hook in st, yo, pull through st, yo, pull through both lps on hook.

Front loop—front lp
Back loop— back lp

Front Loop   Back Loop

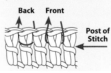

Front post stitch—fp:
Back post stitch—bp: When working post st, insert hook from right to left around post st on previous row.

Back   Front

Post of Stitch

Half double crochet—hdc: Yo, insert hook in st, yo, pull through st, yo, pull through all 3 lps on hook.

Double crochet—dc: Yo, insert hook in st, yo, pull through st, [yo, pull through 2 lps] twice.

Change colors: Drop first color; with 2nd color, pull through last 2 lps of st.

Treble crochet—tr: Yo twice, insert hook in st, yo, pull through st, [yo, pull through 2 lps] 3 times.

Double treble crochet—dtr: Yo 3 times, insert hook in st, yo, pull through st, [yo, pull through 2 lps], 4 times.

Single crochet decrease (sc dec): (Insert hook, yo, draw lp through) in each of the sts indicated, yo, draw through all lps on hook.

Half double crochet decrease (hdc dec): (Yo, insert hook, yo, draw lp through) in each of the sts indicated, yo, draw through all lps on hook.

Double crochet decrease (dc dec): (Yo, insert hook, yo, draw loop through, draw through 2 lps on hook) in each of the sts indicated, yo, draw through all lps on hook.

Treble crochet decrease (tr dec): Holding back last lp of each st, tr in each of the sts indicated, yo, pull through all lps on hook.

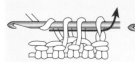

Example of 2-sc dec

Example of 2-hdc dec

Example of 2-dc dec

US	UK
sl st (slip stitch)	= sc (single crochet)
sc (single crochet)	= dc (double crochet)
hdc (half double crochet)	= htr (half treble crochet)
dc (double crochet)	= tr (treble crochet)
tr (treble crochet)	= dtr (double treble crochet)
dtr (double treble crochet)	= ttr (triple treble crochet)
skip	= miss

Special Thanks

Cindy Adams
Charger Place Mat, 16
Raspberry Twist, 134
One Row Afghan, 136
Heather Dawn, 140

Annie Original
Spring Green Rug, 18
TV Time Accessories, 26

Pamela Barker
Jewelry Organizer, 162

Elaine Bartlett
Harvest Rug, 17
Filet Ripple Afghan, 53
Dog Bed, 98
Sand & Sea Afghan, 130
Snakes Alive, 169

Jennifer Borne
Magic Mitts & Ski Hat, 152

Whitney Christmas
Winter Royal Set, 156
Confetti Waves, 158
Strawberries & Kiwi, 164

Cathy Costa
Buttercup Jacket, 62

Judy Crow
Little Boy Blue Edging, 66
Lavender Lace Edging, 67
Sweet Dreams Edging, 67

Beverly Davis
Kitchen Gift Set, 102

Terry Day
Heart Pocket Note Holder, 93

Rhonda Dodds
Shades of Autumn, 132

Nazanin Fard
Hopscotch Lap Throw, 138
Felted Fall Essentials, 160

Holly Fields
Baby Antoinette, 56

Connie Folse
Pot Holder, 40

Debora Gardner
Baby Pocket Afghan, 54

Laura Gebhardt
Beaded Cockleshell
Choker Set, 151

Cindy Harris
Rag Place Setting, 14
Baby Shells Afghan, 68

Kyleigh C. Hawke
Granny's Hangers, 88

Alice Heim
Midnight Blue Pillow, 22

Luella Hinrichsen
Apple, 117

Margaret Hubert
Sunshine t Top, 58
Hooded Beach Towel, 60

Sheila Leslie
Best Friends Treat Holders, 84

Jo Ann Loftis
Towel Edgings, 10

Nina Marsh
Lid Grabbers, 8

Mary Melick
Red Cord Accessories, 150

Maria Merlino
Oxygen Tank Covers, 90
Tooth Fairy Pillow, 94
Slippers for the Family, 166

Marty Miller
Sea Breeze Table Runner, 24
Clutter Keepers, 30
Post Stitch Patchwork, 120

Nancy Nehring
Lace Fan, 142
Crosshatch Stitch Afghan, 144

Barbara Neid
Butterfly, 108
Flower, 109
Heart, 109

Joyce Nordstrom
Harlequin Afghan, 128

Donna Piglowski
Sweet Pea Gown, 50

Nancy Prusinski
Pooch Pullovers, 104

Denise Rothberg
Scrubbie, 13

Barbara Roy
Coat Hanger Hideaway, 155

Jocelyn Sass
Golf Club Covers, 83

Darla Sims
Sonata In Shells Afghan, 124
Easy Tie Wrap, 148

Delores Spagnuolo
Eyeglasses Cases, 100

Kathleen Stuart
Spoil Yourself Bath Set, 80
Catherine Wheel Afghan, 126

Beverly Study
Poke Bonnet, 64

Colleen Sullivan
Bootie Vase, 48

Tara Suprenant
Plastic Bag Holder, 110

Elizabeth Ann White
Autumn Lace, 32
Bouquet Booties, 46
Baby Love Edgings, 67
Easy Elegant Jar Covers, 96

Michele Wilcox
Richly Textured Pillow, 20

Isabelle Wolters
Vintage Fan, 34

Zelda Workman
Candle Mat Doily, 38

Debi Yorston
Nursery Notions, 52

Lori Zeller
Dishcloth, 12
Mocha & Cream, 36